DYLAN THE BARD

A Life of Dylan Thomas

Andrew Sinclair

THOMAS DUNNE BOOKS

ST. MARTIN'S PRESS ❧ NEW YORK

THOMAS DUNNE BOOKS.
An imprint of St. Martin's Press.

www.stmartins.com

ISBN 0-312-26580-8

First published in Great Britain by Constable and Company Limited

First U.S. Edition: November 2000

10 9 8 7 6 5 4 3 2 1

To my inspiration,

SONIA

Hear the voice of the Bard!
Who Present, Past, & Future sees
Whose ears have heard,
The Holy Word,
That walk'd among the ancient trees.

William Blake, *Songs of Experience*

Contents

Illustrations

[11]

Acknowledgements

I must first acknowledge with humility and gratitude the writings of Dylan Thomas himself, for no writer about Dylan can approach his own mocking appreciation of himself: his words have been lovingly preserved by his agents David Higham Associates and his literary executors, and carefully and mainly published by J.M. Dent and Sons. I am most grateful to them for all permissions. I am indebted particularly to extracts from *The Map of Love*, 1939; *Portrait of the Artist as a Young Dog*, 1940; *The Doctor and the Devils*, 1953; *Quite Early One Morning*, 1954; *A Prospect of the Sea*, 1955; *The Poems* (Daniel Jones ed.), 1971, although there was a later edition of the poems. Caitlin Thomas's two books, *Leftover Life to Kill* (London, 1957) and *Not Quite Posthumous Letter to My Daughter* (London, 1963), show both a profound insight into Dylan's character and the greatness of her loss. Again I am grateful for permission to quote from her works because of her letter to me, and those of Vernon Watkins, although Dylan Thomas's letters to him were published in 1957 by J.M. Dent with Faber & Faber. Constantine Fitzgibbon's biography, *The Life of Dylan Thomas* (London, 1965), and his editing of *Selected Letters of Dylan Thomas* (London, 1966), put together some of the material on the poet. Paul Ferris edited an admirable edition of *Dylan Thomas: The*

Collected Letters (London, 1987). His biography of *Dylan Thomas* (London, 1977) was the best to succeed that of Constantine Fitzgibbon, and most intriguing was his *Caitlin: The Life of Caitlin Thomas* (London, 1993).

My own previous illustrated biography of Dylan Thomas, published in 1975 in London and New York, was welcomed by Caitlin Thomas, who wrote to me on 5 November 1975: 'After reading your book I feel you have said the last words on Dylan – with beautiful passionate words – and no more need be said about him. You have picked the plums and touched the living quick of the Dylan situation with penetrating insight. I agree with you that Dylan did what he intended to do – it seems like – in retrospect – he had it all mapped out beforehand the way it came about. What baffles me is from whence first did your passion and your understanding of your subject come?'

In view of the considerable research of the past twenty-four years, which I will acknowledge, and my access to unpublished letters and photographs, I have decided to rewrite my previous biography. For this, I am particularly thankful to Jeff Towns, who also has a passion for the poet in his running of Dylan's Bookstore in Salubrious Passage in Swansea, and his mounting of the Thomas exhibition in the Dylan Thomas Centre there. For I had delivered no last words, as Caitlin Thomas wrote: there are never any last words: there is always something new to be found. My later research on the culture of the 1940s, *War Like a Wasp: The Lost Decade of the Forties* (London, 1989), also added considerably to my understanding of the London background of Dylan's life, as did my biography of the painter Francis Bacon. The further issues of the writings of Dylan Thomas, *The Collected Stories* (London, 1983), *The Broadcasts* (London, 1991), edited by Ralph Maud and Walford Davies, and *The Complete Screenplays* (London, 1994), edited by John Ackerman, made the greater part of the Dylan Thomas material more accessible.

The author further acknowledges with gratitude New Directions Publishing Corporation, the usual American publishers of Dylan Thomas, for permission to reprint extracts from his work published in America, Triton Publishing Company Limited and McGraw-Hill Book Company for an extract from *Me and My Bike* by Dylan Thomas, published in 1965, and Putnam and Company Limited for extracts from Caitlin Thomas, *Leftover Life to Kill*, 1957, and *Not Quite Posthumous Letter to My Daughter*, 1963. While every effort has been made to trace copyright holders, any omissions brought to the attention of the author will of course be remedied in future editions.

Invaluable in my researches have been the following books. Henry Treece, *Dylan Thomas: Dog among the Fairies* (London, 1949); Derek Stanford, *Dylan Thomas* (London, 1954); Elder Olson, *The Poetry of Dylan Thomas* (Chicago, 1954); J. Alexander Rolph, *Dylan Thomas: A Bibliography* (London, 1956), John Malcolm Brinnin, *Dylan Thomas in America* (New York, 1955) and *Sextet* (London, 1982); Lance Sieveking, *The Eye of the Beholder* (London, 1957); *Dylan Thomas, Letters to Vernon Watkins* (London, 1957); Robert Craft, *Conversations with Stravinsky* (London, 1959); Rayner Heppenstall, *Four Absentees* (London, 1960); *Dylan Thomas: The Legend and the Poet* (E.W. Tedlock ed., London, 1960); Robert Graves, *The White Goddess* (London, 1961); David Holbrook, *Llareggub Revisited* (Cambridge, 1962) and *Dylan Thomas: The Code of Night* (London, 1972); William York Tindall, *A Reader's Guide to Dylan Thomas* (London, 1962); H.H. Kleinman, *The Religious Sonnets of Dylan Thomas* (Univ. of California, 1963); John Ackerman, *Dylan Thomas: His Life and Work* (Oxford, 1964) and *A Dylan Thomas Companion* (London, 1990); Aneirin Talfan Davies, *Dylan: Druid of the Broken Body* (London, 1964); Bill Read, *The Days of Dylan Thomas* (London, 1964); Jean Fuller, *The Magical Dilemma of Victor Neuberg* (London, 1965); William T. Moynihan, *The Craft and Art of Dylan Thomas* (Cornell U.P., Ithaca, 1966); Nicolette Devas, *Two*

Flamboyant Fathers (London, 1966); Louise Baughan Murphy, *Sound and Sense in Dylan Thomas's Poetry* (Mouton, The Hague, 1966); Min Lewis, *Laugharne and Dylan Thomas* (London, 1967); Glyn Jones, *The Dragon has Two Tongues* (London, 1968); *Poet in the Making: The Notebooks of Dylan Thomas* (Ralph Maud ed., London, 1968) and *Dylan Thomas in Print: A bibliographical history* (London, 1970); Douglas Cleverdon, *The Growth of Milk Wood* (London, 1969); Dylan Thomas: *Early Prose Writings* (Walford Davies ed., London, 1971); Clark Emery, *The World of Dylan Thomas* (London, 1971); certain of the critics in *Dylan Thomas: New Critical Essays* (Walford Davies ed., London, 1972); Robert K. Burdette, *The Saga of Prayer: The Poetry of Dylan Thomas* (Mouton, The Hague, 1972); Rushworth M. Kidder, *Dylan Thomas: The Country of the Spirit* (Princeton U.P., 1973); Pamela Hansford Johnson, *Important to Me* (London, 1974); Rollie McKenna, *Portrait of Dylan* (London, 1982); A.J.P. Taylor, *A Personal History* (London, 1983); Gwen Watkins, *Portrait of a Friend* (Gomer, 1983): Lawrence Grobel, *Conversations with Capote* (New York, 1985); Rob Gittins, *The Last Days of Dylan Thomas* (London, 1986); John Arlott, *Basingstoke Boy* (London, 1990); Shelley Winters, *Best of Times, Worst of Times* (New York, 1990); George Tremlett, *Dylan Thomas: In the Mercy of His Means* (London, 1991) and with Mrs Dylan Thomas, *Caitlin: Life with Dylan Thomas* (London, 1986).

Of the many newspapers and magazines I have used in this biography, I would particularly like to thank the editor of the *South Wales Evening Post*, also those of the *Adelphi, Adam, New Statesman, Sunday Times, Times Literary Supplement, National and English Review, Daily Herald, Spectator, Observer, Listener, Western Mail, Anglo-Welsh Review, Welsh Gazette, Herald of Wales, London Magazine, Encounter, Horizon, Poetry London, New York Times, Centaur, Los Angeles Times* and *Botteghe Oscure*.

I am also indebted to hundreds of other writings on Dylan and to scores of friends for their accounts of him. By working for the

Acknowledgements

Dylan Thomas Literary Executors on the dramatic version of *Adventures in the Skin Trade* and on the film version of *Under Milk Wood*, I was privileged to hear many stories and descriptions of Dylan. On Dylan The Bard, I was particularly helped by David Annwn, 'Hear the Voice of the Bard!', West House Books, Hay-on-Wye, 1995. It would be invidious to single out any other names from the many who have helped me. I can only thank them all most gratefully for their generous aid over the past forty years.

1

Before I Knocked

Before I knocked and flesh let enter,
With liquid hands tapped on the womb,
I who was shapeless as the water
That shaped the Jordan near my home . . .
My veins flowed with the Eastern weather;
Ungotten I knew night and day.

Dylan Thomas, *Collected Poems*

To begin at the beginning.

In Thomas Gray's ode on 'The Bard', he praised the names of Urien and Taliesin. The first was the ruler of Rheged in the sixth century, the second a following bard from Powys in the Dark Ages. In the seventeenth century *Book of Taliesin* and Aneirin's *Y Gododdin*, the tale was told of the massacre of the young Welsh warriors at the hands of the Angles, as the Druids had been massacred on Anglesey by the Romans. Yet the independent Welsh Lords kept their Bards far beyond the Norman conquests of Wales. Taliesin became a mystic figure, employed by Ceridwen to stir her cauldron of inspiration and science. Recreated after many metamorphoses as animals into her child, Taliesin became the poetic genius in all bards. His name signified the 'bright and shining brow' of the spirit:

[19]

> I was instructor
> To the whole Universe.
> I shall be until the judgement
> On the face of the earth.

After Taliesin, the bards of ancient Wales were either master poets patronised at the Welsh courts or minstrels wandering from village to inn, telling their tales for bread and shelter. The court bards had to undergo a rigorous training in metre and metaphor and Christian allegory. A restricted official vocabulary, carefully vetted for heresy or indulgence, limited the abundance of the Welsh language. A ponderous classicism bound the Welsh tradition of the Middle Ages. Bards competed fiercely for the Chairs of Poetry at the various courts and for the patronage of the Welsh kings; but they were more courtiers than poets, more interested in a safe position than in the dangerous search after poetic truth. At one period, the court bards accepted a metrical code of writing, which restricted them in practice to writing eulogies of the princes and elegies for their deaths. The riches of the full Welsh language and its treasury of myths and romances were abandoned to the minstrels or travelling bards.

These were poets who wandered over the length and breadth of Wales, entertaining and prophesying, divining and telling stories, according to the principles of *The Red Book of Hergest*:

> Three things that enrich the poet:
> Myths, poetic power, a store of ancient verse.

The Norman invaders of the thirteenth century preferred the minstrels to the official bards of the Welsh courts. Thus the Welsh romances of Arthur and of chivalry spread through the Norman courts until they became the popular myths of all Europe. Instead of hymning Celtic resistance to foreign invaders, the folk memories were converted to praising the Norman conquest of France. Geoffrey of Monmouth, the seminal author of *The History of the Kings of Britain*, wrote of a Welsh and Norman alliance at Camelot against Anglo-Saxon intruders. With the crusades, the Celtic bards moved through western Europe and the Near East, chanting their lays. As Widsith in the early English poem of the Far Traveller, they were heard as Dylan Thomas would be, wherever their poems were understood.

> Thus wandering, the minstrels travel as chance will have it through the lands of many different peoples. Always they are bound to come across, in the north or the south, some person who is touched by their song and is generous with his gifts, who will increase his reputation in front of his henchmen showing his nobility of spirit before worldly things pass away, the light and the life. He who works for his own good name will be rewarded on earth by a strong and steady fame.

The Celtic minstrels left their homelands, spreading the legends of Arthur and his companions. Transcendent among them at the court of Poitou was the Welshman Bleheris, also known as Bledri ap Cydifor. He was the 'fabulous translator' of Arthurian legend into Norman French, and he was commemorated by two rivals as someone who knew the history of all the counts and all the kings of Britain, and 'all the stories of the Grail'.

In the fifteenth century, just before the final fall of the independent Welsh princes, the poet Dafydd ap Gwilym won official approval for the Cywydd, a form of poetry that united the traditions of court bard and minstrel. The Welsh bardic tradition, however, collapsed during the English Civil Wars, and its revival in the modern National Eisteddfods was laboured and influenced by Victorian reconstructions of the Druidic past. Even if the competition for the bardic Chair remained as fierce as ever, the winning poems were as circumscribed and mannered as the official court poetry of medieval Wales.

This split bardic tradition was worsened by a split language. North Wales and mountain Wales remained Welsh-speaking and largely unconquered until Tudor times, while South Wales from Pembrokeshire to the English borders was held intermittently by Norman barons, who first spoke in French and then in English. Thus the minstrels patronised by the invaders also learned to rhyme in a foreign language. As the English language spread throughout Wales, particularly with the push of the industrial revolution through the valleys in the nineteenth century, so the common tongue of South Wales became English, the tongue of social advancement and working speech. The spread of nonconformity, too, with its chapels and English hymns, accustomed the people to sing in English as well as to swear at the English. So an economic and religious invasion from over the border led to the cultural dominance of England by the time of the First World War. A new breed of Welsh poets began to desert the tongue of their fathers for the words of the invaders.

One tradition survived in industrial Wales, the respect for the preacher and the poet. Even the coal mines were still situated by the villages, and the new towns and cities filled with people from farm families. Verses were appreciated and needed for burials. In his *Welsh Country Upbringing*, D. Parry Jones told of visits to the local poet, a farm labourer and coal miner called Thomas, who composed churchyard memorial verses for all his part of Carmarthenshire. The elegies, 'though mournful in character and following the fashion and imitating the sentiments of hymns then popular, were full of gospel comfort . . . showing an extensive vocabulary and a mastery of diction, rhythm and rhyme.' As for the rural preacher, he was the actor and judge of the whole community, causing the young Parry Jones to picture God 'as a hard, merciless schoolmaster', able to see through his heart and mind, the cause of agony and fear to him all his life, an Almighty inescapable and ineffable.

This awe of preachers and their methods of spreading the terror of God would be caught by Dylan Thomas in his story 'The Peaches', where he told of his cousin Gwilym preaching about hell-fire and the pit and the ever-watching Eye of God, to end on the words, 'Thou canst see all the time. O God, mun, you're like a bloody cat.' His family came from the villages of the shires of Carmarthen and Cardigan, where the Williams relations farmed the Llanstephan Peninsula between the tidal rivers, the Taf and the Towy, while the Thomases of Johnstown were faithful members and great singers in the Congregational churches. These rural communities, rich with aunts and uncles and cousins as well as cattle and barns and pulpits, would ever remind the poet Dylan of a familiar and biblical Eden, even if his early life would be constricted by the genteel and suburban.

He was to be given the middle name of Marlais by his father. This was to commemorate the most famous member of his branch of the Thomas family, Dylan's great-uncle, William Thomas, whose bardic name was Gwilym Marles, taken from a stream in Cardiganshire, the Marlais. Gwilym was both preacher and bard, a radical and a Unitarian, the champion of Welsh tenants against their landlords, and a leading contributor to the Welsh periodicals of mid-Victorian times. For his support of the poor and the tenants he was evicted from his chapel, but he took his flock with him to a new chapel and achieved fame as a defender of the people. He was 'the towering dead' remembered in one of Dylan's poems, and his influence lay strong on his nephew, D.J. Thomas, who was not to escape the contradictions of Welsh society except through the person of his son.

D.J. Thomas's own father was a guard for the Great Western Railway, but he himself had the determination and many of the talents of the great Gwilym Marles or Marlais. He won a scholarship to the University of Wales in Aberystwyth, where he secured a First Class Honours degree in English. He wanted to be a poet, but he settled at the post of schoolmaster in English at Swansea Grammar School where he taught for nearly all of thirty-seven years. None of his private writings seems to have survived, only his anger at the waste of his talents through teaching, and his railing against God, for he was a lifelong atheist in the manner of G.B. Shaw or H.G. Wells, holding even the weather against heaven and growling, 'It's raining, blast Him!'

D.J. Thomas was the potential poet who lived in the no man's land between the rural bard-and-preacher of the time of Gwilym Marlais and the urban rebellious poet of Dylan's time. His struggle to join the middle class and own a villa and bring up a family was too much for his talent at words, which were still-born. As Dylan's wife was to write, D.J. Thomas had to bear the strain of 'the transition from farm house and railwaymen standards to schoolmaster in a semi-detached suburban matchbox . . . from lavish rough comforts to a pinched penny-pricing gentility.'

His experience was that of much of Edwardian Wales. The urge of many of the Welsh for respectability at any price led to their reputation for hypocrisy. As though in fear of their dark desires, of their natural bawdiness, of their love of drink and chat and copulation, the majority of the Welsh after Wesley seems to have leapt first into a hell-fire puritanism and then into a suffocating respectability that was the condition of that blinkered, boxed, never-to-be-forgotten Swansea society, in which Dylan would be born, from which he would flee and rebel, out of which he would never escape. As he would complain at the height of his youthful revolt against the stuffy values of his home in Cwmdonkin Drive, all his poetry up to the age of eighteen seemed to have a 'terrible lot of priggery in it – intellectual and emotional priggery'. It read 'like a chunk of adulterated Chesterton revised by Sir Edward Elgar'. Young Dylan could and would not renege on the stern strictures of his youth.

Although that proclaimed Welsh poet Wilfred Owen wrote and died of it, the First World War and its horrors were never directly experienced by the schoolmaster D.J. Thomas. Yet surely and slowly, it eroded his life. Usually he kept himself under a tight control, pressing a lid on his steam kettle of a temper. When rarely he exploded, there might be a savage beating of his pupils, particularly on one occasion when a boy giggled during a reading of a poem by Wilfred Owen, perhaps the line, 'Now I am the enemy you killed, my friend.' He seemed to feel the common guilt of the survivors of that first holocaust of the twentieth century, as expressed by J.B. Priestley, who believed that a great generation, marvellous in its promise, had been destroyed. 'Those of us who are left know that we are the runts.' In sarcasm rather than sorrow, D.J. Thomas took out his frustrations on all around him. An austere and pressed figure who wore the disguise of a bank clerk, his social life remained somewhat Welsh, a stout or three downed in the local pub, the Mountain Dew, where he dispensed experience with his rare friend, 'Soapy' Davies, the classics master.

His son Dylan would also avoid fighting in the Second World War, although the influence of that first global conflict seemed to weigh him down. In talking of Wilfred Owen, Dylan would speak of 'the foolishness, unnaturalness, horror, inhumanity, and insupportability of war', in which the martyred Owen showed to all 'the heroic lies, the willingness of the old to sacrifice the young, indifference, grief, the soul of soldiers'. And in his other marvellous radio play, *Return Journey*, Dylan would end with his father's obsession, the trench death which both had avoided. What had become of the people they had known in Swansea? And the park-keeper's answer was 'Dead . . . dead . . . dead . . . dead . . . dead . . . dead.'

[25]

Oddly enough, Dylan would speak no Welsh and be judged by Nationalists as an Uncle Tom, who wrote the language of the conquerors better than they might. He would inherit the contradictions of the history of his country and his family. His father, who did speak Welsh, refused to teach his son the language, and even felt a certain contempt for those who did speak and write it. Without question, speaking Welsh in Swansea was a sign of not having quite arrived yet from the valleys or the mountains. It was somehow a little common. In Cwmdonkin Drive, Dylan's father and mother did not talk in the language of their parents or their youth. As a result, Dylan was steeped in the riches of the English language, although his rhythms and phrasings, his choice of metaphor and odd matchings of words, have that Celtic run and lilt which seem to percolate and press through the greatest writers of Ireland and Wales such as Joyce and Thomas, nightingales in an alien tongue that they charm with the magic of their forgotten one.

If Dylan's father brought with him the urge to deny his Welsh working-class background, Dylan's mother always kept to the simpler standards of the farm. She was talkative, bright, generous, sociable, a worshipper at chapel and a lover of God, a wife who had little in common with her husband and much in common with humanity. She probably read no books except for the Bible and she gave Dylan his unformulated love of God, a half-way house between her warm, chapel-going heart and the conscious atheism of her husband. If Dylan in his late adolescence briefly despised her for being 'stout, safe, confident, buried in her errands', his writings all show the love she brought into his life with her country ways and family, the uncles and aunts of 'A Child's Christmas in Wales', the 'aged, peasant' Annie who lived at Fern Hill, Dosie who married a preacher, and William, the tenant farmer at the old home of Llangain.

Dylan Marlais Thomas was himself born on 27 October 1914, in the house where he would live all his childhood and youth, 5 Cwmdonkin Drive, on the top of a hill by a park in the suburban district of Swansea called the Uplands. He had a sister, eight and half years older than him, called Nancy, who was too advanced to be much of a companion and who represented a new generation that was never to know very well the dream of rural Wales, which Dylan hymned and loved as it was losing ground. In his most rebellious book, *Adventures in the Skin Trade*, the anti-hero Sam Bennet rips up his sister's photograph and 'down went the Girls' School and the long-legged, smiling colts with their black knickers and bows; the hockey-legged girls who laughed behind their hands.' In real life, Dylan seems to have had a remote relationship with his sister, because of the gap in age and sex and interests. She hardly appears in his writings or his life.

Dylan's name was his father's choice and it came from the *Mabinogion*, that Old Testament of national myth. In certain ways, that Victorian translation of Celtic legends by Lady Charlotte Guest, the young wife of the self-made master of the Dowlais Ironworks in South Wales, was the inspiration of modern Welsh poetry. In the text, the son of a magician king makes a maiden, who claims to be a virgin, step over a magic wand. She drops a fine male child with yellow hair. Then the son of the magician says: 'I shall name this child, and the name I shall give him is Dylan.' Once named, the boy makes for the sea and becomes part of the sea, swimming as fast as the swiftest fish. 'And for that reason he was called Dylan Eil Ton, Sea Son of the Wave.' Curiously enough, Dylan's wife was to write that he had a definite connection with the fish family with his heavy hulk-shaped head and elongated, utterly useless hands which she was to call fins.

Dylan himself would claim that his name meant 'the prince of darkness', but this mistake sounds like one of his exaggerations for effect. What was interesting in the choice of the son's names by the father was that both Dylan and Marlais were pre-Christian names, both dealt with magic and myth, both were bardic and both had to do with the mystery of the water, the big seas and the rivers of dreams that were to haunt Dylan's imaginings. By this choice of forenames, D.J. Thomas was electing Dylan Marlais Thomas to the fleshly chair of poetry where he himself would never sit. As the dictum said, those who could did. Those who could not, had children.

This was the heritage of Dylan Thomas. His birthright was a divided country, a divided tradition, a divided language, a divided society, a divided house. As a Welshman, he was born to a land split between the stern nonconformist rural tradition of the nationalist north and the mountains, and the softer English growth of the southern towns and cities. As a bard, he inherited the formal respect for rhyme and discipline of the old court poets, and the opposed gifts of the minstrels, wandering and roistering where they could find ears to hear them.

As a speaker of English, Dylan always had Welsh in his blood and heard the waves of Swansea's 'two-tongued sea'. As a social animal, Dylan was a hidden puritan, who expected women to be as neat as robins' eggs, and was even anxious about his wife's proper dressing when they went to the shops; but, equally, he was the mighty drinker and rioter, heir of the ancient feasts and the dark pubs of Swansea, the pig in the middle between the new middle class and the old ways of farm and railway and mine. And, finally, he was caught at home between the fierce, disappointed education of his father and the warm, gabbing ignorance of his mother, who spoiled him, so that he never could discipline himself to the demands of his 'craft or sullen art'.

These coiled tensions, of course, made the contradictory poet in Dylan, who was indeed 'dressed to die' before 'the sensual strut began'. He was born into conflicts that he could never end except through his work of words, his endless search for a synthesis that was impossible, a unity in divergence, a sweet final resolution of the soul. As he was to write at eighteen, 'To hell with everything except the inner necessity for expression and the medium of expression, everything except the great need of forever striving after this mystery and meaning I moan about. There is only one object: the removing of veils from your soul and scabs from your body.' Dylan was to seek especially in his life that impossible freedom from his self, from the chains of his inheritance, which had willy-nilly helped to determine the poet.

> And time cast forth my mortal creature
> To drift or drown upon the seas.

2

Green as Beginning

This sea-town was my world; outside a strange Wales, coal-pitted, mountained, river run, full so far as I knew, of choirs and football teams and sheep and story-book tall black hats and red flannel petticoats, moved about its business which was none of mine . . . And the park itself was a world within the world of the sea-town.

Dylan Thomas, *Reminiscences of Childhood*

The world of a child is as big as his eyes. The first limits of small Dylan's 'utterly confining outer world' were the front and back of 5 Cwmdonkin Drive, a new narrow semi-detached villa built in 1914, with the plaster still wet on its bricks while his mother's milk was wet on her baby's lips. There was flowered paper on the walls, mock-ebony horses holding up the mantelpiece clock, willow pattern china, tea-cosies and all the furniture of Welsh respectability. Two elements were unusual, D.J. Thomas's brown study lined with books, and the plaster reproductions of Greek statues. There were four rooms up and four down, with a narrow corridor serving them all. Dylan's home was part of the 'ugly, lovely town' of Swansea on its three little hills, 'crawling, sprawling, slummed, unplanned, jerry-villa'd, and smug-suburbed by the side of a long and splendid-curving shore'.

Beyond the house, however, lay the steep slip down to the sea, and the upper windows showed a slope of slate roofs that plunged down to the bay and the harbour, with the Mumbles Head Lighthouse a sentinel to the west. The house itself was perched awry on the hill, threatening to toboggan down on any wild wet day, but facing a reservoir topped with grass and a playing field, beyond which lay the little tree-lined Cwmdonkin Park, 'full of terrors and treasures . . . as many secret places, caverns and forests, prairies and deserts, as a country somewhere at the end of the sea'.

This park was to become the Africa and the Amazon of the small boy Dylan and his rascal friends. His usual approach to its jungles was to force his way directly under the wire that shut the park off from the reservoir, then to crawl through the back into the giant firs, so oddly mingling with palmettos and yuccas and monkey-puzzle trees. Ignored were the respectable parts of the park, the rose garden and the tennis courts and the bowling green. Yet by the fountain where boy Dylan sailed his model boats was the rockery and 'the loud zoo of the willow groves'. There Dylan located the Hunchback of his poem, who

> Made all day until bell time
> A woman figure without fault
> Straight as a young elm
> Straight and tall from his crooked bones
> That she might stand in the night
> After the locks and chains
>
> All night in the unmade park
> After the railings and shrubberies
> The birds the grass the trees the lake
> And the wild boys innocent as strawberries
> Had followed the hunchback
> To his kennel in the dark.

[31]

Into that park the boy Dylan followed the living proof that his family had arrived – Patricia, the servant who lived in the semi-detached house. His story, 'Patricia, Edith and Arnold', described Patricia as a tall, thick girl with awkward hands, with fingers like toes and shoulders wide as a man's, given to spoiling him. And he needed spoiling at times, for he was often ill as a child. He suffered from weak lungs and had to keep to his bed for weeks on end, because of haemorrhages. There he developed a voracious taste for reading, a talent for truancy and avoiding examinations, and a firm conviction that he would die young of consumption. In fact, his scarred lungs healed, and it was asthma and excessive smoking at the age of fifteen that led to his thundering cough and frequent wheezing for breath, even though he liked to claim that he had 'already had twice as much of it as Keats had'.

These bouts in bed did interrupt his early school days at Mrs Hole's School in Mirador Crescent, three blocks down the hill towards the harbour. This was a private school; but some middle-class children were sent there. Dylan's friend Mervyn Levy was at Mirador Crescent at the same age as Dylan and declared that they learned nothing there at all. Yet Dylan wrote of his memories there with affection. The place was 'firm and kind and smelling of galoshes'. And he learned more than boasting and smoking the butt-ends of cigarettes with the other boys. As the First Voice declared in *Return Journey*: 'In Mirador School he learned to read and count. Who made the worst raffia doilies? Who put water in Joyce's galoshes, every morning prompt as prompt? In the afternoons, when the children were good, they read aloud from Struwelpeter. And when they were bad, they sat alone in the empty classroom, hearing, from above them, the distant, terrible, sad music of the late piano lesson.'

Dylan later said that if he was any good as a poet, it was because he was not allowed to go out and play when it was wet. So he stayed inside the house to read, and he gained the love of words

– and Swansea was always raining. His mother concurred, saying that the only way he could be kept from being soaked was to give him paper and pencils as well as books. Then he would vanish into his little bedroom and write and write, a childish dedication to his future craft and sullen art.

Between the dame-school and the park and the house, the small boy lived, unless he was invited away to the farm at Fern Hill or to Aunt Dosie's manse at Newton, where there was too much Sunday School to compensate for the green glories of occasional outings to the Gower Peninsula. At Llangain, however, where the remote farm stood under Fern Hill, Dylan was really 'young and easy under the apple boughs about the lilting house and happy as the grass was green'. The farm in its coat of yellow wash sprawled round three sides of a court, with the farmyard and the outbuildings to one side. Like Cwmdonkin Drive, the farm stood on a slope and the ground dropped away sharply to a lower stream past an old flower-garden. And as the Swansea park, the farmhouse was surrounded by tall old trees, the survivors of that Milk Wood which once used to cover nearly all of ancient Wales. Although the house smelt of rotten wood and damp and animals, the kitchen was lamplit and warm, and Aunt Annie loved Dylan, and he played the summer days away in byre and field, on cart and hill.

> And as I was green and carefree, famous among the barns
> About the happy yard and singing as the farm was home,
>   In the sun that is young once only,
>   Time let me play and be
>   Golden in the mercy of his means . . .

The poem of 'Fern Hill' was the older Dylan's nostalgia for his roustabout country holidays, while his opening story in *Portrait of the Artist as a Young Dog*, 'The Peaches', revealed more of the fears and taints of childhood, the Welsh sense of sin and wickedness that was a hidden anchor always in Dylan's free soul. In this, young Dylan listened to his cousin as he practised his preaching from a farm-cart and then descended to take confessions from his congregation of two small boys, pointing his finger and asking for the worst crime they had done. The boy Dylan catalogued his crimes to himself, letting another boy be whipped for taking his homework, stealing from his mother's handbag, filching library books and throwing them away in the park, drinking his own water to see what it tasted like, beating a dog with a stick to make it lick his hand, looking with a friend through the keyhole to see his maid having a bath, saying that blood on his handkerchief came out of his ears to frighten his mother, pulling his trousers down to show Jack Williams, breaking into a house to pour ink over the bedclothes – all the crimes of a naughty small boy, that weighed him down for fear of being found out, crimes that he would never confess, except to another boy. This was the huge burden of trivial sin so heavy on the young, if hell-fire was threatened as well. This was the awful sense of unnecessary guilt that afflicted the Welsh conscience, young and old.

There was another dark side to the farmhouse at Fern Hill – the story of the Hangman. In legend, a Hangman had lived there with a beautiful daughter, who tried to run away with her lover while he went off to do his killing jobs in Carmarthen jail. The Hangman barred up the lower rooms and made a prisoner of the girl, but at the last she slipped away. So he hanged himself in the kitchen up the hall. Dylan often told this boy-scaring tale with relish later in his life, and it was one of the influences that lay behind his perennial Gothic fantasies, to be revealed in one letter of 1932 when he looked out into the decent Swansea street outside his window and saw 'ghouls, vampires, women-rippers, deflowerers of weeny infants, warted soaks, pimps and financiers pass by.'

Particularly in the stories in *The Map of Love* and in those collected in his *Early Prose Writings* did this excessive, morbid, dark streak appear, a prying after incest, after babies bloodied and burning, after a school of witches learning 'the intricate devil', where a black scissorman 'bent over Gladwys, he healed her wound, she stood his ointment and his fire, she burned at the true altar, and the black sacrifice was done.' Only in the pubs could Dylan later laugh away his fears of witchcraft, claiming to have seen Aleister Crowley sitting in his own bath water.

So much for the visions of glory and damnation from Fern Hill and the manse at Newton. The boy Dylan chiefly lived in the town of Swansea, where the streets and the beach were the escape of the schoolboy, just as the park had been the refuge and battle-yard of the small boy. This was a 'splendidly ugly sea town' to the children, roaming it in search of adventures. As Dylan later declared:

with my friends, I used to dawdle on half-holidays along the bent and Devon-facing seashore, hoping for corpses or gold watches or the skull of a sheep or a message in a bottle to be washed up in the wrack; or where we used to wander, whistling and being rude to strangers, through the packed streets stale as station sandwiches, around the impressive gas-works and the slaughter-house, past the blackened monuments of civic pride and the museum, which should have been in a museum; where we scratched at a kind of cricket on the bald and cindery surface of the recreation-ground, or winked at unapproachably old girls of fifteen or sixteen on the promenade opposite; where we took a tram that shook like an iron jelly down from our neat homes to the gaunt pier, there to clamber *under* the pier, hanging perilously on its skeleton-legs; or to run along to the end where patient men with the seaward eyes of the dockside unem-ployed, capped and mufflered, dangling from their mouths pipes that had long gone out, angled over the edge for unpleas-ant tasting fish. Never *was* there such a town as ours, I thought.

As for the Grammar School, though, it was the same as all other schools to Dylan, except that his father taught English there. From the age of four years old, Dylan had been read Shakespeare by his father in his study, long before the words had meaning, but were only sound after sound, signifying thunders and wondrous nothings. Now in the Grammar School, under a wise and progressive headmaster who did not force the pupils to learn against their grain, but only what seemed of use to them, Dylan studied English and nothing much else. He early found out that he hated academic disciplines, although he later regretted his lack of languages and professional training, and he lived in fear of his ignorance being found out. But while at school, except for some extraordinary victories in long-distance running races, which gave him pride all his life, he was bad at his work and not particularly distinguished among his fellows. He was small and slight, but made up for his size by his boasting and daring. In *Return Journey*, he put a description of himself into the mouth of a schoolmaster:

Oh yes, I remember him well, the boy you are searching for:
he looked like most boys, no better, brighter, or more
   respectful;
he cribbed, mitched, spilt ink, rattled his desk and
garbled his lessons with the worst of them;
he could smudge, hedge, smirk, wriggle, wince,
whimper, blarney, badger, blush, deceive, be
devious, stammer, improvise, assume
offended dignity or righteous indignation as though to the
   manner born . . .
. . . he scuffled at prayers,
he interpolated, smugly, the time-honoured wrong
irreverent words into the morning hymns,
he helped to damage the headmaster's rhubarb,
was thirty-third in trigonometry,
and, as might be expected, edited the School Magazine.

'He was well liked by the boys,' his schoolmate Ronald Cour remembered, 'and was always ready to join in the escapades – such as returning quickly to the form room after a particular lesson in order to barricade the door with desks and resist the onslaught of the boys left outside – supported, of course, by the unheeded protestations of the Master concerned.

'Another such plot, to be an active participant in the planning and execution of, involved the placing of a piece of cotton around the form-room, supported by drawing pins, and which held up the large picture of the village in the French lesson. The highlight of the whole carefully considered operation consisted of the cutting of the cotton in the middle of the hushed translation from one "set book" or other, resulting in the rolled-up canvas picture unfurling with a mighty roar and great pandemonium. The cotton was attached to one of the desks in the front of the form-room opposite the door. Dylan sat somewhere near the front opposite the door.'

There was nothing much else that Dylan did for Swansea Grammar School, or that the school did for him. More important to Dylan than formal work was the friendship he found with Daniel Jones, who was to become his accomplice inspirer and best friend. The relationship began with the fight at the age of fourteen described in *Portrait of the Artist as a Young Dog*. A strange boy pushed Dylan down a bank, they had a wrestle and rabbit-punch, they scratched and bit, they gave each other a nose-bleed and a black eye, then they turned to throw gravel at a man in his garden, egging them on, before walking away together.

Dylan was to leave his own room with his exercise-book full of poems and pictures of Shakespeare, Walter de la Mare, Robert Browning, Stacy Aumonier, Rupert Brooke, John Greenleaf Whittier, Watts's 'Hope' and a Sunday School certificate, which he was too ashamed to take down. He marched over to Daniel Jones's room, impressed by his new friend's claims to be a composer and a poet, the writer of seven historical novels before the age of twelve, and a piano-player and a violinist as well. The Joneses' house, called Warmley, in Eversley Road was to become Dylan's sanctuary, where he and Daniel would play fierce cricket and run a mock radio station between upstairs and downstairs, specialising in such talks as 'Locomotive Bowen, the one-eyed cowhand, will give a talk on the Rocking Horse and Varnishing Industry.'

In a sympathetic memoir of his friend, Daniel Jones made clear that Warmley was a second home to Dylan where he became a member of the family, a third son, another brother or nephew. The atmosphere in the semi-detached large house was unselfconscious and easy-going: there was no chapel or gentility in it. Father Jones was romantic and musical, a believer in God and not in a church, a story-teller and an inspiration to budding writers with large ears. There was also, as Daniel Jones wrote, 'an artistic compulsion in the air'. Since Dylan was writing the School Magazine almost single-handed, while evading all the mathematical lessons that he could, he found in Warmley another academy. He wrote bad poems with alternate lines for himself and his friend Daniel. Yet these exercises were a serious playing with words. The two of them set up a private broadcasting corporation that hardly rivalled the British one, but did introduce the reading of verse – an employment of Dylan in the post-war years.

'Except for the occasional wild games of garden cricket,' Daniel Jones remembered in the *South Wales Evening Post*, 'our time together consisted of an artistic partnership, sometimes in fun, sometimes in earnest, sometimes in collaboration, sometimes apart, but, as it were, still together.'

We tried our hands, perhaps, at every major art, except – thank goodness – architecture. We dug bluish-grey clay from Swansea sands, carried it to Warmley in old biscuit tins, washed it (this was really necessary) and experimented with modelling.

Finding some suggestively 'Gothic' stones in the garden we tried hard with chisels to make them even more Gothic; the result was a display of sparks and a smell of burning. We scraped up money to buy water colours, crayons, even oil paint. Since we couldn't draw, the results were very 'advanced', very 'abstract'. But our literary efforts, though sometimes made in hilarious fun, were more often serious.

The only art which the inseparable friends did neglect was music. That was because Dylan could not play any instrument, although this was no obstacle to their experiments.

Our innumerable four-handed extemporisations on the piano were usually called 'Sonatas' and assigned to a legendary composer, the Rev. Percy, whose biography, 'Percy Droppeth', we wrote with a great deal of laughter. The libretto of our 'opera', 'Blacker Moon', by X.Q. Xumn, consisted of the word 'Heinrich' sung with every possible shade of feeling. But in our musical sessions we were not always alone; Warmley had become a meeting-place for many friends, and these, with members of my family, joined in the general hullabaloo by beating on biscuit tins, blowing recorders and an old motor horn that seemed to have come from somewhere, playing an old 'cello stringed with curtain cord, and so on – this constituted the very variable Warmley Symphony Orchestra.

As Dylan would later write to Daniel, to him Warmley was the only world that had any claims to permanence. Befriended and secure in his home comforts, Dylan lived out his youth in his outer world of Swansea, swaggering and blustering and pretending all the time to be the man he was not yet. He liked putting on many faces to please, the pouting angel when in trouble, the loquacious poet when seeking to impress, the doomed consumptive when asking for sympathy, the bold drinker and smoker among his companions, and the would-be lover among the girls. Later he would mock his pretensions of that time in *Return Journey*, putting in the mouths of the answering girls that he sounded as if he had 'swallowed a dictionary' with his 'cut-glass accent and father's trilby'.

The schoolboy Dylan felt that lonely certainty of talent, that bravado on the face of inexperience, that unnecessary need to impose his manhood on all and sundry, which was the mark of the bright adolescent in his elementary town. Dylan's saving grace beneath his bluster and arrogance was his sense of humour. He never could take himself as seriously as he wished he could. This vein of self-mockery was best shown in the little parody of his life, written to Pamela Hansford Johnson in 1933 from Cwmdonkin Drive, and headed 'A Touching Autobiography In One Paragraph':

I first saw the light of day in a Glamorgan villa, and, amid the terrors of the Welsh accent and the smoke of the tinplate stacks, grew up to be a sweet baby, a precocious child, a rebellious boy, and a morbid youth. My father was a schoolmaster: a broader-minded man I have never known. My mother came from the agricultural depths of Carmarthenshire: a pettier woman I have never known. My only sister passed through the stages of long-legged schoolgirlishness, shortfrocked flappery and social snobbery into a comfortable married life. I was first introduced to Tobacco (the Boy Scout's Enemy) when a small boy in a preparatory school, to alcohol (the Demon King) when a senior member of a secondary school. Poetry (the Spinster's Friend) first unveiled herself to me when I was six or seven years old; she still remains, though sometimes her face is cracked across like an old saucer . . .

So wrote Dylan of himself in this mock-Welsh tract to his new London love. What he said was not quite true, for he embroidered on events for the love of them. A later sentence in this excuse for an autobiography reads, 'A misanthropic doctor, who apparently did not like the way I did my eyebrows, has given me four years to live.' Jeering at his fears, with his tongue in his reader's cheek, self-parodying as well as self-important, Dylan left school at sixteen and a half to earn his bread by his words, or waste of them.

3

A Provincial Bohemian

I *had* to try to learn what made words tick, beat, blaze, because I wanted to write what I wanted to write before I knew how to write or what I wanted to. And as if I knew now.

Dylan Thomas

In Swansea in the depression in 1931, Dylan was lucky to find a job. His refusal to work at school had stopped any chance of going on to a university. Unemployment in his city was high. The great strikes of the 'twenties had led to the closure of many steel mills and coal mines and factories in South Wales. Although Swansea had some specific trades, an industrial slump cut its income. Nearly ten thousand people were out of a job, and two thousand families on the Means Test. The place was full of youths hanging around on the dole, such as the two brothers in 'Just Like Little Dogs', who stood silent for hours under the railway arch, 'statues smoking, tough-capped and collarless watchers and witnesses . . . with nowhere to go, nothing to do.'

Because of his father's influence, the fortunate Dylan was taken on as a copy boy, then as junior reporter, by the *South Wales Daily Post*. For fifteen months, he read proofs before taking to the streets to report local events, such as weddings and fires and funerals. As a reporter, he was both evasive and inaccurate, finding out that all events were much the same, if he left out the list of names of those attending, which he did. The time saved from the working day was spent in the YMCA billiards hall or in the Kardomah Café, where he met his friends and argued the toss, chatting the 'thirties to death. As Daniel Jones later confirmed in the *South Wales Evening Post*: 'Our meetings were not confined to Warmley, of course, but spread to the Kardomah and various pubs. The topics of conversation had an almost limitless range. Art and sex came first perhaps; but we didn't neglect sport, the latest film and the current cricket match at St Helen's.'

Dylan himself wrote in *Return Journey*, he and the young pub lizards talked about: 'Communism, symbolism, Bradman, Braque, the Watch Committee, free love, free beer, murder, Michelangelo, ping-pong, ambition, Sibelius, and girls . . . How Dan Jones was going to compose the most prodigious symphony, Fred Janes paint the most miraculously meticulous picture, Charlie Fisher catch the poshest trout, Vernon Watkins and Young Thomas write the most boiling poems, how they would ring the bells of London and paint it like a tart . . .'

When he was on the job, Dylan used to try and imitate the movie newshound or the senior reporter, Fred Farr, a pub-crawler who knew his way round the prim face and the grim underbelly of Swansea. 'The loose meg of his cigarette burned his lower lip as he failed to open the lavatory door.' In imitation of his teacher of high and low life, Dylan wore 'a conscious Woodbine' on his lower lip, 'a hanging badge of bad habits', also a check overcoat as big as a marquee, a pork-pie hat and a reporter's slouch, as he gathered more beer in his gut than news in his head. His beat was Mumbles and Swansea mainly of the pubs, either the Antelope or the Mermaid or the Three Lamps, 'that snug, smug, select Edwardian holy of best-bitter holies', or the dark dock bars described in 'Old Garbo', a fug of chat and warm drunkenness that was to hold

Dylan all of his life with 'the taste of beer, its live, white lather, its brass-bright depths, the sudden world through the wet brown walls of the glass, the tilted rush to the lips and the slow swallowing down to the lapping belly.'

In that story about Old Garbo, 'who isn't like her, see,' Dylan wrote of making his way through the Swansea crowds:

> The valley men, up for the football; the country shoppers, the window gazers; the silent, shabby men at the corners of the packed streets, standing in isolation in the rain; the press of mothers and prams; old women in black, brooched dresses carrying frails, smart girls with shining mackintoshes and splashed stockings; little, dandy lascars, bewildered by the weather; business men with wet spats; through a mushroom forest of umbrellas; and all the time I thought of the paragraphs I would never write. I'll put you all in a story by and by.

Some of Dylan's friends from Swansea, who also achieved a measure of fame, would write about how it was to know Dylan well. This was the difference between his few true Welsh friends and the hundreds of men and women who later asserted that they were his friends. As the painter Mervyn Levy commented after the poet's end:

> Only a few people really knew Dylan Thomas. He had, of course, hundreds of acquaintances many of whom, since his death, have claimed that they knew him. The mistake is not entirely one-sided. You can meet a congenial pubber only once and feel convinced at the end of the evening that you knew the man, and Thomas was a pubber of genius, warm, generous, humorous, shedding his wit and delectable bawdiness with all the dazzling conviviality of the bubbles winking and bursting

in a glass of lager. He could make any Tom or Dick feel they really knew him. But they did not.

Dylan's most serious critic and companion, the poet Vernon Watkins, would also testify to that quality in him, which imitated Oscar Wilde in putting his life before his art:

It is difficult to explain to anyone who did not know Dylan Thomas why any study of him must remain totally inadequate. It is equally difficult to explain why those who knew him find themselves deeply handicapped in writing about him. The quality he prized most was seriousness, and he was a born clown; but was there any other poet of recent times who could create so quickly an intimacy of judgment, an apprehension of what was valid, in art and in life? That is perhaps one of the reasons why strangers who had met him once for a long conversation felt, after his death, that they had known him all their lives. The entertainer and the intellectual alike were slightly ashamed after meeting him, as he could beat them both at their own game, but if they were humble they quickly recognized that he was humble, too. The prig was his bête noire, the pedant a black-and-white crossword figure whom he didn't despise.

Little of what Dylan wrote as a reporter was worth the paper on which it appeared. The *South Wales Daily Post* was certainly not printing his legend. A series of his pieces, however, did suggest a heredity and future life, 'The Poets of Swansea', which appeared in the *Herald of Wales* in six instalments. Dylan pointed out that he was ignoring poets who wrote in Welsh, patriots who wrote in their national tongue, which he did not admit that he did not know. He started with Walter Savage Landor, but his favourite was Llewelyn Prichard, a poet and an actor with a wax nose, lost in a duel, not through drink. To Dylan, Prichard stood out 'flaming and aloof against the horizon. He failed to be great, but he failed with genius.'

The editor of the *Herald of Wales*, J.D. Williams, remembered Dylan as a reporter on the *Daily Post*. He never mastered shorthand. Did he ever try? His articles on the Swansea poets were so iconoclastic that they had to be watered down. There was a short story submitted, set in a mining valley, which ended with a head in a gas stove: this had to be spiked. To a fellow news photographer, Ronnie Thomas, Dylan was likeable, 'a short lad, plumpish, innocent looking'. Dylan's companion as a proof reader, Bill Willis, recalled him as quite a tidy figure. 'There was certainly no clue in the early days of what was to pour from him in later life. Not for me, anyway. But then I never did take much notice of what it was he was writing among his doodles on our nice clean, white-painted walls.'

In Willis's opinion, Dylan had been introduced to learn the business and become a journalist. That was the idea, and it was hardly to prove successful. The climax was a report from a trial. Dylan 'committed the cardinal sin of omitting the word "not" in a court case. He described someone as being found guilty when they had in fact been declared *not* guilty. For the editor, D.H.I. Powell, a man of strict principles, that would have been the last straw. After all, he had a reputation to uphold that was paramount. Dylan was out.'

Other reminiscences of Dylan as a reporter came from the chief cashier of Lloyds Bank in Wind Street. Not an admirer, Thomas Barlowe recalled Dylan passing to visit the morgue and the police courts to pick up stories. 'Later, people asked: "How could a young man know so much about mortuaries and the language of death in his poems?" The answer is because he saw it for himself.' Barlowe thought that Wind Street was so traumatic that it left a sickness in the young reporter for the rest of his days. 'He saw who had been slaughtered the night before. He heard the language of the police courts. It was bound to have a bad effect.'

In fact, both Dickens and Chekhov had a similar training in the ways of death, and the experience only enhanced their later writing. Yet to Barlowe with his spying and envious mentality, which mirrored so much of the genteel condemnation of Swansea which Dylan sought to escape, a café in Wind Street called Biddles was the poet's downfall. 'Dylan used to spend a lot of his time in there. In fact, the newspaper said he spent too much time drinking coffee in cafés when they let him go. Mind you, he was never too keen on paying. The lady in Biddles used to watch for him trying to leave without paying.'

With language which Dylan would put in the mouths of the disapproving ladies round the Llareggub pump in *Under Milk Wood*, Barlowe declared, 'That time around Biddles is like a great red line down through Dylan's life.' Not only was the Welsh poet a café dodger to the Lloyds Bank cashier, but also a looter. When Castle Street would be bombed in the three days' blitz of the Second World War, Dylan would appear in a pub with his friends, asking for shovels and picks. 'They were going to dig up the basement of a jeweller's that had been bombed, to see if they could find any gold or jewels that had been scattered by the blast. It all came to nothing.'

The gift of a brilliant adolescence, however, is to imagine that all things are possible, even for a Swansea reporter. Dylan also fancied himself as a great performer. J.D. Williams had seen Dylan as a boy acting in the annual play at the Grammar School. Already he was a personality, who 'stood out shoulder-high above the rest of the cast; not alone because his part called for it, but because of a certain distinction of voice and bearing.' While a reporter, Dylan visited with Wynford Vaughan-Thomas the Swansea Empire, where he had the 'entrée back-stage' and took his companion to visit the ageing Nellie Wallace, who knocked out both of the youths with a bottle of gin before going on stage to sing: 'I was after the fox, me boys – but *he* was after *me.*'

Dylan also played the roles of misunderstood writers and artists in the Swansea Little Theatre along with his sister Nancy and her future husband Hadyn Taylor. With another friend and reporter, Eric Hughes, all four appeared in Noël Coward's *Hay Fever.* Dylan was complimented by a local newspaper for his prophetic portrayal of 'an artist with an explosive temper and untidy habits'. In another role, Dylan became a businessman, whose unwritten books haunted him. Yet his apogee and penultimate performance was in Rodney Ackland's *Strange Orchestra*, in which Dylan was told that there was a 'pitiable inevitability' in his portrayal of a self-absorbed novelist in an artistic and neurotic Chelsea and theatreland, 'a powerful forcing house which brings into public view those things which we normally think most decent to hide.' Another performer, Ethel Ross, remembered the reason for his dismissal, one visit too many to a nearby inn called the Cheeses. 'He was always quiet and inoffensive when I met him,' she said. 'But on stage he lost all his inhibitions and was a very good actor. The other side of his character would only come out when he went into pubs with his drinking pals.'

Still in Swansea, not yet in Fitzrovia, Dylan could only pretend to be the Shelley of the docks, a part which he did not yet dare to act. He was writing poetry, yet it was the poetry of his first two *Notebooks*, written on school exercise paper, and imitative and unworked. By the Christmas of 1932, the editor of the *South Wales Daily Post* and Dylan agreed to part, with Dylan contributing occasional freelance articles. His reason for giving up his job had been confessed to his tubercular friend Trevor Hughes in the February of that year. 'I am at the most transitional period now. Whatever talents I possess may suddenly diminish or may suddenly increase. I can, with great ease, become an ordinary fool. I may be one now. But it doesn't do to upset one's own vanity.' Certainly the gap in the *Notebooks* and the weaker Surrealist and drunken poems date from this period, when Dylan was playing a reporter.

Once Dylan had decided to be a poet, impure and unsimple, and to work at little else, he drafted and nearly completed most of the best poems in his first volume, *18 Poems*, and nearly half of those in *Twenty-five Poems*, to be published in 1936, and *The Map of Love*, to be published in 1939. He drew his local encouragement from the writers' circle which met twice a week at the house of Bert Trick, a local Socialist organiser and editor, who actually lived off the proceeds of a small grocer's shop down the hill from Cwmdonkin Drive and 'threatened the annihilation of the ruling classes over sandwiches and jelly and blancmange'. Trick and his wife urged Dylan to read his poems and have them published, if he could. They also developed his talent for the theatrical delivery of his work. Their summer bungalow on the Gower Peninsula was a favourite refuge of Dylan's, where he could walk for miles by the sea and forget the suburban constraints of his home.

This small provincial circle, so important for Dylan in his isolation, was movingly mocked by him in his story, 'Where Tawe Flows'. There the budding writers met like conspirators in the small villa and waited for the wife to go to bed before embarking on their long collaborative novel. Dylan always liked writing prose in company, forced by others to the convivial pen; at various times, he wrote alternate lines or pages of works with Daniel Jones, Vernon Watkins and the wealthy littérateur, John Davenport. The title of his story about the writers' circle was the title of their novel in common, and the plotters were called to order as if at a Labour Party meeting, while the minutes were read by Mr Thomas, being the substance of the book. 'Any questions, gentlemen?' he then asked, and an evening of irrelevant story-telling developed between the comrades.

The comfortable gentility of Swansea life, even among its rebels and would-be artists, was initially a cradle for Dylan's talent although later, in the first days of his Soho rebellion, it would seem as suffocating as the villa home which Sam Bennett destroyed in *Adventures in the Skin Trade* before running away to the big smoke of London. However anarchic Dylan was to be, he could never overcome his gratitude and guilt for that safe, prissy, known Swansea world of dreams in doilies, rebellions in parlours, radicalism in beer-mugs. As with Sam Bennet burning his mother's sunshade to prove his escape from her, Dylan would always feel shame when he denied his puritan upbringing and his appreciation of the niceties of women, tasting his tears like Sam and saying, 'It's salt. It's very salt. Just like in my poems.'

Dylan was born to be a poet. He never doubted that. Words were always his delight and his play. The things that first made him 'love language and want to work *in* it and *for* it were nursery rhymes and folk tales, the Scottish ballads, a few lines of hymns, the most famous Bible stories and the rhythms of the Bible, Blake's *Songs of Innocence*, and the quite incomprehensible magical majesty and nonsense of Shakespeare heard, read and near-murdered' in the first form of his school.

Before Dylan could understand the meaning of words, he loved them for their sound. They occupied his mind, as his boyhood friend Daniel Jones said, to the exclusion even of the things connected with them. Dylan pursued this work of words at school without caring for anything else. He failed every examination in Senior Certificate except English, which his father taught and which he loved. He was truant at all learning that did not have to do with the art of poetry, either writing it or speaking it.

The contrast between Dylan's editorship of the Swansea Grammar School Magazine, in which he wrote bright light verse, and his *First Notebook* of poetry, which he began at the age of fifteen and a half, reflected the split in his nature between the public D.M. Thomas, schoolmaster's son with a social face and the parlour standards of suburban Swansea, and the secret youth of

Dylan, bawdy and bardic in his bedroom alone. His first published poem was called 'The Song of the Mischievous Dog' and read like Lewis Carroll minor. It began:

> There are many who say that a dog has its day,
>   And a cat has a number of lives;
> There are others who think that a lobster is pink,
>   And that bees never work in their hives . . .

The only hint of Dylan's more hidden desires came in the final lines:

> . . . And if I indulge in a bite at a bulge
>   Let's hope you won't think me too vicious.

This facile rhyming for public view was privately contradicted in the groping of the free-style poems of the *First* and *Second Notebooks*. These poems were a curious mixture of imitations from the Elizabethans and Beddoes, Tennyson and Walter de la Mare, Sacheverell Sitwell and the early W.B. Yeats, allied with the wants and despairs and violent obscurities that were to become a feature of the mature poet. While the urge to shock showed everywhere in lines such as 'your thighs burning with pressure' or 'this pus runs deep . . . On every hand the evil's positive', even the blasphemy had a lyrical quality that was to set the later poet in that special green heaven and hell of his, urgent on the themes of love and death and spring and God. He was just sixteen when he wrote the first draft of 'How Shall My Animal'. Except for the first line, little of Dylan's work or self as a terrible youth, the Rimbaud of Cwmdonkin Drive, survived into the final poem, except for his adolescent sexual urge seeking to link religion and women in a fusion of holy lust. This was the youth's version:

> . . . My senses see
> Speak then, o body, shout aloud,
> And break my only mind from chains
> To go where ploughing's ended.
> The dancing women all lie down;
> Their turning wheels are still as death;
> No hope can make them glad,
> Lifting their cheery bodies as before
> In many shapes and signs,
> A cross of legs
> Poor Christ was never nailed upon,
> A sea of breasts,
> A thousand sailing thighs . . .

This was the final version of the adolescent thoughts of sea and crucifixion and lust, published eight years later when Dylan was in his flower:

> . . . I was a living skein,
> Tongue and ear in the thread, angle the temple-bound
> Curl-locked and animal cavepools of spells and bone,
> Trace out a tentacle,
> Nailed with an open eye, in the bowl of wounds and weed
> To clasp my fury on ground
> And clap its great blood down;
> Never shall beast be born to atlas the few seas
> Or poise the day on a horn.

The early poems of the *First Notebook*, indeed, stood on their own. They were merely markers of the method that the poet was to use. Although Dylan wasted words riotously in his speech, he wrought them with labyrinthine care in the drafts of his finished and published and self-chosen *Collected Poems* of

1952, which were all he wished to preserve up until that time, less than one year before his early death. His way of working was both disorganised and elaborate. As he wrote in 1935 to a friend, Charles Fisher: 'My method is this: I write a poem on innumerable sheets of scrap paper, write it on both sides of the paper, often upside down and criss cross ways unpunctuated, surrounded by drawings of lamp posts and boiled eggs, in a very dirty mess, bit by bit I copy out the slowly developing poem into an exercise book; and, when it is completed, I type it out. The scrap sheets I burn . . .'

Later in his life, Dylan would keep the fragments, but he would copy out a poem laboriously in longhand every time that he changed it. He was to show the American critic John Malcolm Brinnin two hundred separate and distinct versions of 'Fern Hill'. This was his way of keeping the poem together, so that it grew like an organism. As he was to tell Brinnin, he carried a phrase in his head for many years, and if it was resonant or pregnant, it would suggest another phrase. So the poem would accumulate through draft after draft, year after year, until at last he found it sufficient.

The *Second*, *Third* and *Fourth Notebooks*, which largely covered Dylan's drafts for poems between 1930 and 1934, were used by him as sources for his poems as late as 1941. They showed a young poet's mind developing from a vocabulary of gloom and imitative Surrealism – probably the product of his first job on the *South Wales Daily Post*. His attempts at protest poetry in the manner of W.H. Auden were failures, with obvious references such as 'the living dead left over from the war' or 'the Western man with one lung gone'. But the surging lines of the future poems were already there, including an early draft of 'And Death Shall Have No Dominion'. His search continued for the antithesis of Welsh puritanism, with its insistence on righteousness and a severe God, who could not be questioned.

Where, what's my God among this crazy rattling
Of knives on forks, he cried, of nerve on nerve,
Man's ribs on woman's, straight line on a curve,
And hand to buttock, man to engine, battling,
Bruising, where's God's my Shepherd, God is Love?
No loving shepherd in this upside life.

Veering between belief and despair, most of the later poems of the *Notebooks* demonstrated Dylan's early search for a mystical fusion of the contradictions that were to torment him all his life. He could not wholly reject the censorious society that loved him, while longing fiercely for the appalling freedom of the poet. He could not spurn God, although he boasted in 1933 that God had been deposed years ago and the Devil reigned. He could only try to resolve the conflicts between the outer obvious world, which had to be lived in and enjoyed and endured, and between his inner vision of some impossible unity in creation. The knowledge of the artist was 'of the actual world's deplorable sordidness and of the invisible world's splendour'. Even Dylan's own poems did not seem satisfactory to him because they dealt too much with the necessary outer world. 'Perhaps the greatest works of art are those that reconcile, perfectly, inner and outer.'

The *Fourth* and final *Notebook* marked the certainty of Dylan with his lifelong preoccupation, an emphasis on the body as the arbiter of all things, a view which would be criticised by his new friend Pamela Hansford Johnson. To Dylan, the body was both meaty and metaphysical as it had been for John Donne and William Blake. 'Every idea, intuitive or intellectual, can be imagined and translated in terms of the body, its flesh, skin, blood, sinews, veins, glands, organs, cells, or senses.' Even the extra-terrestrial could be described by Dylan, because he could not rise to the stars. He had 'to bring down the stars' to his own level. He was the opposite of Plato, who wrote of his lost love:

My Star, you are raised to the stars in the skies.
O, to see you as the heaven does with many eyes.

Dylan preferred his 'unpretty' poems with an 'imagery almost totally anatomical . . . the perhaps wearisome succession of blood and bones, and never ending smiles of the streams in the veins and the lights in the eyes' To him, in the final *Notebook*, there was a 'firmament of flesh and bone'. Jesus Christ, indeed, became the key to this mystery of God in man, even to the agnostic and doubting Thomas, whose poems of the period were awash with the blood and the body and the pain of the crucifixion. Yet, finally, Dylan was always the heretic, the Gnostic, believing that part of the godhead was somehow in every body, that each being was somehow his own suffering Jesus. Spirituality had to be totally comprehended in the experience of living. As he declared at the end of the last *Notebook*, 'Man be my metaphor.'

With Bert Trick's encouragement, Dylan began to have his poems published. Rarely, indeed, did any magazine refuse a Thomas work. His first major poem to be printed was 'That Sanity Be Kept', the second was 'The Force That Through The Green Fuse Drives The Flower' with its terrible Blakeian lines:

And I am dumb to tell the crooked rose
My youth is bent by the same wintry fever.

In all, Victor Neuberg, who ran a poetry half-column in the London *Sunday Referee*, was to print seven of Dylan's poems between 1933 and 1935, along with poems by David Gascoyne and Pamela Hansford Johnson.

This London connection and correspondence with Miss Johnson, then known as a young poetess, would take Dylan to the capital in 1933 on a reconnaissance and in 1934 on a longer stay. The letters between the two young writers showed Dylan at the age of nineteen to be bombastic for fear of seeming provincial, world-weary in case he was thought naïve, tough to disguise tenderness, and sexually aware to hide a probable virginity. Dylan's contemporary, Constantine Fitzgibbon, testified to the poet's masturbation throughout his life, and his early poems certainly revealed that tendency, particularly such lines in the *Notebook* as:

> Jack my father let the knaves steal off
> Their little swag, the gems of life and death . . .

or the more explicit:

> Now that drugged youth is waking from its stupor,
> The nervous hand rehearsing on the thigh
> Acts with a woman . . .

Dylan's intense preoccupation with sexuality was a form of repression until his twenties, as he bitterly wrote to Miss Johnson before he had met her. 'My experience of waking with a woman at my side has been necessarily limited. The medieval laws of this corrupted hemisphere have dictated a more or less compulsory virginity during the period of life when virginity should be regarded as a crime against the dictates of the body.'

If this forced repression had not been true, Dylan would not have made such a vainglorious confession to Miss Johnson of his first known sexual encounter, a weekend in the Gower Peninsula with a friend and a girl called Jane with a loose red mouth. In this letter towards the end of his close relationship with Miss Johnson, Dylan showed the need to boast more than to ask forgiveness, to wallow in the splendour of his sin rather than to declare a deep love for his fellow poet in London.

His drinking, too, was the young provincial poet's other pride. He loved to write of his feats with alcohol, as if somehow boozing was a proof of manhood, a denial of the chapel. An old saying was that the shortest way out of Birmingham was a bottle of gin. To the young Dylan, the best way out of Swansea seemed a bellyful of beer. He liked it when he could 'sedulously pluck the flower of alcohol'. To Pamela Hansford Johnson, he boasted both of delirium tremens and of being doomed to die from consumption within four years. Dylan's adolescent sense of drama crept into his letters from the amateur theatricals in which he loved to perform.

Those poets who are also actors are more popular in their lifetimes, because they can interpret their own works, bravura and pauses and all, to audiences who love rhetoric more than reading. Dylan on the platform was certainly his own best ambassador, although off it he could be his own worst diplomat. In this love of show, he was a poet's poet, a true medieval minstrel. As his friend Richard Burton would declare, all Welsh people were naturally actors, and only the worst ever became professional. Dylan's only interest at school other than English had been acting, where he had delivered a 'fresh and clean' version of the aged Oliver Cromwell, followed by his rumbustious characterisations for the Little Theatre. His friend Bert Trick witnessed how early Dylan's rich and sonorous style of reading poetry was developed, how its spells held its hearers.

Dylan's pride would be to act so well that, whatever the poem, his delivery of its would awe the audience. Richard Burton again would tell of an evening spent with Dylan and Louis MacNeice, in which both he himself and MacNeice recited their favourite and most profound piece of poetry at Dylan's request. When asked for his own, Dylan slowly said, 'This is the best poem in the English language,' and then repeated gravely and with feelings these lines:

I am
Thou art
He, she, it is
We are
You are
They are.

According to Burton, the delivery of the lines was such that the words did seem to be the ultimate in all poetry.

Such was the adolescence of Dylan Thomas, before he began to leave Swansea increasingly for London and discard the image of himself as the tough provincial, to become the fallen angel of Fitzrovia that was captured in Augustus John's famous portrait of him. Luckily, Dylan left an equally notorious portrait of himself at the close of his Swansea youth, the mocking outer cover to the inner poet.

He'd be about seventeen or eighteen and above medium height. Above medium height for Wales, I mean, he's five foot six and a half. Thick blubber lips; snub nose; curly mousebrown hair; one front tooth broken after playing a game called Cats and Dogs, in the Mermaid, Mumbles; speaks rather fancy; truculent; plausible; a bit of a shower-off; plus-fours and no breakfast, you know; used to have poems printed in the *Herald of Wales*; there was one about an open-air performance of *Electra* in Mrs Bertie Perkins's garden in Sketty; lived up the Uplands; a bombastic adolescent provincial Bohemian with a thick-knotted artist's tie made out of his sister's scarf, she never knew where it had gone, and a cricket-shirt dyed bottle-green; a gabbing, ambitious, mock-tough, pretentious young man; and moley, too.

4

Miss Johnson

Hints for Recognition

The gradual shrinking you complain of is chiefly mental, for the more
despondent I become the littler and weaker I feel.

Height – five foot six (about).

Weight – eight stone ten (about).

Hair – some sort of rat-coloured brown.

Eyes – big, brown and green (this sounds as though one were brown & the
  other green; the colours are mixed).

Distinguising marks – Three moles on right cheek, scar on arm and ankle,
  though as I generally wear socks you won't see the little mark there.

Sex – male, I think.

Voice – I suppose it would be called baritone, though sometimes it sweeps
  towards tenor and sometimes droops towards bass. Except in moments of
  hilarity, I believe I speak without an accent.

Size of feet – five (this is not number).

Cigarettes – Players, forty a day stuck in centre of mouth.

Food – hay.

from a letter to Pamela Hansford Johnson by Dylan Thomas,
written in late 1933

PAMELA HANSFORD JOHNSON was a young poet, who was sometimes published by the eccentric Victor Neuberg in the Poet's
Corner of the *Sunday Referee*. In the summer of 1933, she read a
poem by the unknown Dylan Thomas, which began:

That sanity be kept I sit at open windows,
Regard the sky, make unobtrusive comment on the moon,
Sit at open windows in my shirt,
And let the traffic pass, the signals shine,
The engines run, the brass bands keep in tune,
For sanity must be preserved.

Though not a good poem, echoing Auden and Eliot, it was good enough to make Miss Johnson write to Swansea in search of Dylan. His reply was preserved. He dispraised the poems which she enclosed, but he returned to her more of his own poems. He was glad that she was not an aged virgin, but the same immodest age as himself – in fact, Dylan lied, for he was two years younger. His reply was enough to unclench a correspondence between the young writers that was as remarkable as it was one-sided, for Dylan kept none of her letters, while she kept all of his.

Both young poets were frustrated, she by working in an office, he by feeling ignored in Wales. At home, Dylan's friends were leaving Swansea to paint or study music, while his father had cancer of the tongue, and his aunt Annie had just died. Fern Hill was no more for him, only Cwdonkin Drive or a winter cottage at Blaen-Cwm, near Llangain, from where he wrote lengthily and sadly to his new London confidante, exchanging 'insults and compliments, hasty judgements, wisdoms and nonsenses'. Photographs were also exchanged, with Dylan finding Miss Johnson's appearance a little strong for him – he entitled her Wilhelmina.

He professed himself indifferent to her accounts of her previous loves, although his little Welsh ear was open to all secrets. He recommended her to fasten her 'affections on some immaculately profiled young man, and love the swine to death. Love among the angels is a perpetual distemper.' In fact, the evidence and length of Dylan's correspondence shows him perfectly ready to love his

Pamela without passing her off elsewhere, although it took him many letters to confess to that awakening.

Most interesting in the early letters to London was Dylan's need to reveal himself, or rather, to set himself down as he wished to be. He seemed to have had an obsession about proving himself the coming poet, ribald and wise and doomed by death. He admitted to being so far behind Blake 'that only the wings of his heels are in sight'. His search was for the one right word, for there was always one and only one. That was the poet's job, not politics. 'There is no necessity for the artist to do anything . . . He is a law unto himself, and his greatness or smallness rises or falls by that.' Dylan did not want to express what other people had felt, but 'to rip something away and show what they have never seen.' Simultaneously, he was scared of his appearance to the girl he had never met, asking her not to expect too much from 'a thin, curly little person, smoking too many cigarettes, with a crocked lung, and writing his vague verses in the back room of a provincial villa.'

Between his vaunting ambition as a poet and his personal inse-curity, Dylan's letters to Pamela Hansford Johnson rose and slipped. His method of composing them was careful enough, as if he meant them to be preserved as a record of the young dog in his Swansea days. He would jot down random ideas on pieces of paper, hoard them, arrange them, then copy them out in long letters under paragraph headings. Early in the correspondence, there was a description of a Swansea day, the lazy bed-warming and smoking morning of newspapers and shaving and reading the latest periodicals and books, the walk to the pub before lunch at home, the afternoon walk on the Gower cliffs, tea and writing and evening pubs, and so to bed. Contrasted with this sloth, the same letter told urgently of the seed of resolution inside every thinking man, of the mysteries of true poetry, of the country of the spirit called God, of the man who loved as one and the same with the man who hated, for 'a blow can be a kiss out of heaven, and a kiss a blow out of hell'.

Dylan's country cottage life showed an equal contrast between the ills of the flesh and the swoops of spirit. At Blaen-Cwm, Dylan even found a bureau bearing a photograph of himself at the age of seven, 'thick-lipped, Fauntleroy-haired, wide-eyed, and empty as the bureau itself'. After a bus ride there through the industrial towns of South Wales in the grey rain, Dylan protested that he had had enough of his own bloody country, that he wanted 'out of the narrowness and dirtiness, out of the eternal ugliness of the Welsh people, and all that belongs to them'. But in contrast to his depression, he later retired 'like an emancipated Cupid with pen for arrow, to a bleak, unmaidened bed,' there to write out, 'Thomas: HIS IDEAS'. These were his attacks on sexual conventions and hypocrisy, containing perhaps a grain of hope for his future relationship with Pamela; 'the honest friendship of boy & girl' was to be allowed 'entire freedom and culmination', without any agreement between their families. His was a dream of a society where boys and girls were free to have as many lovers as they wished until they found a lover with whom they could be for a longer time, or for ever. Such was Dylan's vision in constrained wet Wales, where he often felt 'so utterly and suicidally morbid' that his letters should read like an excerpt from the *Undertakers' Gazette*.

Dylan's way out of Swansea was through voice as well as pen. He recommended to his poetess the speaking of her poems. He himself chanted aloud in a sonorous voice every poem he read. 'The neighbours must know your poems by heart,' he insisted, 'they certainly know my own, and are bound to be acquainted with many passages of Macbeth, Death's Jester, and the Prophetic Books. I often think that baths were built especially for drowsy poets to lie in and there intone aloud amid the steam and boiling ripples.' He continued in his letters to write parodies of poems and mockeries of himself, and he began to show a touching opening in the hedgehog points of the prickly young poet, saying how important to him was the freedom of his writing to her, and asking her forgiveness for his vulgarity and attacks on her poems. He promised not to run himself down any more; 'by this time you know as many of my faults and shortcomings as I do myself.' This was the first and last time he had ever written in confession and appreciation.

So Dylan moved, in the correspondence, from self-defence into self-mockery and on to a tentative trust. As he accused her from her photograph of bristling with individuality, 'images of a herd of porcupine', so he blunted his own quills. He found her a terribly accomplished person, while he could not sing or play music or draw, and even his acting was only of madmen, neurotics, nasty modern young men and vulgar comedians. He could not, however, give up his low style for her high style. He was damned if he could swap his 'warmy wombs for all the fairy bubbles this side of St Paul's. We're extremists, girl, one upstairs in our lady's chamber and the other downstairs in our lady's chamber-pot.' He urged his Pamela not to be a successful neo-Georgian poet, but to follow her 'selfspring; everything comes out of yourself, and darkness, despite what you say, has infinitely more possibilities than day.' His own poetry was not facile, but written at the speed of two lines for each 'painful, brain-racking and sweaty' hour. And as for present times, civilisation was the murderer, the coming revolution the hope, everything wrong that forbade the freedom of the individual.

So Dylan began to take off the hard mackintosh of the tough youth around town and show himself as naked and vulnerable as he was. His letters to Miss Johnson started with the urge to shock and outrage, and they ended with the need to love and be loved. His criticism of D.H. Lawrence in them was most interesting. He attacked Lawrence for his paganism and sex-and-sun loving – something that had appealed to the seventeen-year-old Dylan and was now becoming meaningless. 'A born writer is born scrofulous; his career is an accident dictated by physical or circumstantial disabilities.' Lawrence was weak and diseased, but insisted on writing of the struggle of the ideas of the pagan strong, thus making his writing 'a *lie* from start to finish'. Dylan now confessed that his own early defence of the body being all was unsatisfactory. The life of the body was terribly limited, while the life of the non-body was capable of realising infinity, of getting somewhere.

By giving up his defences, by admitting himself to himself in letters to another, Dylan did not claim to become free of his obsessions. In fact, he gloated over his complexes. They gave him an 'immense, if unholy, joy . . . like a dead man exulting in the company of his beetles'. He tried staring at his friend Daniel Jones across a room until optical distortion made him see new features on the other's face, 'the antlers of a deer, or a cloven foot, or the fingers of a hand, or a thing no words can ever describe, a shape, not beautiful or horrible, but as deep as hell and as quiet as heaven'. This was an invoking of devils, and by God, they came. Yet from the dead flesh that obsessed the young Dylan, he would build up a living flesh through his faith. Some day, however, he would try to write 'something altogether out of the hangman's sphere, something larger, wider, more comprehensible, and less selfcentred'. One day he might even come up to her expectations.

So ended the year of 1933, with Dylan setting himself good resolutions. He would think nothing in the world ugly, not even the dung of a pig. He would not label the brain into separate compartments, differentiating between the poet in himself and the need to eat lunch. 'It is said to be mad to write poetry and sane to lunch at one o'clock; but it is the other way about.' He wanted to believe in dragons and a new colour, so much whiter than white that white was black. He wanted to forget all that he had ever written and start again, 'informed with a new wonder, empty of all my old dreariness, and rid of the sophistication which is disease.' Above

D.J. Thomas –
Dylan's father and early literary mentor

William Thomas –
'Gwilym Marles',
Dylan's paternal great uncle –
a renowned preacher, poet,
politician and schoolmaster –
and the source of Dylan's
middle name.

Young Dylan with his older sister Nancy
on Swansea Sands.

D.M. Thomas
as Oliver Cromwell.

Dylan as depicted in his School Magazine
acting Oliver Cromwell in Drinkwater's play.

Cwmdonkin Park – Dylan's magical playground full of 'secret places,
caverns and forests, prairies and deserts' [Rem. Of Childhood].

THE SONG OF THE MISCHIEVOUS DOG.

There are many who say that a dog has its day,
 And a cat has a number of lives ;
There are others who think that a lobster is pink,
 And that bees never work in their hives.
There are fewer, of course, who insist that a horse
 Has a horn and two humps on its head,
And a fellow who jests that a mare can build nests
 Is as rare as a donkey that's red.
Yet in spite of all this, I have moments of bliss,
 For I cherish a passion for bones,
And though doubtful of biscuit, I'm willing to risk it,
 And love to chase rabbits and stones.
But my greatest delight is to take a good bite
 At a calf that is plump and delicious ;
And if I indulge in a bite at a bulge,
 Let's hope you won't think me too vicious.

D. M. THOMAS 3A

'The Song of The Mischievous Dog' – Dylan's first ever publication,
a humorous light poem in the S.G.S.M. Dec. 1925.

'The young Actor' – a break from rehearsals.

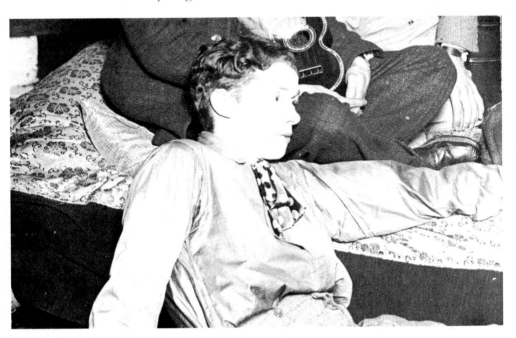

18
POEMS

DYLAN THOMAS

Published by
THE SUNDAY REFEREE and
THE PARTON BOOKSHOP
PARTON STREET, LONDON, W.C.1

18 Poems – The elegant title page to Dylan's first book,
only 250 copies were published in 1934.

'The Young Dog' Dylan playing croquet
in Vernon Watkins' garden on the Gower peninsular.

Dylan and Caitlin – newly-wed and back in Wales.

Dylan and Caitlin relaxing on the beach in Dorset.

Caitlin enjoys the pleasure of nature.

all, in the shape of a boy 'and a funny boy at that', in the very short time he thought he had left, Dylan wanted 'to live and love & be loved; I want to praise and be praised; I want to sleep and wake, and look upon my sleeping as only another waking; I want to live and die.'

So in a few months of correspondence with someone he felt to be his equal and on the side of his angels, Dylan largely matured and gave up some of his posturings and rantings for a simplicity that was to inform and illuminate his best poetry. He wanted to be free to confess himself and not feel condemned for it. He sensed the surge of potential so strongly that it induced wonder rather than self-disdain. Above all, he no longer was alone in his sprawling, dreaming youthful ambitions. If he was not certain, if he never would be able to resolve the contradictions within his society and himself, yet he could hope now, 'a short, ambiguous person in a runcible hat, feeling very lost in a big and magic universe', wishing his Pamela 'love and a healthy new year'.

The meeting between the two young poets, already half in love with each other and their own correspondence, took place in February 1934. Dylan was nineteen, Pamela Hansford Johnson was twenty-one, both were nervous. He arrived at her mother's place in Battersea in a pork-pie hat, polo-necked sweater and a raincoat with bulging pockets. He had prepared his opening remark. 'It's nice to meet you after all those letters. Have you seen the Gauguins?' He stayed for a week on that visit to London, for six weeks on his next visit, and on and off during the following year, walking with his Pamela on Clapham Common or taking the bus to Chelsea, seeing a Sean O'Casey play and trying to get a literary job. His appearance, according to Miss Johnson, was very lovable.

He revealed a large and remarkable head, not shaggy – for he was visiting – but heavy with hair of the dull gold of three-penny bits springing in deep waves and curls from a precise middle parting. His brow was very broad, not very high: his eyes, the colour and opacity of caramels when he was solemn, the colour and transparency of sherry when he was lively, were large and fine, the lower rims rather heavily pigmented. His nose was a blob; his thick lips had a chapped appearance; a fleck of cigarette paper was stuck to the lower one. His chin was small, and the disparity between the breadth of the lower and upper parts of his face gave an impression at the same time comic and beautiful. He looked like a brilliant, audacious child, and at once my family loved and fussed over him as if he were one.

Although Dylan found no work to keep him in London and had to go home to Wales – seen off by Pamela in a mood of supreme depression – he soon wrote to her that he loved her. This letter and its successor were not published, only a third one in which Dylan said that he regretted his famous love letter with all the conviction of his murky conscience, also the pathos of the second folio. He promised now to 'keep clear of the emotional element', even though he knew nothing could be spoilt between him and Pamela.

He showed himself resilient and back to his old bad jokes. He also saw a future in London opening before him, with letters from Stephen Spender arriving, and T.S. Eliot asking him to call, although he confessed to Pamela that he was 'not half as brave, dogmatic & collected in the company of Literary persons' as he might have led her to believe. His recent poem in the *Listener* had even caused Sir John Reith and the British Broadcasting Corporation to print a public apology for its obscenity, particularly for the lines:

A candle in the thighs
Warms youth and seed and burns the seeds of age . . .

Dylan claimed to Pamela that his poetry had now been banned from being broadcast, all for three other lines, not about copulation, but about a metaphysical image of rain and grief:

> Nor fenced, nor staked, the gushers of the sky
> Spout to the rod
> Divining in a smile the oil of tears.

Pamela's luck along with her love had begun to rub off on Dylan. The *Sunday Referee* offered as its Poetry Prize the printing of a book of poems. Her work had been the first book printed; his work would be the second. The editorial staff on the newspaper felt that it was impossible for so young a man to write such extraordinary poetry and sent him his train fare, in order to see if he really was the author. They were satisfied, and Dylan spent the Easter of 1934 with Pamela and her family and a future opening out in front of him; he even attended his first literary lunch at the Café Royal.

Both Dylan and Pamela were preparing to write prose now, he his *Red Book* of short stories, she her first successful novel, *This Bed Their Centre*. Dylan contributed the title to her. Even back in Swansea, he no longer felt beset by enemies on all sides, but safe in a ring of love, in the protection of Pamela's understanding. He only hated being solitary in his bedroom at home, like any young lover. 'Why aren't you here with me, in my little circle, holding my hand & braving the wicked world with me? Don't tell me – I know. The world is so wickedly wicked it won't let you brave it with me.'

Yet Dylan remained solitary and thin-skinned, living within his own pride, fierce and vulnerable, even fearful of his new love. 'How horribly easy it is to be hurt,' he wrote to Pamela. 'I am being hurt all day long & by the finest & most subtle things. So on goes the everyday armour, and the self, even the wounded self, is hidden from so many. If I pull down the metals, don't shoot, dear.'

He pulled down the metals to her in nearly every line. He wrote that he believed they would live together one day 'as happily as two lobsters in a saucepan, two bugs on a muscle, one smile, though never to vanish, on the Cheshire face,' even if their idyll ended with tax collectors, him nuts and her gaga. But in the meantime, he needed an anti-mercenary job in London. He despaired that he was 'as green as ever as to what I must do in this dull, grey country, & how one little colour must be made out of you and me.'

An exile at home, Dylan polished his *18 Poems* throughout the early part of 1934 yearning for his 'Pamela and a Chatterton attic'. He found the writing of poetry very difficult now, complaining of working on six lines as hard as a navvy, only to find that he had picked and cleaned them of all except their barbaric sounds. He decided that he was 'a freak user of words, not a poet'. He thought his lines abstruse and meaningless, not the words he wanted to express. In the end, he went away to stay at Laugharne with a new friend, Glyn Gower Jones, in 'the strangest town in Wales'.

At Laugharne, indeed, Dylan acted as if under a black spell. The whole mood of his letters changed. He wrote of working as a Symbol Simon on a novel as ambitious as *The Divine Comedy* with a chorus of deadly sins, the incarnated figures of Love and Death, an Immaculate Conception, a bald-headed girl, a celestial tramp, a mock Christ, and the Holy Ghost. He felt tortured 'by every doubt and misgiving that an hereditarily twisted imagination, an hereditary thirst and a commercial quenching, a craving for a body not my own, a chequered education and too much egocentric poetry, and a wild, wet day in a tidied town, are capable of conjuring out of their helly deeps.'

He had lost faith in his work. 'There is torture in words, torture in linking & spelling, in the snail of their course on stolen paper, in their sound that the four winds double, and in my knowledge of their inadequacy.' He agreed with Buddha that the essence of life was evil. He wrote on a 'hopeless, fallen angel of a day'. And although Dylan ended the letter with protests of his love for Pamela and disclaimers of his rantings and rumblings, yet he sent the letter to show his black-dog mood that was to end in his deliberate destruction of his intellectual love affair.

Dylan's next missive revealed his adolescent urge to swank and his puritan conscience; it contradicted the new maturity of his poems. He described, in a prose so simple and a handwriting so bad that it seemed to come straight from his sense of sin, a weekend in Gower with a reporter friend and his fiancée. All three got drunk, the girl left the friend to spend four nights in Dylan's bed, and everybody was swilling all the time. Dylan's confession continued, 'Oh darling, it hurts me to tell you this but I've got to tell you because I always want to tell you the truth about me. And I never want to share. It's you & me or nobody, you and me and nobody. But I have been a bloody fool & I'm going to bed for a week. I'm just on the borders of D.T.s darling and I've wasted some of my tremendous love for you on a lank, redmouthed girl with a reputation like a hell.' So the outpouring of shame, mixed with pride, continued to the end of the letter, with a demand that he must come to London to be with his Pamela, if she would ever see him again.

Dylan so wallowed with guilty luxury in his sense of sin and manhood and truth at all costs, that he did not calculate on Pamela's reaction. Predictably, she was mortified, writing probably about this letter in her diary on 27 May, 'Appalling distressing letter from Dylan. I cried lustily nearly all day and had to write telling him it must finish. So an end to that affair.' There was no end to that affair, since affairs of the mind as well as of the heart do not end like theatrical exits on a note of drama. Miss Johnson saw Dylan again on 12 June in London, when he stayed with her for two weeks. In her delight of getting him back and his delight of being forgiven, he pressed her to marry him, and she nearly accepted.

[69]

She had second thoughts, perhaps about the Gower episode, and the love affair was allowed to peter away in another visit of Dylan to London and in her visits to Wales to meet his family. At last she saw the room where Dylan wrote most of his poems, and which he had described to her as 'a tiny, renovated bedroom, all papers and books, cigarette ends, hardly any light. *Very* tiny. I really have to go out to turn around. Cut atmosphere with a book-knife. No red cushion. No cushion at all. Hard chair. Smelly. Painful. Hot water pipes very near. Gurgle all the time. Nearly go mad.'

The visit to Wales was not a great success for Miss Johnson and her mother, who found the garrulous Florence Thomas rather tiresome. Dylan's true age came out, a mere nineteen years old, and Miss Johnson began to realise the impossibility of the situation. Fairly conventional herself, she would not live with Dylan before marriage, and he was too young to marry and too sexually pressing to wait. His demands on her had become urgent since the Gower escapade and had led to appalling rows on his last trip to London, where he had often spent the August nights drinking in order not to come back sober to the same house where his unattainable love was sleeping. In modern times, the sexual and social barriers between Dylan and his Pamela might have been lifted with ease; but the age of permissive families was decades away from the relationship of Mr Thomas from Cwmdonkin Drive and Miss Johnson from Battersea.

So the relationship ended in a formal letter, which explained nothing, and yet had to be written. This was dated spring 1935. Dylan wrote: 'I should have written what's much too long a time ago, because there's so much to explain and so much that, perhaps, will, and should, never be explained – it means such a lot of belly rubbing and really tearful apologies on my blasted part. But never mind that. Britons never will be slaves, and I'm a rat.'

He was not. He had merely gone through a first strong passion, and he had shown the contradictions of his nature and of his society. He adored the free love of an intellectual affair with a poetess; but the free love of their bodies was impossible in the suburban surroundings of the depression years. He enjoyed the pleasures and remorses of his drunken weekend with the loose red-mouthed girl in Gower; yet his primary sense of Welsh sin, his elementary vision of a hell of poisoned drink and Jezebels, sent him to the confessional and half-way to the registry office with his Pamela within three weeks.

He was liberated by finding out that he was acceptable and lovable to the young poets of London; but he was bound by the provincial and middle-class necessity to earn enough money to set himself up in London, if he wanted to live there with a respectable wife. He could never escape the warm spoiling of his youth, the safe fug of his 'womb with a view' on to a wall and the far Welsh sea. He was too young to look after himself, let alone another. Only his poetry denied his lack of years.

5

From Chelsea to Donegal

This is the quarter of the pseudo-artists, of the beards, of the naughty expressions of an entirely outmoded period of artistic importance and of the most boring Bohemian parties I have ever thought possible.

Slightly drunk, slightly dirty, slightly wicked, slightly crazed, we repeat our platitudes on Gauguin and Van Gogh as though they were the most original things in the world. There are, of course, scores of better people that I do meet, but *these* little maggots are my companions for most of the time. I think I shall change my digs quite soon.

from a letter to Bert Trick by Dylan Thomas,
December 1934

In Dylan's unfinished novel, *Adventures in the Skin Trade*, his surrogate hero Sam Bennet spoiled his father's examination papers and dirtied his parents' house in Swansea before running away to sinful London. In actual fact, Dylan left with his father's blessing and his friend Fred Janes in a car in November 1934, to begin his independent life off the Fulham Road on the borders of Chelsea in a large room in Redcliffe Street. Their first lonely postcard of 17 November 1934, read: 'Arrived. Canvas, paper, book, no money . . . We are free most of the time and whether it would be easier to meet . . . Anywhere, or here, or there, we shall be here or there. Write soon to the poet Janes or the painter Thomas who

[72]

would wish – the mannered pigs – to see your hand in the RETURN POST.'

Dylan found it hard to work in such muddled and messy surroundings. For yards around him, he could 'see nothing but poems, poems, poems, butter, eggs, mashed potatoes, mashed among my stories and Janes' canvases. One day we shall have to wash up, and then perhaps I can really begin to work.' Winter conditions did not improve his outlook or output. By February, he was excusing his lateness in replying to a letter, because of

the abominable cold cramping the fingers, elongating the sweet hours of bed, and forcing, eventually, the tired half sleeper to erect a small fire in an insufficient grate; the skin of laziness, cancelling the positive virtue that regards sin and virtue lazily, equally and equably; the lack of ink . . .; the worries of a life that consists, for the most part, in building the brain on paper and pulling down the body, the small and too weak body to stand either the erection of a proper brain or the rubbing of saloon counters: the pressure of words, the lack of stamps; flu in embryo . . .

From the point of view of Fred Janes, Dylan was not the easiest of flatmates. There was a strange contrast between their habits. He was glued to his easel-cum-chair, experimenting continually, while

Dylan would disappear for days – perhaps weeks on end; on one occasion he went out to get a haircut and the next time I saw him was in Swansea, months later: he'd been staying in Ireland somewhere! He was undoubtedly tremendously restless coming and going at all times. Now a furious burst of work, often sitting up in bed with his hat and coat on to keep warm, then a complete disappearance from view only to turn up with

[73]

some new friend – a down and out from the embankment – a broken down American boxer, a Communist in hiding from Fascists, after one of Mosley's meetings at Olympia – they would stay for a while, maybe hours, days or weeks, then disappear for good.

Dylan wished to crash into London, or the Bohemian part of it, which had taken over from the steady values of Bloomsbury. Oxford Street split the artists' ground into a northern and southern Fitzrovia. In the north was a marginal area of hospitals, the rag trade, small business, good pubs and ethnic restaurants flanking Charlotte Street. Southern Fitzrovia lay below Oxford Street and carried the name of Soho after a hunting call 'So-ho', once shrieked to Jacobean hounds. In the 1930s, northern Fitzrovia became the Bohemia of London, snatching the reputation from Chelsea and attracting to its pubs and restaurants many of the artists and writers and provincial aspirants of the time. The converging and swirling and splitting groups in the Fitzroy Tavern and the Marquis of Granby, the Wheatsheaf and the Bricklayer's Arms, the Eiffel and the White Towers, were the Bohemians of the city and period. They were what the poet John Heath-Stubbs called them – the overspill from Bloomsbury.

The life of urban Bohemians was first described by Henri Mürger, whose scenes of their life in Paris in the 1830s were used as the libretto for Puccini's *La Bohème*. In his introduction to his book, Mürger distinguished between amateur Bohemians, who liked the style of life but were rich enough to avoid the consequences, and deluded Bohemians, who were not dedicated to the arts but to their own self-destruction for a chimera. Their axiom was that Bohemia was not a way, but a cul-de-sac. True Bohemians were called or elected to the arts. They lived between two abysses – poverty and doubt. Their everyday survival was a work of genius, a daily problem that they managed always to resolve with the help of audacious mathematics. The American poet George Sterling agreed in his definition of the two elements essential to the true Bohemian. 'The first is devotion or addiction to one or more of the Seven Arts; the other is poverty. I like to think of my Bohemians as young, as radical in their outlook on art and life, as unconventional.'

The kings and queens of pre-war Fitzrovia attracted the young and the radical and unconventional, who provided their bed-fellows and beer-money. When he was not roistering in Chelsea, the ageing painter Augustus John often went to the Wheatsheaf, where he mesmerised the young Dylan Thomas up from Wales and would introduce him to the ravishing Caitlin Macnamara, later the poet's wife, but immediately his passionate mistress at the Eiffel Tower hotel with the bill charged to John. The aged painter paid £43 for his next lunch at the Eiffel Tower. 'Little Welshman with curly hair,' the proprietor Stulik explained. 'He stay two weeks and eat. He says you pay.' And John did pay, swearing to settle the score with Dylan.

'John, a great fornicator,' the poet John Gawsworth wrote in his diary, 'is disgusted at the betrayal by Dylan Thomas who, he says, robs his £3-in-Post-Office mistresses of their honest earnings, drinks the cash, and leaves the c—t . . . Sexually speaking and economically, I suspect A.J. in his early days went further than the absurd Thomas: i.e. spent the contents of the P.O. Book but, being far from impotent, presented a bastard in exchange . . . A.J. is a God, D.T. is verbal D.Ts, anaemic diarrhoea, a Welsh slag-heap.'

There was competition and judgement between the *habitués* of Fitzrovia. One denizen, Philip O'Connor, declared that the uprooted artists were babies, prattling themselves into worlds of great achievements. Yet they never delivered anything except disasters, while they watched, sportingly, out for each other's blood. A queen of the Wheatsheaf, the painter Nina Hamnett, described the decline of the area before the outbreak of the Second World War. The news circulated that it was the only quarter in London where drinks were cheap and people amusing. The old inhabitants did not like being gazed at like so many wild animals, and Nina resented the competition of grubby medical and art students sketching the regular drinkers so that she could not.

The reputation of Fitzrovia, however, attracted wealthy young misfits from Oxford and Cambridge, and O'Connor remembered the regulars clustering round the undergraduates like wasps round a jam-pot, driving them away quickly with needs and stings. He thought there were two neighbouring Bohemias with Bloomsbury representing the rich one, even though there was no true Bohemia for the rich, only the illusion of playing the gypsy artist over a safety-net of privilege set firmly in place. One of the wealthy players was Peter Watson, the heir to a margarine fortune, who became the bankroll of the Fitzrovian artists and poets. In Stephen Spender's words, everyone loved Watson and 'he paid for everything', even giving money to David Gascoyne and Dylan Thomas, who made it all disappear 'quick as a sardine'. To O'Connor, income was the frontier of Bohemia. 'Fitzrovia was a national social garbage centre. But its inhabitants had the sweetness as well as the gameness of humanity gone off. They lived a life of pretence among themselves, and the successful ones pretended also to become outsiders, leaving the district to slander it.'

Coming to London had the virtue of making Dylan better known to the London poets and editors, and the vice of making it hard for him to do more than hack-work, reviewing books. The condition of his future life already began to be formed on this first independent stay, the excitement of the city leading to a physical collapse that sent him away to the convalescence of Wales, where he would write poetry and become bored to death. Certainly his reviews in the London literary magazines showed little depth and much invective. The provincial bombard thundered overmuch.

Even Stephen Spender was accused of lines, passages, and clusters of images of an uncommon facility and ugliness.

Dylan dressed down Thomas Moult, the unfortunate editor of *The Best Poems of 1934*, for selecting the worst poems of the year. Anthologies were, anyway, 'pernicious to the intelligent reading of poetry; one poem sucks the blood of another; two or more similar varieties of talent are apt to cancel out.' As for two books of verse by two young men, actually Lyle Donaghy and John Lehmann, Dylan started his review with the line: 'It can be said, with the utmost sympathy, that a poet should have his bottom kicked every week.' As a young reviewer, this might more aptly have been done to the bumptious Dylan, so vulnerable to criticism of his own poetry. To a Swansea reporter, he declared that most writers today moved about in gangs. 'They haven't the strength to stand and fight as individuals. But even as "gangsters" their machine guns are full, not of bullets, but of dried peas.' Life was hard for Dylan: he claimed that sometimes he would give much to be a bank clerk. Yet he liked difficulties – 'just as I like things that are difficult to write and difficult to understand . . . No poet ever understood everything he wrote himself.'

In fact, the slim volume of Dylan's *18 Poems* was fortunate in its reception, receiving praise from Rayner Heppenstall, Edwin Muir, and finally from Edith Sitwell, whom Dylan had recently called in a private letter 'a poisonous thing of a woman' who wrote 'virgin dung'. This first book of Dylan's was actually published on 18 December 1934, in an edition of two hundred and fifty copies, some of the cost provided by an avant-garde bookshop run by David Archer, a young man in revolt from his public-school and Cambridge values. Dylan was becoming a little known, mainly due to the championship of Stephen Spender, in spite of the review of his work. Even those who were wary of him and whom he often disliked, such as Geoffrey Grigson, the editor of *New Verse*, befriended his talent without accepting his nature.

[77]

An account of Dylan by Grigson in 1934 was most revealing, stating that Dylan had not yet sloughed off enough of lowest-middle-class Swansea. 'He was not so cocky. He needed assurance with which he was never generously and liberally supplied . . .' He was uncertain of the part he was acting, the Rossetti angel-poet or Rimbaud. His features were 'still unpoached at this time'. But London quickly intimidated Dylan less and was entered by him more, until he soon found that it preferred 'to aesthetic debauch, or its uniform, the Toughish Boy, the Boy with a Load o' Beer, in and out, so boringly, of the pubs'.

A contemporary and biographer, Constantine Fitzgibbon, went at length into the reasons for Dylan's continual drunkenness. Some were psychological; he simply had no head for drink and became drunk far too easily. Part lay in his Welsh background; drunkenness was a denial of his Welsh chapel education. Another cause for drinking was his insomnia; as he wrote in one letter to Miss Johnson, at times he did not sleep for a fortnight and tried everything, pills and counting sheep, getting drunk and staying sober, but nothing worked.

Dylan was not, indeed, an alcoholic. He did not crave drink, only the ease which it brought to his overworking brain and the facile company that relieved his solitude. As Fitzgibbon testified, Dylan went for weeks of his life only sipping weak tea for enjoyment, and he was no more of a true alcoholic than an outgoing woman might be a true nymphomaniac. 'Dylan drank as a woman may be promiscuous, for many of the same reasons.' And as his friend from Swansea, the artist Mervyn Levy recalled, they used to get drunk at the Royal College of Art to affront members of the Christian associations. Their heroes were Oscar Wilde and Dowson, 'gutters and drink'.

During these first London years after his drift from Miss Johnson and before his attachment to Caitlin Macnamara, Dylan's encounters with women were more casual than lustful, more for company than sensation, more passive than active. Fitzgibbon again suggested that Dylan seldom, if ever, went to bed with women before his marriage, except if he had been drinking. He was continually short of sleeping-places near to his pubs, and he would find himself in a convenient bed more often than a chosen one. If his life at the time was like Captain Cat's sea-life 'sardined with women', yet he could complain to Rayner Heppenstall one night as he sidled along to Bloomsbury and his probable fate, 'Oh God, I'm so tired of sleeping with women I don't even like.'

Many writers are bad at being promiscuous with women, from the certainty of knowing how the affair will end before it has even begun. After the deprivations of his Swansea youth, Dylan was often too weak to resist an opportunity in the glad-eyed pubs of London; but his enjoyment was always tempered by his sense of waste. And once the first desperate denial of the Welsh chapel was over, the final reason of Dylan's generous exposure of himself to drink and women in London was more through timidity than aggression, more through tolerance than attack.

In *Adventures in the Skin Trade*, he gave his young Welsh hero Sam Bennet the curious quality of attracting adventures to him by accepting life in every position, 'like a baby who had been given self-dependence'. People would come to Sam Bennet, bringing life, and he would go on. As Dylan once said, when asked why he drank too much, 'Because they expect it of me.'

Dylan's defence of himself in his novel as an innocent and his accusation of others as the inveiglers might not have been totally true, but it was partially so. Dylan was too lazy and too passive to resist temptation, particularly in London pubs; there he found social convention edged him on to excess, whereas small-town Wales had haltered him. His trouble was to find a balance and a moderation, which he never did. And if his role of the *enfant terrible* was essentially false, yet he played it to its death and his own.

[79]

Richard Burton described one other seduction in Dylan's drinking. While every man who met him loved the extraordinary warmth of his natural personality and wit, Burton said that Dylan was only the most magical and wittiest spell-binder in the world between the third and the eighth drink. Before that, he was morose. After that he was uproarious or maudlin. But in that middle ground of alcohol, that every man's land of gab, when his fears and inhibitions were gone, the actor met the poet in a riot of fancy and words.

Dylan's early ménage with Fred Janes was joined by Mervyn Levy in a new bare room nearer the transplanted heart of Chelsea – as Dylan once objected, 'this bloody land is full of Welshmen.' Levy played the Bohemian artist, while Janes played the serious one, even collecting Dylan's rent by holding Dylan's trousers (with him inside them or not) upside down until the coins fell out on the floor. Levy liked playing the clown, Groucho Marx to Dylan's Harpo – a role which Dylan could play very well with his halo of yellow curls and eyes full of innocence and deceit.

Moreover, Levy encouraged the fantastical vein in Dylan as well as begging on the pavement for beers, if necessary. As he wrote, 'Wandering the streets . . . we wove incredible fantasies as we so often did when we were together for a while. How many mice would it take to pull the London to Glasgow Express? Half a million? A million? Oh! More, lots more! Don't forget they'd have to pull it at the same speed as it normally goes. Anyway, if you had *enough* mice you could do it. It stood to reason.'

This was the time that Dylan was more waif and stray than plump and bully, the period of the famous Augustus John painting of him which hangs in Cardiff. This was described by Dylan as 'that dewy goblin portrait frog-goggling . . . out of the past'. In the memoirs of the London Bohemians of the 1930s, indeed, Dylan did wander on and off like a Robin Goodfellow. To the poet George Barker, he was small and thin, with a dirty wool scarf wound around himself like an old love affair, looking like a runaway schoolboy. To the impressionable Sheila MacLeod, he was 'a handsome cherubic youth, crowned with an aura of thunderous power and doom'. To another observer of the young poets who clustered around the Archer bookshop, 'young though he was, he seemed old: a strange grubby figure, dressed in a skimpy, green sweater, with tousled hair and bitten nails,' a forerunner of the Angry Young Men. 'Some of his admirers likened him to Chatterton. Others expected him to commit suicide quite soon; his enemies described him as a boor.'

His later friend Vernon Watkins, eight years older than Dylan, had not bought a copy of *18 Poems*, because he had known Dylan only as a child. Then they met in Wales. 'He was slight, shorter than I had expected, shy, rather flushed and eager in manner, deep-voiced, restless, humorous, with large, wondering, yet acutely intelligent eyes, gold curls, snub nose, and the face of a cherub. I quickly realized when we went for a walk on the cliffs that this cherub took nothing for granted. In thought and words he was anarchic, challenging, with the certainty of that instinct which knows its own freshly discovered truth.' As a Welsh reviewer of *18 Poems* had already noted: 'It is like no poetry that ever came out of Swansea before. Strange, compressed, tortuous, exciting by its wild leaps of imagination, and tantalizing by its equally strange lapses into baffling obscurity, it will puzzle, irritate, and yet, we venture to say, grip the interests of the reader as few modern poets do.'

Such was Dylan's manner and reputation in his first long stay in London. He could get away with any excesses, because he appeared elfin and his work was promising. Yet nothing is further from performance than promise. Dylan found that London was not a place to work in, only to fritter and bluster away his talent for words. At the beginning of March 1935 he was back in Swansea, writing to Glyn Jones that the trials of his life had proved too much for him, the courts had found him guilty, and that he had come home for a few weeks rather hollow-eyed and with little real work to his credit. He had to go to the country to get on with his poems. Even Swansea, especially Swansea, was no womb now, for the few old friends who remained had jobs and marriages, and the writing Dylan had no time for too much beer in the evenings – 'at least temporarily'.

So Dylan left soon for the ultimate seclusion, a cottage in Donegal converted by the American artist Rockwell Kent into a studio. Despite their caginess towards each other, Dylan met with Geoffrey Grigson, for his first week there. Grigson described him as the Swansea Changeling, translated to the side of an Irish 'cold, soul-tightening ocean', chanting 'We are the Dead' to the echoes reverberating 'We are the Dead, the Dead, the Dead, the Dead.'

Peat fires and potheen, potatoes and buttermilk healed Dylan on his own, once Grigson had gone. The poet described his impressions to Bert Trick, saying he was as lonely as Christ some-times in a poor, dirty land, where 'the pits rut and scrabble in the parlours', and the people were superstitious or mad, whining or boring, and the blood sports were blood sports. Naturally, the west coast of Ireland was beautiful and wild, but it could not cure Dylan's restlessness. Like the swallow in the hall of the Old English poem, *The Wanderer*, Dylan felt he had to pass on, even if he was to come back to Wales. 'I wouldn't be at home if I were at home. Everywhere I find myself seems to be nothing but a resting place between places that become resting places between resting places themselves . . . the body and the brain, all the centres of movement, must shift or die. It may be a primary loneliness that makes me out-of-home. It may be this or that, and this or that is enough for today. Poor Dylan. Poor him. Poor me.'

If Dylan was full of self-pity about the intolerable essence of his craft, the solitude needed to write poems, he was perfectly inconsequential about his method of escape. Having announced that he would stay until September, he walked off early over the hills and far away without paying his bills to the local farmer and his wife, who had looked after him. One of Dylan's friends finally settled the matter, but Dylan was merely pouting and unrepentant, 'acting the injured Suckling'.

These were the repetitive extremes of Dylan's life, the interminable reactions of his later days. Excess in the city sent him off to boredom in the country. After a little rural work at words, he had to scuttle back to the city, leaving his peace and his bills behind him. As he wrote at the end of 1935, he had spent most of the summer in Donegal and had done a lot of good work there, but 'a wave of rather alcoholic laziness' had set in since at home in Swansea, and he was only just beginning to put words together again. 'The poetry machine is so well oiled now it should work without a hitch until my next intellectually ruinous visit to the bowels of London.' Poor Dylan. Poor him.

That ruinous and repetitive visit to London was confessed in his unfinished work, *Adventures in the Skin Trade*. Although it was not written until the first years of the war, and although it was set down after his loving memories of Swansea collected in *Portrait of the Artist as a Young Dog*, it represented the full imaginative rebellion of Dylan from his secure childhood and youth, swaddled by villas. As Vernon Watkins explained, *Adventures in the Skin Trade* was meant by Dylan to be 'an extended story, not strictly autobiographical, but bearing a relation to the two parts of his experience, his own actions and the actions of his dramatised self'. The hero would actually do what Dylan dreamed of doing and never did; he would make a total break with the past before taking the same train to unknown London which Dylan had actually once taken.

In its conception, the novel was ambitious. Dylan intended his passive young hero, Sam Bennet, to lose each of his seven skins to one of the seven deadly sins until finally Sam would be left naked, after a comic journey through the circles of the Inferno of

London. In a short piece entitled 'Prologue to an Adventure', published in the first number of *Wales* in the summer of 1937, Dylan's thoughts of flaying London were already beginning to form. His narrator was himself, walking through the wilderness of this world, the strange city of a 'mister lonely', beckoned by 'ladies on their own, . . . naked as new-born mice'.

Heaven and hell shifted up and down that city: and the night-club he entered was explicitly called the Seven Sins. There two little girls danced barefoot in the sawdust, and a bottle splintered on their legs. A negress kissed him, but he escaped into the night and the rocking city, where 'the seven deadly sins wait tidelessly for the moon'. Now he went in at the door of the Deadly Virtues, where the sea of faces parted, and he stumbled forward to the fiery bottles. 'Brandy for the dreamer,' a wooden voice said, and he got drunk before lurching out again into a city where the pavements were mazes dragging down the drinkers from a world of light into a crawling sea-bed.

The confessional themes for the later novel remained in the structure of *Adventures in the Skin Trade*. Dylan did not begin that work until 1941, and he dismissed his intentions as merely 'a mixture of Oliver Twist, Little Dorrit, Kafka, Beachcomber, and good old 3-adjectives-a-penny belly-churning Thomas, the Rimbaud of Cwmdonkin Drive.' He wrote the first three chapters of the novel quickly, carried along by the comic fantasy and anarchy of its surface, almost unconscious of its obsessive basis.

Vernon Watkins thought that Dylan abandoned the novel half-done because the greater and crueller anarchy of the war, which distorted London beyond measure, took the place of his night-mare city. The black-out made London even more of a pit than Dylan's imagination could dig for it. In fact, the novel stopped because he became a screenwriter later that year, and somehow he never got back to his fragment, even though he was trying to con-tinue the novel as late as the year before he died.

The first obsession of the novel was escape, the break with Swansea. Sam Bennet silently and ineffectively destroyed his parents' home in Mortimer Street, off Stanley's Grove, with his eyes still heavy from a dream of untouchable city women. He wanted to cause so much destruction that he would never be *allowed* to come home again. Fearing his own ignorant, lazy, dishonest and sentimental character, easily influenced by anybody, he wished to prevent himself from returning by an unforgivable act of wanton destruction. So, when his family saw him off to the train – still unaware of the minor havoc in Mortimer Street – Sam Bennet could turn for a last look and see 'three strangers waving'. He had cut his family wholly from his future. Dylan in his fantasy wanted to escape completely from Swansea; but he never did, and never could.

The second obsession of the novel was the total acceptance of the world and the refusal to manipulate one's own life. Dylan, in fact, used his contacts with poets and editors of poetry magazines to further his career; but Sam Bennet's first act in the train lavatory was to flush away the helping names, the influential numbers, the addresses that could mean so much in London. Sam only kept his money and the number of an unknown girl. His first act on arrival was to sit in the railway buffet and have a beer, although, sadly enough, Swansea was already there in the person of the insufferable Ron Bishop, also up in the smoke. Yet Sam accepted the encounter with Mr Allingham, the furniture dealer, only too ready to help drink away the money of any new arrival, rattling his fortune, fresh as Copperfield, straws in his hair. Sam's belief that something would happen, must happen to him, finally annoyed Mr Allingham into shifting him from the buffet with a bottle stuck on to his finger. Sam had to 'give London a chance'.

The third craving of the novel was Dylan's love of a secure and overstuffed disorder. His own bedroom in Cwmdonkin Drive was a ragbag of clutter, while Mr Allingham's room was a pyramid of unsaleable junk – and the best room Sam had ever seen. People disappeared in the fullest room in England. They remained lost and easy and safe. Anyone could do anything in the room, nobody could see anyone. The perfect anarchic world.

At the High-Class tobacco shop, however, Dylan's fear of strict female authority surfaced, the terror of the cruel and precise women that were to rule Dylan's pages, from Mrs Dacey with her head so prim that it might spill to Mrs Ogmore-Pritchard who shoo'd away the old sun for fear it might spoil the polish. In these comic gorgons, there was always a suppressed lust that was even more terrifying than their schoolmistress morality. Mrs Dacey mothered the fainting Sam about the hair and the mouth, while creaking like a door; she was all lechery and fingers cold as lizards; her hand ached on his thigh, five dry fishes drying on a cloth. The chapel dress on the bawd, the holy face fronting the suppressed desire, these Welsh habits clung to some of Dylan's own actions as well as informing his perceptions.

In Sam's bath scene with Mrs Dacey's daughter, Polly, Dylan's sexual passivity was revealed. Sam was conned by Polly into stripping naked and getting into an ice-cold bath in the dark. Polly said she was undressing; but she did not. She fed him eau-de-Cologne instead of brandy, knocked him out while she disappeared. So the simple provincial was made bare and broken by the promises of loose city women, while he actually had no sex and a split head for his trouble. Above all, Sam did not choose debauchery; its deceitful disaster inflicted itself upon him.

Now Sam Bennet reached the fundamental obsessions shown in 'Prologue to an Adventure'. Mr Allingham, Mrs Dacey, and the homosexual George Ring took him on an infernal drunken plunge into the dives of London in a chapter headed 'Four Lost Souls'. They danced in the rain in the wet Edgware Road; they drank in a bar called the Antelope where they talked fiercely of sex; they took a taxi to the West End to call at the Gayspot, which was like a coal cellar, the bottom of the pit. 'This was a breath and a scar of the London he had come to catch. Look at the knickerless women enamouring from the cane tables, waiting in the fumes for the country cousins to stagger in, all savings and haywisps, or the rosy-cheeked old men with buttonholes whose wives at home were as lively as bags of sprouts.' Then the women spoke and disillusion set in. Pub talk was pub talk anywhere. 'London is not under the bedclothes where all the company is grand and vile by a flick of the cinema eye, and the warm linen doors are always open.' The knickerless women, first seen as enamouring shapes, were really 'dull as sisters, red-eyed and thick in the head with colds; they would sneeze when you kissed them or hiccup and say Manners in the dark traps of the hotel bedrooms.' The way to hell was still paved with good conventions.

The dive into the semi-depths ended with a fracas in the Gayspot, with a bounce out on to the pouring pavements, and a final plunge into the Cheerioh, which was the ocean bed of London. There the drinkers and dancers were the older brothers and sisters of those in the Gayspot. 'There were deep green faces, dipped in a sea dye, with painted cockles for mouths and lichen-ous hair, sealed on the cheeks; red and purple, slate-grey, tide-marked, rat brown . . .' They were, as Mr Allingham said, 'the foul salt of the earth'. And on this profound and briney observation, *Adventures in the Skin Trade* came to an unfinished end, half-deep in the bowels of the infernal tides of London.

The reasons why Dylan never finished his comic novel were many. Factually, the war and scriptwriting intervened; psycholog-ically, Dylan lost over the years the fine salacious wonder of the Swansea Youth meeting the first shock of London – he had been there too often by the time he tried to complete the novel. Also Dylan despised his comic writing, however serious it was at base, for being done with relative ease and interfering with the hard drafting of his poetry. Not until the critical success of *Under Milk*

Wood in his dying days could Dylan rate his prose as highly as his verse. Humorous writing was a paying and enjoyable interlude, not his craft or sullen art.

There was a deeper reason for *Adventures in the Skin Trade* remaining unfinished. Dylan was perhaps too young and unaware to chronicle his own self-destruction in London. Although his poetry throughout was permeated with the wish for death and the love of death, it was still poetry. A factual, even if amusing, description of a disintegration of a fantasy self through the seven deadly sins might need a certain detachment from the process, in which Dylan was far too involved.

In a letter to Vernon Watkins of 1936 in which Dylan declared himself a man of the aspidistra, he also boasted that he had been in London for over a week, 'and the same things happened there that always happen: I kept roughly a half of my appointments, met half the people I wanted to, met lots of other people, desirable and otherwise, and fully lived up to the conventions of Life No. 13: promiscuity, booze, coloured shirts, too much talk, too little work.' There was an involvement with the city, which was inescapable and slowly fatal to Dylan. He could mock that involvement and describe it, but he could not end it or describe his end from it.

Adventures in the Skin Trade remained fresh because provincial boys were always arriving in the 'capital punishment' of the great city, expecting signals and wonders and debauches, and finding wet pavements and insecurity and disillusion. Another Welsh writer who arrived in London at much the same time as Dylan, Gwyn Thomas, also described his first impressions, so similar to Sam Bennett's.

The minute I got off the train my feet seemed to be perched on rolling boulders. And I have never landed there since without a sense of malignant insecurity. My mood has always been that of

[88]

the man in whose wake I once left the station. He was walking up the ramp that leads into Praed Street. He was with his wife. He was lugging a large, scuffed suitcase. There was a look of crumpled innocence about them both. She was looking around her edgily, without gladness. He pointed at a newspaper poster. It said: *Nude Blonde Found Strangled In Paddington.*

'See?' said the man. 'They're at it all the time.'

Whatever he boasted, however much Dylan seemed a tiddler in the London depths, or indeed a chicken in a country Eden, he was always in his nature the boy from the Uplands, safe only in Swansea, whose adventures in the skin trade might result from the stripping of his skins by the deadly sins, but who would always grow those skins again as a defence of his own private world, in the way that the villas of the suburbs put on fresh coats of paint each spring to keep up with the Joneses.

6

Soho and Surrealism

═══════

The word is too much with us. He raised his pencil so that its shadow fell, a tower of wood and lead, on the clean paper; he fingered the pencil tower, the half-moon of his thumb-nail rising and setting behind the leaden spire. The tower fell, down fell the city of words, the walls of a poem, the symmetrical letters.

Dylan Thomas, 'The Orchards'

CAITLIN MACNAMARA, who was later to marry Dylan, lived much the same Bohemian youth, since the old painter Augustus John was her neighbour in England. In her *Not Quite Posthumous Letter to My Daughter*, she told of that frivolous age of the talented and creative youth of the 1930s, with its 'trivially crazy idea that it was *clever* to drink to extinction; and *clever* to be promiscuous to dulling the discrimination of the flesh.' Anyone who did not join in these clever pastimes was considered drab and boring. Later on in life, Caitlin lamented that she was hypnotised by these commands to do wrong, that she had never raised herself by as much as an aspidistra or a potted palm into the enviable ranks of accepted uniformity.

The trouble was the old romantic and decadent notion that every orgy of excess was permitted to the Artist. In fact, in

Caitlin's opinion, Dylan had a longer life than he might have had, because of his poverty and relative lack of fame in his early days. Success, and early success, was the tomb of the writer. 'Luckily to Dylan the tomb came late, and he solved the issue of integrity quite simply; whenever in town, and confronted by the easier joys of telling endless stories to buddies in pubs from morning till night, by not working at all until he was back in the penitence of the country.'

Such was the Soho and Fitzrovian background of Dylan's drinking days for twenty years, from the first time he came to London until the keg-of-bitter end. He never escaped his simple pleasure at the wickedness of London compared with Swansea or Laugharne. He knew it was a fraudulent wickedness, froth on the same old brew. Yet the city was bigger and the conversation was better and the big names more exciting. And there were his literary cronies, Norman Cameron and Geoffrey Grigson and William Empson, Rayner Heppenstall and Ruthven Todd, as well as his personal companions, Fred Janes and Mervyn Levy, in whose rooms he would sleep on a mattress on the floor, never possessing even a room of his own, but always in those of other people who paid the rent.

Soho and Fitzrovia were to Dylan a state of mind, with companions without boundaries, the escape from any need to do more than beg money and entertain. As he wrote in apology to a critic he had failed to see in 1936, 'When I do come to town, bang go my plans in a horrid alcoholic explosion that scatters all my good intentions like bits of limbs and clothes over the doorsteps and into the saloon bars of the tawdriest pubs in London.'

Yet London did provide for the young Dylan one of his more intense influences, from which he also had to escape – Surrealism. The obscurity of his earlier poems, the strange and intense juxtaposition of adjective and noun, and the violence of the imagery, made many critics confuse Dylan's youthful work with that of

English Surrealist poets such as David Gascoyne. The first and most important of these was Richard Church, who was the poetry editor at J.M. Dent and Sons, and who had agreed to publish Dylan's second book of verse, his *Twenty-five Poems*. Church was a poet himself, who preferred Dylan's simpler efforts and criticised him for the Surrealism of his current and more obscure poems, stating that he had been 'caught up in the delirium of intellectual fashion of the moment'.

This stricture was denied by Dylan, since many of the poems had originated in his earlier *Notebooks*. He wrote back on 9 December 1935 that he had very little idea what Surrealism was and had never even read a page of Surrealist literature. Anyway, his poems were not Surrealist. A friend of his had replied to his enquiry, saying that Surrealist writing need not have any meaning at all. And while his own writing did suffer from 'immature violence, rhythmic monotony, frequent muddle-headedness, and a very much overweighted imagery', every line was meant to be understood. The reader should comprehend each poem 'by thinking and feeling about it, and not by sucking it in through his pores, or whatever he is meant to do with Surrealist writing'. Anyway, in a later letter to Church, Dylan wrote he hoped that an understanding of him would not be confined to his simpler poems, and that the day might come when none of his poems would be 'indecently obscure or fashionably difficult'.

Richard Church did accept the poems for publication in September 1936, and Dylan became caught up in the latest intellectual fashion. He went to the Surrealist Exhibition held in the New Burlington Galleries in the June of that year. Although Dadaism and André Breton, Salvador Dali and Paul Eluard had become commonplace in smart Paris, they were hardly known in London. The attack of Surrealism on established values in art was still shocking across the Channel. And to a provincial youth like Dylan, this international subversion of all artistic traditions made his own defiance of conventions look no more important than a dog lifting its leg against a lamp-post.

At the exhibition itself, which Dali attended in a deep-sea diver's suit, Dylan is said to have handed out boiled string in cups, enquiring politely, 'Weak or strong?' As a young and rebellious poet, the richer circles of the Surrealists took him up briefly; he could be guaranteed in his role as an *enfant terrible* to add to the sensationalism of the moment. A unique Surrealist sketch signed by Dylan has survived. Created for the children of John Davenport, it showed a figure in a red suit on top of a ladder, balanced on a bicycle on a beach, delivering 'A PETITION TO THE GOVERNMENT', which was a white woolly giraffe of total goofiness.

Constantine Fitzgibbon stated that the Surrealist Exhibition led to Dylan's final débâcle before his marriage. He was introduced to a call-girl at a private view, who wore over her face a wire cage covered entirely with roses. Later at her Mayfair house, Dylan caught a venereal disease. The treatment for it was long and painful in the days before penicillin. He had to retire to bed in Swansea for eight weeks, taking the salvarsan cure, which his mother did not know about. He begged Geoffrey Grigson not to talk about his illness, for such news 'might ruin his lecherous chances'. His absence led to Caitlin Macnamara's return to Augustus John, yet Dylan's conscience was pricked. A sense of guilt led him to confess to her for the first time that he loved her. He also had to give up alcohol during the cure, and the effect on him was melancholy.

Yet if Dylan's physical brush with the international Surrealists was painful, their influence on his prose for four years was undeniable. Some of Dylan's stories were being published in Roger Roughton's Surrealist magazine, *Contemporary Poets and Prose*, and they were also to be published in his next work to be printed, *The Map of Love*. While the stories of this period have occasional images of power such as 'night came down, hand on thigh', they

[93]

are dense and clotted, full of mysticism and lack of clarity, violence and a striving for the unusual.

There were intimations of themes to come in some of the tales, particularly in suggestions for the future Captain Cat of 'In the Direction of the Beginning', lines such as 'he was a shoreman in deep sea, lashed by his hair to the eye in the cyclop breast, with his swept thighs strung among her voice; white bears swam and sailors drowned to the music she scaled and drew with hands and fables from his upright hair . . .' None of the stories succeeded in themselves; they were knotted in their own webs of words, unlike the poems of that period, which were not wilfully obscure, but 'a string of words stringed on a beanstick'.

The stories did, however, link Dylan to his bardic roots, although the Surrealist techniques of the prose were not disciplined or clear enough to create a popular myth. In 'The Orchards', the hero's name was significantly Marlais, Dylan's own middle name, taken from the bardic name of his great-uncle. In the tale, the hero 'sharpened his pencil and shut the sky out, shook back his untidy hair, arranged the papers of a devilish story on his desk, and broke the pencil-point with a too-hard scribble of 'sea' and 'fire' on a clean page. Fire would not set the ruled lines alight . . . nor water close over the bogy heads and the unwritten words. The story was dead from the devil up.'

So it was. No incantation of complex prose could make the Druidic pages blaze in Dylan's surreal period, except perhaps in 'The Burning Baby', which is the best of the overcharged efforts of this time. Basing himself on the true history of Dr Price of Llantrisant, a self-declared Druid and the apostle of cremation, Dylan wrote of his costumed old man burning the body of his dead illegitimate baby on the top of a hill at Caerlan. Dylan distorted the truth to make the baby incestuous, conceived of the old man's daughter, while the old man himself was changed to the vicar Rhys Rhys in order to shock opinion still more. In his sermons, the vicar preached of the sins of the flesh and prayed to God in the image of our flesh. Later 'merry with desire, Rhys Rhys cast the bible on the floor.'

Dylan's early prose suffered not only from the obscurities of Surrealism, but from the need to offend gratuitously. In addition, his overt concentration on Welsh myth rather than on the Welsh present and people made these first stories somewhat unreadable. Richard Church might have been wrong in criticising Dylan's early poems for the influence of Surrealism, but he certainly seemed to have put Dylan's prose on the right path. He suggested that Dylan write stories about his original world of Swansea, something that Dylan was to do in his first successful prose writing, the stories collected in *Portrait of the Artist as a Young Dog*. These stories did, indeed, put an end to the surreal fever in Dylan's prose of the late 'thirties and get him finally to work on what he had promised Church, a Welsh idea which 'would clear up nearly all vaguenesses and leave me something practical and (almost) commercial to work upon.'

Throughout this period, a poet and critic called Henry Treece was working on articles which would become the first major evaluation of Dylan's poetry, although it would have to wait until 1949 to be published after the war. Treece would begin his study with a defence of Dylan from the charge of being a Surrealist poet. He would compare poems of Dylan's with those of David Gascoyne, but he would prove fairly conclusively that Dylan's images came from the subconscious controlled by logic rather than from the spontaneous subconscious. To Treece, a Surrealist line such as 'the strident crying of red eggs' had little value beside wrought lines of Dylan's such as:

Which is the world? Of our two sleepings, which
Shall fall away when cures and their itch
    Raise up this red-eyed earth?

In his pre-war letters to Treece, Dylan thanked him for his early
defence and praised him for his critical method. Treece's lucid
comparisons convinced Dylan once again that 'my own sane bee
in the bonnet can never be a pal of that French wasp forever sting-
ing itself to a loud and undignified death with a tail of boiled
string.' Dylan had recovered from his fashionable bath in claptrap
and clap. So much so, that when Treece's study of him did finally
appear, Dylan inscribed a copy, 'To hell with this stinking book.'
He ended by stating his profound disagreement with the Surrealist
manifesto. 'To them, chaos is the shape and order. This seems to
me to be exceedingly presumptuous; the Surrealists imagine that
whatever they dredge from their subconscious selves and put
down in paint or in words must, essentially, be of some interest or
value. I deny this.'

The forty-three of Dylan's poems collected in book form and
printed in 1934 and 1936 had an impact at the time. Treece called
the publication of *18 Poems* 'a wordy revolution' against the *fin de
siècle* period of disillusionment and disintegration in contemporary literary circles, with all political statements seeming suspect
on the Right and the Left. The slim volume assaulted the chaos
and melancholy in poetic circles. How different were these poems
by a nineteen-year-old from 'Mr Eliot's *Waste Land* depression,
W.H. Davies's leisurely perusal of sheep and cows, Mr [Herbert]
Read's Great War reminiscences and Auden's telegraphese'.

Later in an acute article on Dylan called 'Druid of Her Broken
Body', the author and critic John Wain was to support Treece in
his view of his times. Wain corroborated that Dylan grew up in a
bad literary period, in some ways worse than more modern days.
In the 1930s, there was a general assumption that the regions were
dead and London was the source of all thought and intellect.
Roots had to be chopped off, heritage denied, accents clipped to
the standard speech of the metropolis. Dylan did not conform to
the conventions of his time, neither to the social-conscience

verses of Auden and his followers, nor to the wilful obscurities of the imported Breton school.

As Wain wrote, logically applied Surrealism was as sure a recipe for mediocrity as logically applied Social Realism. Dylan looked resolutely into his inner adolescent world of symbol and myth, of sex and God and death. As he wrote to Treece at the time, enclosing his first draft of 'How Shall My Animal': 'I hold a beast, an angel and a madman in me, and my enquiry is as to their working, and my problem is their subjugation and victory, downthrow and upheaval, and my effort is their self-expression.'

Treece found *18 Poems* far superior to Dylan's next book of *Twenty-five Poems*. There was some merit in his judgement. The first volume represented the reworking of many of the best poems from the four Swansea *Notebooks*, while in the second volume, at least sixteen of the poems can be traced back to the same *Notebooks*. These versions were thus Dylan's second selection from the extraordinary outpourings of his adolescence. They often represented, perhaps as sops to Richard Church, the more simple poems of Dylan's youth, written before the first published work.

When Treece attacked Dylan for apparently printing two styles of poetry in his second volume, and when he called the result 'a poetic scrapbook', Dylan admitted to the charge. He had reworked 'the straight poems' of his earliest period of the *Notebooks* and had leap-frogged them over the back of the volume of 1934 to appear for the first time in 1936. 'Both books contain poems written over about eight years,' Dylan wrote; 'there is still no definite sequence.'

Yet the simplicity of some of these poems and the championship of Edith Sitwell, who roundly declared that no other young poet showed so great an achievement, led to an unusual success for the second volume. Four editions were printed of *Twenty-five Poems* and three thousand copies were sold. Although other critics carped at Dylan, they could not detract from his unexpected success.

[97]

Geoffrey Grigson might later declare that this minor celebrity in London was due to a confidence trick played by the poet on the public, but Treece and Wain would disagree. Dylan's limited success with his contemporaries was due to his unique gift for dealing with fundamentals in the lives of most people, with birth and death, with God and the Devil, with love and decay. Despite the obscurity of many of his poems of this period, a quality rooted in human nature always structured each poem, as the bones the body.

The 'straight' poems of the second volume became some of the more famous of Dylan's work. Perhaps, as Treece said, the first *18 Poems* had a 'foetal unity' and were preoccupied with sex, at its most intense in 'I See The Boys Of Summer In Their Ruin' and 'The Force That Through The Green Fuse Drives The Flower'. Yet none of them had the urgent cadences, the sense of bardic incantation mixed with biblical memories, that lay in Dylan's modern psalm against dying, 'And Death Shall Have No Dominion'. If the ten sonnet-like sequences of 'Altarwise By Owl-light' were more wilfully obscure than anything in the first volume, yet the final versions of Dylan's earlier 'straight poems' made him at last seem a true people's poet in 1936. 'This Bread I Break' was worthy to rank beside Dylan's denial of death in his *Twenty-five Poems*; these were the two great songs of the new bard of Wales at last reaching his true wide audience and flock.

> And death shall have no dominion.
> No more may gulls cry at their ears
> Or waves break loud on the seashores;
> Where blew a flower may a flower no more
> Lift its head to the blows of the rain;
> Though they be mad and dead as nails,
> Heads of the characters hammer through daisies;
> Break in the sun till the sun breaks down,
> And death shall have no dominion.

Three times in his life, Dylan answered a set of questions about his attitude to poetry. The first, at the age of nineteen, was written for *New Verse* and demonstrated much of his ambivalence at the time. While he strongly asserted that his poetry reflected his individual struggle from darkness towards some measure of light and thus declared his distance from the socially committed poetry of Auden and his school, yet he put himself on the side of a form of Marxist control of the means of production, in order to make possible communal art. He supported the narrative poem from tradition, justifying it by reference to T.S. Eliot and rejecting any form of Surrealist poem by association. He also rejected spontaneous creation, pointing out the hard labour of his craft. His claim to the influence of Freud was probably lip-service. Dylan's images at the time seemed largely the product of his subconscious without benefit of self-analysis on the Freudian model.

1. Do you intend your poetry to be useful to yourself or others?
To both. Poetry is the rhythmic, inevitably narrative, movement from an overclothed blindness to a naked vision that depends, in its intensity, on the strength of the labour put into the creation of the poetry. My poetry is, or should be, useful to me for one reason: it is the record of my individual struggle from darkness towards some measure of light, and what of the individual struggle is still to come benefits by the sight and knowledge of the faults and fewer merits in that concrete record. My poetry is, or should be, useful to others for its individual recording of that same struggle with which they are necessarily acquainted.

2. Do you think there can now be a use for narrative poetry?
Yes. Narrative is essential. Much of the flat, abstract poetry of the present has no narrative movement, no movement at all, and is consequently dead. There must be a progressive line, or theme, of movement in every poem. The more subjective a

[99]

poem, the clearer the narrative line. Narrative, in its widest
sense, satisfies what Eliot, talking of 'meaning', calls 'one habit
of the reader'. Let the narrative take that one logical habit of
the reader along with its movement, and the essence of the
poem will do its work on him.

*3. Do you wait for a spontaneous impulse before writing a poem; if so, is
this impulse verbal or visual?*
No. The writing of a poem is, to me, the physical and mental
task of constructing a formally watertight compartment of
words, preferably with a main moving column (i.e., narrative) to
hold a little of the real causes and forces of the creative brain
and body. The causes and forces are always there, and always
need a concrete expression. To me, the poetical 'impulse' or
'inspiration' is only the sudden, and generally physical, coming
of energy to the constructional, craftsman ability. The laziest
workman receives the fewest impulses. And vice versa.

4. Have you been influenced by Freud and how do you regard him?
Yes. Whatever is hidden should be made naked. To be stripped
of darkness is to be clean, to strip off darkness is to make clean.
Poetry, recording the stripping of the individual darkness, must
inevitably cast light upon what has been hidden for too long,
and, by so doing, make clean the naked exposure. Freud cast
light on a little of the darkness he had exposed. Benefiting by
the sight of the light and the knowledge of the hidden nakedness, poetry must drag further into the clean nakedness of light
more even of the hidden causes than Freud could realise.

*5. Do you take your stand with any political or politico-economic party or
creed?*
I take my stand with any revolutionary body that asserts it to
be the right of all men to share, equally and impartially, every

production of man from man and from the sources of production at man's disposal, for only through such an essentially revolutionary body can there be the possibility of a communal art.

6. As a poet what distinguishes you, do you think, from an ordinary man?
Only the use of the medium of poetry to express the causes and forces which are the same in all men.

7

Peace before War

I think a squirrel stumbling at least of equal importance as Hitler's inva-
sions, murder in Spain, the Garbo-Stokowski romance, royalty,
Horlicks, lynchlaw, pit disaster, Joe Louis, wicked capitalists, saintly
communists, democracy, the Ashes, the Church of England, birth
control, Yeats' voice, the machines of the world I tick and revolve in,
pub-baby-weather-government-football-youthandage-speed-lipstick,
all small tyrannies, means tests, the fascist anger, the daily, momentary
lightnings, eruptions, farts, dampsquibs, barrel-organs, tinwhistles,
howitzers, tiny death-rattles, volcanic whimpers of the world I eat,
drink, love, work, hate and delight in – but I *am* aware of these things
as well.

from a letter to Henry Treece by Dylan Thomas,
6 or 7 July 1938

DYLAN met Caitlin Macnamara at the Wheatsheaf in Charlotte
Street in April 1936, and they began an impassioned affair.
Although Augustus John had introduced his young mistress to the
Welsh poet, he did not know immediately of her new love, even if
most of Fitzrovia did. Dylan was her own age, and his lethargic
and intense character fitted marvellously with her own alternating
rhythm of laziness and violent energy. She had trained as a free-
style dancer in the mode of Isadora Duncan, and her flight from

her parents' broken marriage and the decaying charms of the family mansion in Ireland had taken her to the passions and liberties of the John household, Paris and Soho. Now she returned to Augustus John, while Dylan went through his Surrealist fever and fell sick of it and decided that he loved Caitlin, after all.

The next meeting between the two of them led to a confrontation with Augustus John, who glossed over the affair in his autobiography. The three of them had met again at the Georgian house of the writer Richard Hughes, which was called the Castle because it adjoined the ruins of the old fortifications at Laugharne. They set off to visit the National Eisteddfod, which was being held in Fishguard that year near the circle of ancient Druid stones overlooking the old harbour. Caitlin and Dylan's public attraction for each other led finally to a drunken fight in a car-park between Dylan and Augustus John, in which the old painter knocked the young poet down and drove off with Caitlin into the night.

Dylan, however, kept on writing to Caitlin the love-letters of his joy and intentions. 'I don't want you for a day', he wrote . . . 'a day is the length of a gnat's life: I want you for the lifetime of a big, mad animal, like an elephant.' His language then became that of one of the first of the flower children. 'We'll always be young and unwise together. There is, I suppose, in the eyes of the They, a sort of sweet madness about you and me, a sort of mad bewilderment and astonishment oblivious to the Nasties and the Meanies; you're the only person, of course, you're the only person from here to Aldebaran and back, with whom I'm free entirely; and I think it's because you're as innocent as me.' Naturally, they knew the lust and the dirty jokes and the dirty people, and they could count their change and cross the road, but their innocence was truly deep, so that they knew nothing much of the ways of the world, and did not care about that ignorance.

Such innocence of the ways of the world was assumed. Both Caitlin and Dylan had other lovers and entanglements to shuck, before they could come together. Dylan had been living with Emily Holmes Coleman, who was in love with him. She was an American friend of Djuna Barnes and the secretary of Peggy Guggenheim. She had also published an autobiographical novel, *The Shutter of Snow*, in 1930, telling of her confinement in an asylum after the birth of her baby. She had been attached to the poet George Barker, who was attracted to another neurotic writer Antonia White, who was a friend of David Gascoyne. So when he met Dylan with Caitlin on 13 April 1937, he was taken aback. They were off to see *The Golem*, but in Leicester Square, Dylan got a lump of dust in his eye and had to be taken to a chemist's shop. 'Really rather repulsive as he sat there with his inflamed eye and ugly nose, his face thrown back, the boracic dripping between his corduroyed knees; but one did not feel repulsed, all the same.'

Gascoyne was shocked to hear that Dylan meant to marry Caitlin within a few days' time. 'She is small – florid in miniature, with an incipient Roman nose – blonde, *almost* fluffy, wearing a brick-red coat and skirt. She says very little. My first impression was of a hard innocence, obtuse, hermetic, and a concealed but very precise knowledge of how to deal with anyone she might want to deal with.' After passing on the news, Gascoyne met his usual literary gang in Fitzrovia that night:

> The usual blurry chaos ensued. Ruthven Todd arrived, very drunk, with a long story about fighting a gang of toughs; and Nina Hamnett, of course, also drunk and with long stories about everybody one has ever heard of; odd lesbians; vaguely literary young men; a rather nice sculptor called Richard Hughes; a young upper-class Cambridge friend of apparently everybody – and God knows who else! One's head went round. George [Barker] very wisely left less than half way through the evening. When the pub closed we all went

to another, then in a taxi to the Café Royal, then to some Soho café-bar place, Ruthven getting more and more maudlin and incoherent, and the subject of Emily and Dylan and Kathleen M. [Caitlin] incessantly recurring. Emily seems to be 'bearing up under the strain' marvellously well, as they say, but Tony [Antonia White] seems to think this is a danger signal.

This sort of thing usually overwhelms me, I get more and more depressed and dumb and finally go home feeling quite dead. But this evening I somehow managed to keep my head and to take in everything that was going on all around. It was extremely complicated. For once, I even quite enjoyed it all, in a detached and wondering way.

The whole point being:

a) the impingement of worlds;

b) the illusion of human intercourse ('There is no conversation').

What Gascoyne was doing was giving a profound picture of the drunken aimlessness and complexities of Fitzrovian life, from which Dylan had to escape, if he ever wanted to produce his best poetry. As Gascoyne reflected the following morning:

It is really shocking to see how everyone collides about in their own world, completely oblivious, almost all the time, of everyone else's. What impressed me most last night was the way everyone was so utterly at cross-purposes, unable to understand anyone else's objective even for a moment. Emily and Tony misunderstanding one another, Emily not really understanding Dylan or he Emily, Barker unable to understand Ruthven, and everyone else around making the most fantastic mistakes at every moment, and nobody, except Tony, having even the faintest idea about me . . .

Over the next two months, Dylan did decide to put a temporary end to his Fitzrovian shenanigans and to go to Cornwall for the summer to marry his Caitlin Macnamara. The last sight that Gascoyne had of him was in May, when he met Antonia (Tony) White at Heneky's and became involved with her in an evening with Norman Cameron and Dylan, all ending in a gruesome scene in Antonia's flat, with she and Dylan 'pretending to play "wolf-dogs" on the carpet and altogether getting on each other's nerves in a bad way, till I blunderingly tried to stop them and succeeded in putting Dylan's back up. "Where are the halo and the wings," he asked, "of Tony's guardian angel?" ("He is *not*", she remarked, of Dylan, "a child of light." We none of us felt like one. It was very miserable).'

If not a child of light in London, Dylan became so with Caitlin in Cornwall. Both were penniless and free and in love. They were married suddenly on 12 July, in the Penzance registry office, 'with no money, no prospect of money, no attendant friends or relatives and in complete happiness'. The reasons for the marriage seem to have been contradictory – a mutual latching on to a passion to last a lifetime; Dylan's fear of losing his girl again to Augustus John or another; his residue of Welsh puritanism and respectability that made him want to show his wife proudly to his family at home; and finally the absurd belief at the heart of all first marriages for love, that the ceremony would magically end all problems instead of beginning them.

After such a glad beginning, the young lovers were lodgers at the mercy of family and friends. A visit to the new Thomas home at Swansea ended in the disapproval of Dylan's mother at Caitlin's gypsy dresses, so she and Dylan moved to her mother's house near Augustus John in Hampshire. There Dylan wrote to Watkins, 'Caitlin & I ride into the New Forest every day, into Bluebell Wood or onto Cuckoo Hill . . . We are quiet and small and cigarette-stained and very young.' As always, Dylan was living on nothing and looking to his friends for financial help. In a letter to Henry Treece, he wrote that he had suffered from living from his neighbours' hand to his mouth. 'I have achieved poverty with distinction, but never poverty with dignity; the best I can manage is dignity with poverty.' If he was going to go on writing any longer, he would have to give up living, and live in a vacuum.

Dylan's alternatives seemed limited to him. They were either the slow debts of the country or the quick debts of the city. Even in London, he could still be living in penury and in doubt. 'In London, because money lives and breeds there; in penury, because it doesn't; and in doubt as to whether I should continue as an outlaw or take my fate for a walk in the straight and bowler-treed paths.'

Of course, Dylan could never have measured out his days by commuter trains. He was no T.S. Eliot or Wallace Stevens, to fit his verses to his regular hours. He even laughed at his own bombast in thinking he could be a daily worker for bread or wages. 'The conceit of outlaws is a wonderful thing,' his letter continued. 'They think they can join the ranks of regularly-conducted society whenever they like.' He certainly could not.

As Caitlin later testified, Dylan never suffered from the usual doubts about his craft or the form of it. 'From the minute he saw daylight: he had no choice but to write.' All that seriously bothered him was the arrangement of patterns of words, 'and which particular word, out of his glorious riches of words, was the most apt. That, and a continuous headache of debts.' Between money and muse, poverty and craft, Dylan's marriage skimped and bloomed. Some money did somehow trickle in, from a poem here, a story there, from an occasional review, and even from the United States, where James Laughlin of New Directions was persuaded to buy up the rights on Dylan's next five books for a reasonable sum in dollars, to be paid weekly in a form of allowance. This income was enough to help him move on to Laugharne, where Richard Hughes found Caitlin and him a fisherman's cottage for themselves.

So began Dylan's long association with Laugharne, which he had first seen in the black mood before his original sinful Gower affair. Then he had noticed its curious Englishness in manners and accent, although it was surrounded by hundreds of miles of Welsh countryside. Laugharne had seemed to him populated by a race of thick-lipped fools sweating their lives away cockling on the deadly sands.

This was a church town rather than a chapel town with a polyglot population of Welsh descent, mixed with Dutch and English and Spanish blood. Occupied rather than lived in, it was beleaguered as well as beguiling, with its chief function waiting for something to happen and living on the dole. As Dylan remembered later, it was an island of a town, where some people started to retire before they started to work, and others seemed 'like Welsh opium-eaters, half asleep in a heavy bewildered daze'.

With Caitlin pregnant in the summer of 1938, Laugharne was a haven for Dylan. The only worry, as always, was the bills. Although his publishers gave them a little regular money and his friends like Lawrence Durrell contributed the occasional pound, 'crisper than celery and sweeter than sugar', he failed to get a grant from the Royal Literary Fund. Debt drove him back to Caitlin's mother's house for her to have the baby there; but pride brought him back to Laugharne again in the spring of 1939 and in the last seasons before the war.

Although Laugharne was cheap and comforting for Dylan, London could provide the only solution for his poverty. Yet in this country bliss of his, the skin-stripping capital had become hateful. As he wrote to Watkins after three dark days in London, it was an insane city of the restless dead. 'Every pavement drills through your soles to your scalp, and out pops a lamp-post covered with hair. I'm not going to London again for years; its intelligentsia is so hurried in the head that nothing stays there; its glamour smells of goat; there's no difference between good & bad.'

Even if Laugharne was bitter and cruel because of small debts, yet he and Caitlin were happy there. If only it were not for money, and tiny sums of money at that. 'The garret's repugnant,' as Dylan complained to Treece. 'I can't keep a steady hand and wag a wild tongue if worry like a bumbailiff sits silently nagging by my side. Poverty makes me lazy and crafty. I'm not a fineweather poet, or a lyrical tramp, or a bright little bowl waiting for the first fine flush, or a man who cuts his face with a grand phrase while shaving; I like regular meals and drink and a table and a ruler – and three pens.'

So Dylan remained at heart roomed and domesticated. He wrote best when living within his comforts and spoiling by his women. In those early days of marriage, as Caitlin wrote, 'Dylan may have been a skinny, springy lambkin, but I was more like its buxom mother then.' She managed the little house and the baby Llewelyn on almost no money. She provided Dylan with his interminable stews, which he liked in his stomach before the solace of the pub, where she also went with him throughout the country years.

Rural living did not mellow Dylan's arrogance about his fellow writers. He was not one of those authors who find that a little fame of their own makes them able to forgive the abilities of their contemporaries. Dylan's book reviews in the pre-war years showed a continuing disrespect for the great names of the past and present. Emily Dickinson's poetry, arguably as good as William Blake's, was dismissed by Dylan as an oddity, 'the curiosity of a narrow abstract vision interpreted in legal, commercial, financial and mathematical phraseology, furnished with the objective commonplaces of a life lived between the sewing basket and the bird bath, the Bible and the account book.'

To Dylan, the preliminary novel of genius by Samuel Beckett, *Murphy*, appeared to be the product of an Irish comic journalist forced to write in an advanced Paris-American quarterly, or of an old-fashioned music-hall character-comedian trying to alter his act for a pornographer's club, 'and always it is Freudian blarney: Sodom and Begorrah.' William Carlos Williams's reputation was built up like a pack of visiting cards, while his *Life Along the Passaic River* was ruined by 'the affected *and* insipid convention of trying to write like an enemy of writing'. H.G. Wells was a specimen of 'the boy who never grows up; a sort of Peter Bedpan'. John Dos Passos's masterpiece, *U.S.A.*, was the uncondensed material for the Great American Novel, 'that ton of a dry dream which has ruined beyond repair such a number of ambitious men', while the structure of the novel opened, like a bolstered bosom, to let us all in. Even Kafka's *Amerika* had a beginning and a tail, no middle and no sting. Only Flann O'Brien got a pat on the head for his *At Swim-Two-Birds* and for not being at the forefront of modern Irish literature among several others, whose names Dylan pretended not to remember.

On the eve of war in 1939, Dylan published his third book, *The Map of Love*. He included some of his mythological and Surrealist stories, which he had hoped to publish under the title of *The Burning Baby*. The title also included the last of the overworked poems taken from his four Swansea *Notebooks*. Of the sixteen poems in *The Map of Love*, eleven seemed to date from his adolescence, of which eight were merely pruned rather than rewritten. While 'How Shall My Animal' was completely worded anew except for the first line, Dylan only actually wrote five new poems in the two and a half pre-war years at the beginning of his relationship with Caitlin.

These new poems showed Dylan consciously trying to be simpler and stronger. In 'After The Funeral' at last he admitted to the reality and melancholy of his loved aunt's end.

> ... her death was a still drop;
> She would not have me sinking in the holy
> Flood of her heart's fame; she would lie dumb and deep
> And need no druid of her broken body.
> But I, Ann's bard on a raised heart, call all
> The seas to service that her wood-tongued virtue
> Babble like a bellbuoy over the hymning heads ...

Dylan no longer showed the bombastic and self-conscious pretence of uncaring for family death, chronicled in his youthful letter to Trevor Hughes of January 1933, when he had tried to ignore his aunt dying of cancer of the womb. Then he had boasted of 'the pleasant death-reek at my negroid nostrils', and had declared that he had not the faintest interest for her or her womb, and would only miss her biannual postal orders. Now that he had grown into love of Caitlin, Dylan had also grown into a respect for death, including his own.

That respect also showed in his powerful new poem, beginning:

> Twenty-four years remind the tears of my eyes.
> (Bury the dead for fear that they walk to the grave in
>   labour) ...

Dylan remained obsessed by the fact that his end was natural and inevitable, but at the moment he was more occupied with his sensual strut. Yet even the delights and sloths and respectabilities and commitments of marriage had their price. They kept him away from his true calling. The best poem in *The Map of Love* was Dylan's lifelong cry from the heart at his failure to write more poems.

> On no work of words now for three lean months in the
>   bloody
> Belly of the rich year and the big purse of my body
> I bitterly take to task my poverty and craft.

To take to give is all, return what is hungrily given
Puffing the pounds of manna up through the dew to heaven,
The lovely gift of the gab bangs back on a blind shaft . . .

When the timeless time-wasting days of first marriage began to
be counted in babies and hours, the war would have begun. The
lovely gift of the gab was not to work much on poems for a
decade, only at the warm running pieces of memory that began in
the stories of *Portait of the Artist as Young Dog* and ended in the nos-
taligic BBC pieces of his last years. Dylan's friend Vernon Watkins
noticed how suddenly Dylan began to write about people as they
actually were and behaved. As for the stories of Dylan's youth,
'very Welsh they were, more true to Swansea than Swansea itself'.

This collection of autobiographical pieces gave the exaggerated
essence of the place, a reality that could be recalled rather than seen.
The nostalgia was mixed with both comedy and irony. If the title of
the book owed something to James Joyce's *A Portrait of the Artist as
a Young Man*, Dylan always denied that he had read a word of the
Irishman's memoirs before writing his own book – but then, as
Caitlin always said, Dylan had a congenital passion for lies.

These Swansea tales were Dylan's most coherent work in prose.
Although each story was self-contained, taking Dylan from Fern
Hill in his boyhood to the pubs of Swansea beach of his young
manhood, yet they served as the ten windows of an upbringing
that was as solid and semi-detached as an Uplands villa. Dylan's
wicked observing of Welsh observances, both social and Sunday
ones, made the stories a comic delight. In the first story, 'The
Peaches', where plump Mrs Williams with the big car visited the
poor farm-wife Annie, she refused the hoarded tinned delicacy of
the title with the squashing and self-revealing remark, 'No, no, Mrs
Jones, thanks the same . . . I don't mind pears or chunks but I can't
bear peaches.' Such small-town snobbery was a gift to Dylan's
sense of mimicry and skill at word-play.

The other themes of the poet sounded through the stories. The boy Dylan staying at his grandfather's cottage dreamt of 'heavenly choirs in the sticks, dressed in bard's robes and brass-buttoned waistcoats', while his grandfather went off to be buried in his ancestral ground at Llangadock before his time, 'like a prophet who has no doubt'. Sex showed its fumblings and misdirections and impossibilities in the triangle of Patricia and Edith and Arnold, in the bullied calf-love of 'Extraordinary Little Cough', in the unmeant squalor of 'Just Like Little Dogs' where the brothers exchanged girls on the night sand, and finally in the climb through the labyrinth of the guest-house stairs to the lost Lou of 'One Warm Sunday' in which Dylan mourned the unapproachable pub women of his adolescence who later smothered him in his London years.

Schoolboy humour and cheeky jokes, pub chatter and mock-tough talk, made real the adjectival paragraphs of the overblown descriptions of self and place, with Dylan remembering when 'the eccentric ordinary people came bursting and crawling, with noise and colours, out of their houses, out of the graceless buildings, the factories and avenues, the shining shops and blaspheming chapels, the terminuses and the meeting halls, the falling alleys and brick lanes, from the arches and shelters and holes behind the hoardings, out of the common, wild intelligence of the town.'

The advance and the declaration of the Second World War in the late summer of 1939 led the London poets and artists to personal decisions, some wise and some silly. The luckier ones were excused the moral choice of being combatants or conscientious objectors by physical disability. Of the neo-Romantic poets who went to Fitzrovia as their wartime university, John Heath-Stubbs was half-blind and the South African poet David Wright was deaf. Many tried to avoid call-up for as long as possible, including the editor Julian Symons and the alcoholic art historian Ruthven Todd, but above all they felt that the war had been declared against each man individually. Like Muslim fanatics, most of the Fitzrovians thought that a German bullet had their name on it, something which gave them a good reason to avoid going near flying bullets. As Todd wrote:

Time may have answers but the map is here.
Now is the future that I never wished to see.
I was quite happy dreaming and had no fear:
But now, from the map, a gun is aimed at me.

The quiet desperation which afflicted England on the outbreak of the conflict threw nearly all the artists out of work – if they had any. The orchestras had no bookings, the theatres went dark. The resting actors congregated in the Duke of Wellington near the Globe Theatre and the White Horse near the Apollo and the Salisbury near the Coliseum where they met the disparate group of poets published by Julian Symons in *Twentieth Century Verse*, Roy Fuller and Gavin Ewart, D.S. Savage and Ruthven Todd, Keidrych Rhys and Lynette Roberts, who later married each other. The little magazine's successor *Now* was edited by George Woodcock, who moved the regular drinking spots of its contributors to Soho and the Swiss Tavern and the York Minster, usually called the 'French pub', which Woodcock and the eclectic editor with the paper supply, Tambimuttu, used as virtual offices.

Up the Soho streets were the Highlander and the Crown and Two Chairmen, where the film-makers trained by the four luminaries of the pre-war documentary cinema, the ex-painter Humphrey Jennings and the realistic John Grierson and Basil Wright and Cavalcanti, all had beer-money falling from their pockets because of the multitude of newsreels and propaganda shorts demanded by the Ministry of Information. Documentary films were to be a lifeline to many of the unemployed writers such as Dylan Thomas and the actors and the artists, mixing in Soho where the theatres and casting agencies and film cutting-rooms and editorial offices and small publishers clustered round a hurly-burly of restaurants and cafés, clubs and pubs. Although the members of the various professions and trades used to stick together and talk shop, they were thrown into each other's company by the circumstances of the war, the shortage of drink, the loss of many of them to the armed forces, and the curious camaraderie which hardship and the blitz were to create among different groups and classes.

For young men waiting for call-up or on leave from the forces, Fitzrovia was a heady education. What drew the young poet Michael Hamburger there was not only his Oxford friends, John Heath-Stubbs and David Wright, but the feeling that the Soho pubs broke down class and nationality. Though predominantly upper middle class or parasitical on it, 'that war-time and pre-war bohemia could accommodate the Welshness of Dylan Thomas, the Scottishness of W.S. Graham, of John Burns Singer and of the two [artistic] Roberts, Colquhoun and MacBryde, the East End Jewishness of Willy Goldman. Paul Potts was a Canadian, Tambimuttu a Ceylonese.' There were painters like John Banting already out of fashion; and others – like John Craxton, John Minton, Keith Vaughan, Lucian Freud or Francis Bacon – recently established or not yet at the height of their reputations. Hamburger was unaware of any professional envy or competition among these drifting configurations. He did not know what people did by day, if anything at all. There were quarrels, but nothing to do with the intrigues that beset most literary groups or magazines. The cult of success was considered vulgar, and Hamburger was too young yet to see the objections to the cult of failure.

The literary heir of Gawsworth, who was reviewed favourably in comparison with T.S. Eliot before the war, knew the attraction of the lack of success to Fitzrovian drinkers. Jon Wynne-Tyson was attracted to the Soho pubs, as most nascent writers were.

The war came and gave them a form of camaraderie. They were potential victims of a holocaust which destroyed people, young minds trying to find their way and an identity. None of them had a real amount of output behind them. They talked about art and themselves rather than got on and did their own thing – only fragmented things without a background which was destroyed by the war. They were struggling for a background which they found difficult to realise. The war produced the Bohemia which was the death of art and identity. It was a decade of fragmentation.

Yet this very fragmentation would create the opportunity for a democratic and real culture within the Churning of Fitzrovia and its outlying stamping-ground, Chelsea. Five categories of artists were bound to meet there during the war: the home Fitzrovians, who avoided conscription or worked for the government or the forces stationed near London; those escaping from provincial exile in training camps or on conscripted duties working on the land or in factories; those on leave from service overseas; the refugees from Europe or the voluntary exiles driven back to England by shame or the belated urge to serve their country; and, finally, the Commonwealth and American artists and journalists, shipped by the tides of war to London. 'Even if you steer clear of Piccadilly with its seething swarms of drunks and whores,' George Orwell would write after the invasion of foreign allies, 'it is difficult go anywhere in London without having the feeling that Britain is now Occupied Territory.'

Before he was thrown into this seething maelstrom, Dylan had to avoid conscription. In truth, this was more a matter of cowardice than conviction. He wrote to his new patron and friend, John Davenport, that he was desperate to get a job because all the unemployed were going to be conscripted. 'My one-&-only body I will not give.' He did have his name put down for work at the

Ministry of Information, on the 'crook list' with 'all the half-poets, the boiled newspapermen, submen from the Island of crabs, dismissed advertisers, old mercuries, mass-snoopers'; but nothing came of it.

The outbreak of war seemed to Dylan to be a deliberate attack on himself and his powers of poetry. He complained of the beginning of 'Dylan-shooting' in a copy of *The Map of Love* dedicated to Pamela Hansford Johnson. He had not the means to flee to neutral America like W.H. Auden and Christopher Isherwood. So he chose the path of trying to become a conscientious objector, not from religious scruples, but simply from a distaste for the disruption of his own life. As he wrote to Bert Trick, 'I can't raise up any feeling about this war at all. And the demon Hitlerism can go up to its own bottom. I refuse to help it with a bayonet.'

Friendship and physical incapacity luckily solved the problems of Dylan's selfish pacifism. When he tried to encourage his literary acquaintances to contribute to a symposium in support of his objector's position before he was called to a tribunal, he usually received a cold shoulder or a hot reply to his effort to form 'a common or rarefied front or backside'. When his time for the tribunal came, however, Dylan found he could not stomach a plea of religion as an excuse not to fight, so he did not plead at all. Instead, the army medical examiners in their mercy diagnosed him as an acute asthmatic and he was graded at the bottom level of those fit to soldier. If war was not Dylan's concern, those who ran the war were equally unconcerned about him.

So Dylan's pacifist blunder ended in a whimper. More real was the problem of debt. He had to raise £70 to stop himself and his family from being turned out of their cottage in Laugharne, with all their possessions seized. Stephen Spender organised an appeal which was sent to leading literary figures. The money soon was found, with a small surplus. This was a tribute to Dylan from a group of writers whom Dylan rarely praised and was to parody to literary death in his libellous novel, *The Death of the King's Canary*.

The work was written during 1940 on a drunken stay in the Cotswolds with John Davenport at the Malting House, where Davenport used to entertain writers and musicians seeking escape from the war. Alternate chapters and even pages were written by the two collaborators, but the manuscript was unfunny without being ironic, harsh without being penetrating. The plot dealt with the choice of a successor to a dead Poet Laureate, and it lampooned the bad behaviour of most of the living authors whom Dylan envied. One person not caricatured in the manuscript was the blond and attractive William Glock, the Controller of Music at the BBC, who managed to have affairs at this time both with Davenport's wife Clement and with Caitlin who was flattered with such attention. Their literary husbands hardly noticed.

The one affectionate portrait in *The Death of the King's Canary* was naturally reserved for Dylan's fantasy self, who was a young and handsome Welsh poet called Owen Tudor with a dark and subtle look, as thin as Dylan was now becoming stout and beer-bellied. One line only from Owen Tudor prophesied the self-mocking comedy of Dylan's later style: 'When I am a rich man with my own bicycle and can have beer for breakfast, I shall give up writing poetry altogether and just be absolutely disgusting.'

The war, however, and lack of riches stopped Dylan from writing poetry and set him on the absolutely disgusting search for a job. He had to earn money by doing something. Scrounging in wartime was almost as bad as treason.

8

The War at Home

The home was to Dylan, more especially, a private sanctum, where for
once he was not compelled, by himself admittedly, to put on an act, to
be amusing, to perpetuate the myth of the Enfant Terrible: one of the
most damaging myths, and a curse to grow out of. We lived almost separate lives, though physically close, and passed each other with a
detached phrase on strictly practical matters; as though we were no
more than familiar landmarks, in the furniture of our minds. Excluding
the times, more frequent at night, when the house rattled, and banged,
and thudded, and groaned with our murder of each other.

Caitlin Thomas, *Leftover Life to Kill*

THE forced gregariousness, the necessary intimacy of writers and
artists in the war years, discovered its milieu in the pubs, which
also had their golden age. As Theodora Fitzgibbon explained in
With Love:

They were the only places in wartime London where one could
entertain and be entertained cheaply, and find the companion-
ship badly needed during the war. For people of our age with
no solid, regular accounts behind us, it was difficult to come by
even a bottle of sherry. Food was very scarce indeed, and food
for the occasional dinner party had to be hunted for and often

took many hours and much traipsing about. Many middle-aged people used to drinking at home found their only source of supply was the pubs. Bombs dropping on London could not be so easily heard when one was in them, and the company lessened apprehension. I loved pubs, they were new to me and I liked being able to find friends I wanted to see in a certain place at a certain time. Dylan had previously pointed out to me that the link between host and guest was a tenuous one, but that it never arose if one met in a pub.

Dylan Thomas, indeed, was one of two wartime Fitzrovians who would rise to international fame without rejecting his pub past; the other was Francis Bacon. But as the Irish writer and Fitzrovian Anthony Cronin observed, their success was a result of a defiance of the world and its fashions rather than a cultivation of them. For most Fitzrovians, success passed them by or they lost interest in it. But 'none of these people made a virtue or a life-style out of rejection or bohemianism . . . They knew that artists as well as many other people had been poor and that some people must accept poverty as preferable to the waste of time and the corruptions inherent in the struggle to avoid it.' The uncreative, Cronin believed, were most likely to confuse a mere life-style with a creative discovery. Those who clustered round the real artists and poets frequently did.

Fitzrovia was an initiation for young men and women, a world of sought encounters. 'One unlearned a lot and developed social skills,' John Heath-Stubbs said. 'It was a school of life which lasted till the late 'forties. In a night, how many distinguished people you met.' When the fledgling novelist Peter Vansittart wanted to win some sort of reputation without earning it, he roamed the statutory Soho pubs. He stepped over the drunken Dylan Thomas. From a safe distance he watched the two unpredictable artists, Robert MacBryde and Robert Colquhoun. He dodged for weeks buying Julian Maclaren-Ross a drink as he held court, using his silver-knobbed cane as a sceptre and a truncheon.

David Wright found Tambimuttu and Michael Hamburger, then on leave, in the Swiss pub and was introduced to Dylan Thomas, drunk and helpless and woebegone, nattily dressed like an unsuccessful commercial traveller. At the French pub, where old Gaston Berlemont presided with his grey handlebar moustache beneath the photographs of famous prize-fighters and music-hall stars, Dylan met everybody who would buy him a drink, just as the crown princess of the Wheatsheaf, Nina Hamnett, jingled her money-box at anyone who could fill her glass and then said, 'Have you the mun, deah?' Graham Greene was drinking in the Horseshoe with friends during the 'great blitz' of Central London, and he found all the Soho restaurants closed except for the Czardas in Dean Street. He ended on fire duty all night in Bloomsbury and, unshaven in the morning, was berated by a chemist when he asked for razor-blades: 'Don't you know there's a war on?'

Encounters proliferated in Soho pubs and drinkng-places throughout the war. Stories of meetings in them were legion. But the questions were these. The meetings, were they inspirational? Did they produce better music or writing or painting, or were they merely a relief from the disciplines demanded by the arts? In Maclaren-Ross's case, he wrote after midnight and after drinking, and his early material came from his army days; only at the end of his life did he write his *Memories of the Forties* about his times in Fitzrovia. What was clear from that book was that pub life was full of fun and games, verbal and physical, like Maclaren-Ross's own match game called Spoof. Yet also clear was the convenience of the pubs for young and unknown writers, particularly those from the armed forces on leave, in meeting their peers and their editors.

After their time inside military psychiatric hospitals, the discharged Fitzrovians joined those who avoided serving because of physical disability, such as Nina Hamnett's friend who came back to the Wheatsheaf, saying, 'None of the fighting forces will have me so I have returned to the old corps, the "Saloon Barrage".' Even John Lehmann, cruising on the last night of the blitz in the Fitzroy Tavern, bought Nina Hamnett several drinks before he picked up a sardonic young man in uniform, who spent the night chuckling macabrely as the bombs crumped down. He tended to remain on the outskirts of the pub groups, his eyes narrowing over his cigarette-holder, assessing 'the relative pleasures of company against the nuisance value of unwanted or rejected contributors to *New Writing*'.

Those who were excused military service because they were already serving the BBC or the Ministry of Information could also congregate in Soho, Louis MacNeice and Cecil Day Lewis and George Orwell, who resented being made to put out propaganda, wasting his brains on war and feeling mean because other men were dying. And finally, littérateurs like Lehmann and Connolly were exempt because they were leading magazine editors, considered a reserved occupation for the very few.

As war broke out, Dylan had begun looking for both a way not to die and a way to keep alive. The film industry seemed a possibility. Dylan wrote to John Davenport from Laugharne: 'Does the film-world want an intelligent young man of literary ability, self-conscious, punch-drunk, who must (for his own sake) keep out of the bloody war, who's willing to do any work – provided of course that it pays enough for living? I'm not expecting plums from the war . . .' John Davenport could not help Dylan; but in 1940, Dylan met Ivan Moffatt, the son of the actress Iris Tree. Moffatt was working for Strand Films, a company run by Donald Taylor and deputed by the Ministry of Information to make many of its short films, which were designed to boost morale on the home front. Taylor recognised the need for good writers of prose as well as efficient scriptwriters. In the film-struck Dylan, he found a marvellous journeyman with words and a pupil at film technique.

As a boy, Dylan had always loved the cinema. In *Return Journey*, he wrote of 'the flea-pit picture-house where he whooped for the scalping Indians with Jack Basset and banged for the rustlers' guns'. With his café friends in Swansea, films were always part of the gossip and gibble-gabble, as they talked about 'Augustus John, Emil Jannings, Carnera, Dracula, Amy Johnson, trial marriage, pocket-money, the Welsh sea, the London stars, King Kong . . .' In his spoof play written for Pamela Hansford Johnson, *Spajma and Salnady: Or Who Shot the Emu?*, Dylan explained his nineteen-year-old cinema taste as particularly influenced by German Expressionism, including: *The Cabinet of Dr Caligari, Atalante, The Student of Prague, The Edge of the World, Vaudeville, Waxworks, The Street, M,* and *The Blue Angel* with *Sous les Toits de Paris, Potemkin, The Gold Rush, The Three Little Pigs,* and the Marx Brothers' comedies thrown in for good measure. Otherwise, he claimed rarely to go to the pictures, as the vast majority of films were notoriously bad. As for Norma Shearer, Lionel Barrymore, Clark Gable, George Raft, Joan Crawford, Uncle Tom Navarro and all, he preferred 'abstruse poetry, symbolical fiction, discordant music, and beer'.

In fact, Dylan was far more serious about the cinema than he pretended. He had revealed his interest in the subject while still at school. There he had contributed to the Swansea Grammar School Magazine an article on the development of the modern cinema from D.W. Griffith to the coming of sound. If his judgements were adolescent, his sense of the future of the medium was evident. Sound was all-important, both to him and the film industry. The article ended: 'Even film-pioneers must start at the beginning of sound-film production, and learn what there is to be learnt.'

The good fortune of Dylan was the revival of the British cinema with the war documentary, subsidised by the state. Co-director of the blitz film, *London Can Take It*, the former painter Humphrey Jennings would achieve a poetic authenticity in *Fires Were Started*, his depiction of the London Fire Brigade and Auxiliary Fire Service, in which so many writers and artists were enrolled. The documentary techniques spilled over into a distinguished series of war films; one of them was Cavalcanti's chilling work of the imagination, *Went the Day Well?*, in which Graham Greene recounted the occupation of an English village by Nazi paratroopers wearing British Army uniforms.

The apogee of the cinema of the early war years was *In Which We Serve*, produced by the Italian refugee Filippo del Giudice, with Noël Coward playing the role of his friend Lord Louis Mountbatten almost as well as Mountbatten played it, and showing a restraint and power of observation that denied his usual mannerisms. The careful social delineation of the characters of the sailors on the doomed destroyer made the film a lighthouse to the new British cinema with its strong documentary tradition. 'It took a war to compel the British to look at themselves,' a contemporary critic wrote, 'and find themselves interesting.'

The documentary film meant pay and salvation to some of the Fitzrovians, particularly those attached to Donald Taylor at Strand Films in Golden Square. The Highlander in Dean Street was one of the Soho pubs frequented by technicians and continuity-girls from the Films Division of the Ministry of Information. There Taylor met Julian Maclaren-Ross, who had already been recommended to him by Dylan Thomas. The two fledgling scriptwriters soon encountered and appraised each other:

Dylan wore a green porkpie hat pulled down level with his slightly bulging eyes: like the agate marbles we used as Alley Taws when I was a boy in France, but a darker brown. His full lips were set low in a round full face, a fag-end stuck to the lower one. His nose was bulbous and shiny. He told me afterwards that he used to rub it up with his fist before the mirror every morning until it shone satisfactorily: as a housewife might polish her doorknob or I the silver-topped malacca cane that I affected in those days.

Instead of writing a script on the Home Guard, they used to spend their time drinking Irish whiskey in the back bar of the Café Royal, Scotch ale in the Wheatsheaf, gin in the Highlander, and whatsoever passed for drink in the Horseshoe Club. Dylan used to attack Maclaren-Ross for his dandy airs, stating, 'Sordidness, boy, that's the thing,' although Dylan's friends suggested that his girth should make him do his war work as a tank.

A new art form developed, the documentary with staged scenes, which was to become a mainstay of post-war television — that remarkable British invention was shut down abruptly by the British Broadcasting Corporation in the first week of the war with the tart remark that as so many things were closing, television was not singled out for neglect. The acted documentary film, however, *Target for Tonight* reconstructed realistic scenes in the fuselage of a grounded Wellington bomber, F. for Freddie, to simulate an air raid over Germany. Its propaganda value was great, showing to seventy million people in Britain and the United States. Its success led to a new confusion between the actual and the artificial, the documentary and the feature film, the truth and the forgery, that corresponded to the privations and the hopes of those waiting to go to war.

The ageing critic Robert Herring went to one party crowded as usual with the young makers of documentary films. A director was complaining that he could not find a suitable crater to shoot, although there were thousands in the bombed streets. They did not look like craters. 'We shall probably have to make one,' the director said earnestly, 'and I did so want to have no faked stuff.'

Herring found the film-makers too earnest and patronised them. This was their first war, and his second. The tedious trivialities of rationing, gas masks, uniforms and economy were second nature to his generation of older people, who had made a mess of peace because they had not met it before.

Five kinds of film were being made during the war years: instructional films on every subject from putting on gas masks to avoiding venereal diseases, all of them sponsored by the government or the armed services; short and long propaganda films like *Desert Victory*, again supported by the government; propaganda feature films like *The Way to the Stars* made by commercial production companies, but encouraged by the government, which allowed only films 'of national importance'; indirect propaganda films such as *The First of the Few* which needed the co-operation of the armed forces; and escapist films ranging from *Fanny by Gaslight* to *Brief Encounter*, which the government finally permitted because these filled the British quota and were good for civilian morale. In detailing such categories, the producer Michael Balcon stressed that there were no government plans for film-making at the beginning of the war and never any for commercial feature films.

Yet he did attribute the renascence of the British cinema to the stimulus of adversity on the creative mind. This was England's gain and America's loss. British films had direct human impact, even if they lacked the technical gloss of the Hollywood product. And at last there was widespread state patronage of the most expensive medium of all, the cinema. 'You can write poetry and make sketches in a fox-hole, but film production is a clumsy, laborious, collaborative, mechanical business. The film producer's atelier is given the courtesy title of studio, but to the layman's eye it resembles much more what it very nearly is – a factory.' Only the creative process of the manufacture of films saved the studio from the moral degradation of the conveyor belt. 'And then, and even then, not always.'

Dylan started as a film-pioneer in sound film production at £8 a week for Strand Films, later increased to £10 a week. Since he was alarmed by the bombing in London, he was allowed to write wherever he wished. On his visits to London, most of the script conferences were held in pubs or in the Café Royal at the producer's expense, so Dylan felt a new ease as well as a new career opening in front of him. His old existence as a poet seemed expendable. As he was to write in one of his screenplays, 'when one burns one's boats, what a very nice fire it makes.' His arson was at Bertram Rota, the rare-book seller, who bought off Dylan in 1941 his four *Notebooks*. Since Dylan had used this material as the quarry for more than half of his published poetry, it was an act of suttee.

Constantine Fitzgibbon suggested that Dylan's act was an imitation of Keats, long Dylan's mythical hero. Dylan had not died young of rotten lungs as Keats had. Now at the age of Keats's death, twenty-six years old, Dylan could kill poetry for ever in himself, and, like the young Rimbaud, he could seek his future in the golden Abyssinia of Wardour Street. As his friend and co-screenwriter Maclaren-Ross wrote of Dylan: 'he was extremely interested in the film-medium,' though he did not have 'the true Documentary Mind'.

At first, Dylan not only wrote documentary scripts, but he also provided the voice behind the sound-tracks. In Basil Wright's *This Is Colour*, he spoke with Valentine Dyall and others. He was the sole scriptwriter in *New Towns for Old*, which dealt pleasantly with the problems of commentary by throwing this plea for the reconstruction of industrial towns after the war into a dialogue between two voices – the later technique of the opening of *Under Milk Wood*. He co-operated with Ivan Moffatt on *Balloon Site 568*, a propaganda film encouraging recruits in the barrage balloon service with its 'floppy elephantine charges'. He also worked on documentaries about the Council for the Encouragement of Music and the Arts, *The Conquest of a Germ* by penincillin, and on a deflation of Nazism called *These Are the Men*. In this, Dylan's ironic verse was super-imposed on a shortened version of Leni Riefenstahl's *Triumph of the Will*; Hitler and Goebbels and Goering and the Nuremberg Rally leaders were made to confess their errors, as if injected by a truth drug. The anonymous critic of the contemporary *Documentary News Letter* praised Dylan for verse which 'frequently cuts like a knife into the pompously bestial affectations of this race of supermen'.

For the Fitzrovian writers, particularly Dylan, screenwriting and radio work were meant to be the drugs which prevented them from achieving their better work. In Thomas's case, this was doubtful. He had always had a passion for the cinema, sharing it with many of his generation. In the words of Cecil Day Lewis's 'Newsreel':

> Enter the dream-house, brothers and sisters, leaving
> Your debts asleep, your history at the door:
> This is the house for heroes, and this loving
> Darkness a fur you can afford.

Dylan and his friends were always in the dream-house; but the actual discipline of writing simple scripts for radio and screen documentaries refined Thomas's language and clarified his sentences. His letters to his friend and fellow Welsh poet, Vernon Watkins, showed him still writing a few and good poems including 'A Refusal to Mourn the Death, by Fire, of a Child in London' and 'Fern Hill'. Dylan never did blame his work in other fields as a way out of his responsibilities. He did not think that living by writing more than poetry was a waste of himself. As he testified to *Horizon* in answer to questions on 'The Cost of Letters': 'Shadily living by one's literary wits is as good a way of making too little money as any other, so long as, all the time you are writing

BBC and film-scripts, reviews, etc., you aren't thinking, sincerely, that this work is depriving the world of a great poem or a great story.'

Dylan's work on ten documentary films might well have influenced the lines of his later and greater verse. All art of whatever sort interpenetrates and informs all other art from the same source. No artist can put his different styles into little boxes: they spill over. That was why so much richness came out of the meetings of such diverse minds and crafts in Fitzrovia. Dylan's waste of words may well have been in his pub performances, where he spoke like a genius between his third and eighth drink, but it was not in his commissioned work. All he wrote enriched all else he wrote. What he spoke spilled over and was lost. In that failing, he was like his friend, the poet George Barker. As John Minton said of him, 'If you haven't heard George performing at the Windsor Castle on Saturday night, I doubt if you know what poetry is. Odes and elegies by the dozen. They sweep them up after closing time.'

Some documentaries with scripts by Dylan were completed by Strand Films including *Green Mountain, Black Mountain,* in which he celebrated Wales at war, not the ancient war against England, but the terrible near war that had united Wales and England against a common enemy. This concluded bitter memories of dole queues and slag heaps with the refrain: 'Remember the procession of the old-young men. *It shall never happen again!'*

In his loose and lingering look at wartime Britain, *Our Country,* wandering through the Liverpool docks and blitzed London, the hopfields and airfields of Kent, the mines of South Wales and steel works of Sheffield, to end up in some strange West Indian lumber yards in Scotland and on a bottle of rum in an Aberdeen trawler, Dylan's words did not impose themselves on the visuals. Through the medium of Jo Jago's camera and the narrator, a merchant seaman who wandered around wartime Britain, Dylan and the director John Eldridge produced a propaganda documentary which one critic in 1944 thought 'the sole and successful experimental film of the war period'. Its success went to Dylan's head and his two last documentaries were never released. *Is Your Earnie Really Necessary?* was suppressed by the Ministry as a lampoon after its first screening, while *Where Are They Now?* was never shown at all.

Dylan was always thought by Caitlin and his literary friends to be wasting his time and his genius as a scriptwriter. Yet he himself chose to be connected with films. He was not conscripted, he volunteered. If his asthma had not prevented his conscription into the army, he would have wasted out the war as a clerk in some camp. As it was, the writing of documentaries was his war work and his wages. For the first time in his married life, he earned a regular salary in a job that did not prevent him from writing poetry, if he had wanted to do so.

He did sometimes object to the conditions of the work with 'dishonest men with hangovers', saying in one letter that he was writing from 'a ringing, clinging office with repressed women all around punishing typewriters, and queers in striped suits talking about "Cinema" and, just at this very moment, a man with a bloodhound's voice and his cheeks, I'm sure, full of Mars Bars, rehearsing out loud a radio talk on "India and the Documentary Movement".' Yet Dylan, in fact, was a talented scriptwriter who improved from documentary to documentary, who was contributing both to the war effort and to his family's upkeep, and finally, who was escaping from that dreaded solitude that was the necessary confinement of poets.

For film-making was a sociable trade. It solved the problem of the writer, that desperate seclusion with blank pages, which, even if covered with words, had no audience until they lay dead on the printed page years after the event. The social animal in Dylan as well as the actor in him adored the quick translation of words to screen through the medium of the actual life of people that the British wartime school of documentary tried to capture. If Dylan was only a craftsman at films and not an artist, yet even its despised techniques helped him as a poet.

Commentaries, by their nature, had to be clear. They had to be unobtrusive behind the visuals. Dylan's early verse style tended to obscurity and exaggerated metaphor. His stint as a documentary writer for Strand Films taught him economy, precision and simplicity of expression. His major post-war poems such as 'Fern Hill', 'In Country Sleep', 'Lament', 'Do Not Go Gentle Into That Good Night', and 'Prologue' appeared to benefit from that workaday wartime need to communicate with the people of Britain in as clear a voice as possible.

At the birth of his first son Llewelyn, 'a fat, round, bald, loud child, with a spread nose and blue saucer eyes', Dylan had felt a surge of Welsh feeling and named the boy after a historical hero. As he wrote to Bert Trick of the baby, 'he sounds militantly Welsh, and, though this is probably national pride seen through paternal imagination or vice-versa, he looks it too.' The baby at first led to a closeness in the marriage with Caitlin, but soon the pressures of the war and living from friends' room to parents' home, from hand to debt and month to mouth meant that Llewelyn stayed with Caitlin's mother, while the new baby, Aeronwy, named after the Welsh river, stayed with Caitlin and Dylan in their single Chelsea room in London, their only secure base in the war years between a succession of makeshift homes in Swansea and Cardiganshire and even in Sir Alan Herbert's empty studio in Hammersmith. To say that the Thomases travelled light would be to exaggerate; they wandered with hardly a thing. In 1942, Dylan summarised his possessions as not enough to fill a mouse's home. 'It is very good sometimes to have nothing,' he wrote with bravado; 'I want society, not me, to have places to sit in and beds to lie in; and who wants a hatstand of his very own?'

His wife did, and so did he. Their Chelsea studio was occupied by a large double bed, a baby's bassinet, a gramophone and records; on the walls, there were reproductions of Henry Moore's drawings of people sleeping in air-raid shelters, which were put up alongside Dylan's own efforts at scratching pictures. In these cramped conditions, Dylan made himself comfortable enough, spending his days with the film men in Wardour Street and his evenings in the Chelsea pubs, sometimes insulting soldiers for the hell of it, and excusing his own lack of doing much for his country by pretending that he did not care much about what his country was doing.

His war poems, few as they were, contradicted his public attitude of cynicism and alienation. In particular, 'Ceremony After A Fire Raid' showed a profound grief at the shock of war and its outrageous murder of an innocent baby.

> . . . Into the centuries of the child
> Myselves grieve now, and miracles cannot atone.

Yet the tragedy of dying never translated itself in Dylan into the catharsis of hating an enemy, a people, Germans. He would rather drink the war away, work on his short films, and pretend a detachment which concealed his inward preoccupations and obsessions that did not change.

Even Caitlin at the time, although not in retrospect, was deceived by Dylan's deliberate waste of himself in London life, by his pose as the world-weary pub-crawler, disgusted with life. In an extraordinary memoir, a friend called Jack Lindsay told of going to the Chelsea studio to find that Dylan had torn up all his poems the night before and had thrown them into the rubbish-bin. To Lindsay, Caitlin's job was to rescue the poems from the rubbish when life got too much for the poet. Yet she refused, saying it was the last thing she would do. 'Dylan's corrupt. Corrupt right through and through. It's not for me to save him from himself. If he can't do it himself, let him rot.'

Naturally, Caitlin knew her man and naturally he had to salvage his poems himself. To throw them away had been an act of self-drama, not one of self-despair. Although the sale of the four Swansea *Notebooks* to Bertram Rota had ended Dylan's body-snatching of poetry from the corpse of his youth, he did not stop working on the new poems of his manhood, which were usually published in the one literary redoubt of wartime, Cyril Connolly's *Horizon* magazine. Connolly spoke of Dylan at that time, before he was mobbed to death in America like Orpheus by the Thracian women: 'In the war years he could still look very fresh and attractive, although his cynical *persona* had descended on him. He really preferred to enclose all literary conversation in a kind of capsule of ridicule and parody. I used to buy his poems spot cash from his wallet as if they were packets of cocaine.'

In the distress and chaos of the conflict, there was a curious security in Soho and Fitzrovia. There was army pay to stand drinks to those artists on leave or avoiding military service. 'I'm Dylan Thomas, and I'm f——ing skint,' the poet with lips like Michelin tyres said to Joan Wyndham in the Wheatsheaf. 'Be a nice Waafie and buy me another Special Ale.' Later, she avoided his beery kisses — it was like being embraced by an intoxicated octopus. There was now little threat of darkness falling on the bars from the air. For those in uniform starved of intelligent company or intellectual excitement, in search of the pick-up of fellow souls as well as bodies, the allure of Fitzrovia grew into a potent musk of beer, gin, chatter and encounter. Alan Ross remembered:

A perpetual waiting for darkness at Rainbow Corner, lonely groups of GIs, chewing or staring or making passes at adolescent girls, painted and screaming like parrots; Bloomsbury girls and writers, drunks and sergeants and itinerant queens in

Soho pubs; artists and military ex-stockbrokers and middle-class girls doing their bit at the Antelope; non-alcoholic excesses at the Astoria Ballroom and Palais de Dance, sailors and Waafs spilling out into unlit streets to catch last trains from sand-bagged, gaping stations. They played 'Deep Purple' and 'Jealousy' and 'Lili Marlene' at Naafi's and Other Ranks' Clubs. They linked arms in the streets and sang 'Yours Till the Stars Lose Their Glory' and 'Frenesi' and 'She'll be Wearing Silk Pyjamas When She Comes'. It was a time of Vera Lynn and the Stage Door Canteen . . . There had been earlier, more haunting songs like 'A Nightingale Sang in Berkeley Square' and 'Room 504' and 'That Lovely Week-End'. But the specialists in nostalgia were drying up; everyone was getting tired of the war, of uniforms and drabness. Manners deteriorated; imagination sagged; it took an extra two drinks to come up to par.

Everybody was expecting the war to be over soon, and it never was – the Second Front had to begin, and it never did. In the spring, the *New Yorker* correspondent noted, a young or old Englishman's fancy lightly turned to thoughts of invasion, this time towards France, not from it; but D-Day was conspicuous only by its postponement. There was a certain gloating from the BBC carolling about the tonnage of bombs dropped on Berlin rather as if rugby scores were being announced; but this counting did not alleviate the general fatigue.

James Pope-Hennessy, now posted to a cellar in the War Office, found London shabby and stale with crowds milling round Piccadilly, 'pleasure-seeking men on leave, who find no pleasure because it no longer exists in this tarnished city'. There was a frightening increase of an evil atmosphere, which approved to haunt the tube stations day and night. London seemed to be in a doldrum, secure and adequately fed and paid, waiting for something momentous or disastrous to happen, and certainly expecting the end of the war.

The pre-war literary feuds reared up their hydra heads once more. What the blitz had lopped off, the All Clear renewed. Lacking a common enemy overhead, the artists found the enemy in each other roundabout. Class divisions were again apparent. The left-wing and grammar school and regional writers resented the dominance of those Old Etonians on *Horizon* and Penguin *New Writing*. Julian Symons found the battle of 'players against gentlemen, puritans against hedonists, Goths against silver-age Romans' a permanent one in twentieth-century Britain. The war had camouflaged it, not ended it. Julian Maclaren-Ross agreed. An internecine war between various schools of poetry and individual poets was breaking out. Dylan Thomas might say that poetry was not a competitor, but with competitive poets around such as the Scots W.S. Graham, the light of battle glowed in his glaucous eyes. He would not be called a regional poet, only an international one. The latest theatre of war was in the bar-rooms of Fitzrovia. In spite of the truce which the blitz had induced, there had always been a conflict among the people whom A.S.J. Tessimond described as 'The Lesser Artists':

> We that are ill-assorted, arrogant, petty,
> Incompetent-at-living, glib-at-comment,
> Destructive, self-destructive, self-divided,
> Restless, rootless, faithless, faith-demanding,
> Unsatisfied, unsatisfiable crew
> Whom the ironical gods in a casual moment
> Chose for their gift of tongues and touched with fire.

When the danger dropped from the sky once more with the flying bombs, Caitlin moved herself and the children out of London to a cottage at Bosham on the Sussex coast, then to

Beaconsfield in the cocktail belt, then back to Wales with the parents at Llangain, and finally on to a summer bungalow called Majoda outside the small town of New Quay in Cardiganshire, at a rent of a pound a week, which Dylan could almost afford. The rooms were tiny, as Dylan complained, the wood and asbestos walls as thin as bumpaper, and a howling baby enough to put any poet off his stroke of words.

London, however, could never be abandoned before VE and VJ Days, and the end of the interminable war in Europe and Asia. Dylan came up to be the best man at the wedding of Vernon Watkins, but he never reached the church on time, lost in his usual alcoholic inefficiency, writing back apologetically on the train to Wales 'in the windy corridor, between many soldiers, all twelve foot high & commando-trained to the last lunge of the bayonet... Reeking & rocking back from a whirled London where nothing went right, all duties were left, and my name spun rank in the whole smoky nose.'

Drinking, the threat of random violence, sudden death from the air, the company of fellow poets and artists, the tarts and the Lost Girls – these were the lures of Fitzrovia in the last years of the war. This was the place for the wounded to be healed nightly, the violent to assuage their anger, the disturbed to feel creative without needing to produce anything very much. In his letter to the deaf David Wright on his sixtieth birthday, the blind John Heath-Stubbs recollected their youth at the end of the conflict in those convalescent homes of the unquiet spirit that were the Wheatsheaf and the Fitzroy Tavern, the Swiss and the French pubs:

> But our friendship really began in Soho,
> Our second university – so many lessons
> To learn and to unlearn – days of the flying bomb,
> The hour of the spiv and the wide boy.

Passing through those streets was rather like
The jaunt that Dante took through the Inferno;
Yet we discerned there an image of the City.
A certain innocence coinhered with the squalor.
I doubt if it does so still, even for the young.

9

Deeper in Debt

━━━━━━

On top of bills & writs, all howlingly pressing, I must get out of here
& find somewhere else to live at once. And that will take money, which
I haven't got. All I earn I spend & I give to past debts. I'm in a mess all
right. But I *know* I could write a good new script. And I wish Redgrave
& Rank would pay me to do it.

from a letter to Graham Greene by Dylan Thomas,
11 January 1947

POETS have one paradox in common with monks. Their practice and way of life depend on being solitary and gregarious.
They must be alone to write poems, even if serving as swaddies
in a desert army. But they must also meet other poets and
editors to celebrate their work and arrange for it to be published. They must write elegies for the deaths of their peers and
eulogies on encounters with their comrades and employers.
Dylan Thomas might not have practised his lonely craft for
ambition or bread, but he could not have survived or have seen
his work printed without a subsidised war decade spent around
Fitzrovia. Contacts and commissions in London kept the artist
going, particularly the British Broadcasting Corporation and its
gang of wordsmiths.

[138]

To secure a living wage after the war, the writers and the poets were already making for Portland Place like drakes drawn to a duck. 'When the writers formed and clustered again,' Dan Davin noticed, 'it was about the knees of the BBC.' In August 1946 *Picture Post* ran an article about the poets already working for the broadcasting corporation, which was called 'A Nest of Singing Birds'. The antagonists, Louis MacNeice and Roy Campbell, were featured along with William Empson, now a news reader on the Eastern Service. Although George Orwell had left his position running 'Talks to India', Patric Dickinson was in charge of the poetry programmes. He held himself to be the best producer of verse for public performances in England and employed many of his peer group including Dylan Thomas, who was a regular reader and writer, although not on the staff, because of a certain prejudice against his occasional drunkenness while live on microphone.

The Yorkshireman Rayner Heppenstall also took to the BBC after demobilisation as tripe to onions. His autobiography, *Portrait of the Artist as a Professional Man*, was a salutary lesson in how a Fitzrovian writer might be changed by a spell of army duty into a fit servant of a media corporation. He himself did not take to his colleague Roy Campbell, who seemed like a huge limping ram under his South African felt hat. Campbell repaid him in invective, once saying to him, 'Rayner, you look like a bald-headed gnome who has swallowed an acid-drop the wrong way.'

By virtue of the power of patronage, Heppenstall did much to shift the beerholes of Fitzrovia from Charlotte and Dean Streets to the purlieus of Portland Place. He hymned the qualities of broadcasting pubs, the intimate Stag's Head with only a saloon and a public bar, the Windsor Castle and the Whore's Lament, the George or Gluepot and Shirreff's Wine Bar, and the between-hours Colony Room of north-west Fitzrovia, the 'M.L.' or Marie Lloyd, where afternoon drinkers forgot their microphones in a basement near the Gluepot. Heppenstall preferred the Stag's

Head and brought there C.P. Snow and Pamela Hansford
Johnson, now married to Snow after her odd engagement to
Dylan Thomas. Rose Macaulay came and Norman Cameron, Sean
O'Faolain and Angus Wilson, Laurie Lee and Henry Reed and
Muriel Spark. George Orwell returned as an outside writer of
feature scripts, forsaking the George for Heppenstall's chosen bar.
Yet the other leading writers and poets, W.H. Auden and
Theodore Roethke when in England, and George Barker and
Dylan Thomas, usually drank with Louis MacNeice, while the
poets from Cairo, Lawrence Durrell and Bernard Spencer, drank
with Terence Tiller, another poet who had become a BBC producer, but, as with so many of his fellow poets, working for the
broadcasting corporation doused the fire of his creation.

The ultimate Fitzrovian, Julian Maclaren-Ross, complained in
the Wheatsheaf that everybody had gone, and tried to move crab-
like to the west and the Stag's Head. Yet as he entered, conversa-
tional groups ceased. He was considered 'a grinding, egoistical
bore', and when Heppenstall tried to defend his merits as a writer
and a critic, he talked to deaf ears. Anthony Cronin saw him in the
George 'like a scarecrow among seagulls'. In the new kingdom of
the airwaves, the man with the monologue and the silver-topped
cane was read out.

Just as military service was held to shackle the war poet, service
for the broadcasting corporation was considered a creative death
by a thousand programmes. The writer Jocelyn Brooke, who left
the army to become a producer there, found the strain of the job
could be mitigated by alcohol, which caused a chronic hangover.
His sense of guilt and his solitary nature could be assuaged only
by a progressive increase in social activity: he was a fish out of
water and soon resigned. In his five years of war duty in Portland
Place, William Empson wrote only three short poems. He
explained his inability to produce in one piece of six lines, entitled
'Let it go':

It is this deep blankness is the real thing strange.
The more things happen to you the more you can't
Tell or remember even what they were.

The contradictions cover such a range.
The talk would talk and go so far aslant.
You don't want madhouse and the whole thing there.

The wars of the poets added some gore to much bile. As
Rayner Heppenstall noted, there was a lot of literary hitting at this
time. Dylan Thomas, now subsidised by the BBC, went on being
a boozer and a brawler in his new drinking-places, the George and
the Stag's Head, which he left one evening to have a fight in
Hallam Street. His subsequent bloodshot eye was said to have
been caused in scratching the ball with the thorn of a rose, a
romantic explanation that invited disbelief. He broke his fragile
bones easily in accidents; he was never happy unless he was wandering around as the walking wounded.

Yet among the poets working for the BBC, Dylan's writing,
which seemed to be penned to be read and heard, developed
into the finest English language ever broadcast by the medium
across the world. As Dylan declared of a Festival of Spoken
Poetry, 'Known words grow wings; print springs and shoots;
the voice discovers the poet's ear; it's found that a poem on a
page is only half a poem.' Stephen Spender agreed that Thomas
had gained more than any other poet from his war work,
writing scripts and broadcasting, which had given him 'the
sense of a theme, without taking away from the forcefulness of
his imagery'.

Dylan now wore a continual cigarette on his mouth, and his
face and his belly were bloated. His old friend from Swansea,
Charles Fisher, described how Dylan could always be found at the
time, if enough bars were combed to trace his willing progress.

Ah. Here is the green man at the height of his acclaim. He sits in a corner propped up by two walls, a smouldering, soggy firework sending up stars of singular lucidity. His admirers surround him. What will he do next? They wonder. Will he burst or explode? A long silence. Dylan moves his head. A dozen necks crane forward to gather crumbs of irreverence or, perhaps, to learn how to write a poem. 'A pint, I say,' he rumbles in that deep belly-voice that makes audiences shiver. The pint is quickly fetched.

So the *enfant terrible* grew into the *célébrité choquant*. Dylan played his role of performer and poet more morosely now, as the accumulating alcohol slowed his responses and darkened his perceptions. He was less ready to suffer fools gladly, although always willing to take another drink from them. Rosalind Wade had first met the young poet in 1934 and had found in him the elementary desire to shock, 'rather as a certain type of child will scribble on a clean wall'. Then, he had attacked everything and everybody, 'interlarding his comments with any and every swear word', but he had totally failed to disrupt the carefully-tolerant liberal gathering in evening dress through which he had sat like a malignant gnome. By 1946, however, when she met him again at a literary dinner, he came under protest and went out to get a drink, unable to bear the chit-chat before eating.

This horror of formality and small talk was an utterly genuine reaction. Finally he reappeared and sat through the meal, throwing pellets of bread at the other diners. But when the 'talk' began it was good to see his boredom and indifference drop like a mask from his face, as he listened attentively to every word and afterwards congratulated his speaker with spontaneous enthusiasm. It was in this mood that he delivered commentaries and broadcasts, once the crust of resentment and seeming rudeness had been broken through.

[142]

Dylan hardly finished the few poems he wrote in London, except when he was on his own. His most fertile period was at the end of the war, when he managed to find a bungalow for his family at New Quay, a tidy retirement seaside town in Wales that was to provide the geography for *Under Milk Wood*, even if much of the essence of the play came from memories of Laugharne. There at Majoda, Dylan once again proved what Caitlin always fought for and fought him for, that he could only write his best poems in the dull, contentious close bosom of his family – and recover from them in the everyday evenings at the pub, where Caitlin had to join him to keep him near.

Pubbing, she was to discover, also became easy for her like most pernicious habits. She welcomed 'the noisy, tapped and lamped cosiness . . . the burning upward rush to the head; then the lulla-bying coma of the alcohol.' In the end the pub became for her almost what it was for Dylan, 'home; more homely than our own; from home.' She could not remember one isolated evening that she had spent with Dylan at their house; there may never have been one. 'To contemplate living without a pub to go back to; was homelessness indeed. A long, homeless blank to fill up; like a sheet of blank paper with no inspiration. With no boozing pals in it, to fill it with homely life.'

The particular pub in New Quay, which was their home from home and the refuge from the blank pages that might become poems or film-scripts, was the Black Lion. This place was recorded by Dylan in one of his rhyming parodies of verse sent to his friend T.W. Earp. The poem was called 'New Quay' and held echoes of the Llareggub to come, from No-good Boyo to the prurient Jack Black and Evans the Death.

> . . . No-good is abroad. I unhardy can
> Hardly bear the din of No-good wracked dry on
> The pebbles. It is time for the Black Lion . . .

[143]

I sit at the open window, observing
The salty scene and my Playered gob curving
Down to the wild, umbrella'd, and french lettered
Beach, hearing rise slimy from the Welsh lechered
Caves the cries of the parchs and their flocks. I
Hear their laughter sly as gonococci.
There stinks a snoop in black. I'm thinking it
Is Mr Jones the Cake, that winking-bit,
That hymning Gooseberry, that Bethel-worm . . .
Sniff, here is sin! Now he must grapple, rise:
He snuggles deep among the chapel thighs,
And when the moist collection plate is passed
Puts in his penny, generous at last.

Although such poems were largely foolery, they did hold the seed of Dylan's best comic writing to come; and at New Quay, Dylan also toiled at some of the finer poems in his next volume, *Deaths and Entrances*. If he had a literary conscience at the time, it was Vernon Watkins. Although Watkins was serving in the air force and lost Dylan's letters to him in the mid-war years, enough letters from Dylan survived to show that the serious poet was begging to be let out of the paunchy cynic of the bar-room. The correspondence demonstrated Dylan at his most warm-hearted and open, with all his adolescent defences dropped to his friend. He sent to Watkins from Wales copies of 'Poem In October', 'Holy Spring', 'A Winter's Tale', 'The Conversation of Prayer', 'This Side of the Truth', and 'A Refusal To Mourn The Death, By Fire, Of A Child In London'. Soon afterwards in 1945, Dylan wrote his two masterpieces, 'Fern Hill' and 'In My Craft Or Sullen Art'. The year of the end of the war and Dylan's return to Wales brought about the flowering of his genius as a poet.

As Daniel Jones commented, the style of Vernon Watkins was

at the opposite pole to that of Dylan Thomas. T.S. Eliot greatly liked Vernon as a man and a poet and equally disliked Dylan as a man and a poet. As literary editor of Faber and Faber, Eliot 'published many volumes of Vernon's poetry, and whatever one's personal taste may be, there is no doubt that the work is of consistently high quality. Vernon was very active as a translator of French and German verse; the translations of Heine and Holderlin are particularly good.' Yet if Eliot was overcome by the refinement of Watkins rather than the romanticism of Thomas, the loss was to Faber and Faber, which never published the greater Welsh poet.

A reading of the poems in *Deaths and Entrances*, which was printed in 1946 and set the seal of critical approval on Dylan's reputation, showed how Dylan's hackwork on film-scripts and reviews and occasional prose pieces for broadcasting had wonderfully improved the clarity of his verse. The balance and ease and sensuousness of 'Poem In October' and 'Fern Hill' were the true labours of a man who had grown out of the wilful obscurities of youth into the careful simplicities of age. The young Dylan would not have dared to be as direct and romantic as the mature poet in his contemplation of his work.

> In my craft or sullen art
> Exercised in the still night
> When only the moon rages
> And the lovers lie abed
> With all their griefs in their arms,
> I labour by singing light
> Not for ambition or bread
> Or the strut and trade of charms
> On the ivory stages
> But for the common wages
> Of their most secret heart . . .

If Dylan had written very few poems in the war years, yet his disgust at his experiences then allowed a pent love of country Wales to well out of the poems of that year of his return to a sea-town in Cardigan. Perhaps Dylan did need to be deprived by the conditions of life from writing poems in order to let them concentrate and clarify inside him. Vernon Watkins, for instance, wrote that Dylan's 'Poem In October' had been contemplated for all the three unproductive London war years before it was set down finally and sent to Watkins in 1944 from Llangain, Dylan's old haunt by Fern Hill and by his dead aunt's farm. Even when he was temporarily free of debt or concern, which was rare enough, Dylan showed no great urge to write more poetry; in fact, the pressures upon him might well have contributed to the coming of the poems, while his enjoyable paid work on other forms of words might have aided the actual forming of the lines of verse. His whole life enriched his later and greater poems.

Dylan grew more and more to be the family man now, and Caitlin's portrait of him was illuminating. He remained very much the uncontrollable child, even with his children. He would flood Caitlin with torrents of words, since there was no fury like the weak against the weak. Because of his Welsh hypochondria, which he wanted lovingly nursed and spoiled, he hated real illness in his own children, because they sprang from him and seemed tainted by him. 'He was never his proper self till there was something wrong with him; and, if ever there was a danger of him becoming "whole", which was very remote, he would crack another of his chicken bones, without delay, and wander happily round in his sling, piling up plates with cucumber, pickled onions, tins of cod's roe, boiled sweets; to push into his mouth with an unseeing hand, as they came, while he went on solidly reading his trash.'

Caitlin admitted that Dylan was better than she was at living the simple, or moronic life. She thought it was because he was literally 'out of this world'. His habits had hardly changed from his adolescent Swansea days, when his own mother had been his early Caitlin in the arranging of him. Late out of bed, early to the lunchtime pub. Back to a heavy lunch, eaten apart from the children and their noise. Then away to a shed or an office, 'and bang into intensive scribbling, muttering, whispering, intoning, bellowing and juggling of words; till seven o'clock prompt' and it was opening time in the pubs all over Wales and the British Isles.

The one worm that gnawed at Dylan's innards and swallowed his muse was debt. Here again, Caitlin understood and could not help. She herself liked no more to look for a job than Dylan did; her work was the children and the nursing of him; his puritanism, anyway, would have prevented him from allowing her to go out to find work to support them all. In temperament also, despite the appearances, Dylan cared more about money than Caitlin did.

> Poor nervous Dylan, who had inherited, besides his father's hypochondria, his acid pessimism for always anticipating the worst, suffered sleepless nights more than me. I had developed, through never having any, and my mother's lofty teaching, that it is vulgar to speak of money, a happy detachment from it, and, though nobody enjoyed the spending of it more, it was a solemn duty with me, yet I could never make myself feel it really mattered, or appreciate the value of it. And of course it was Dylan had the job of making it.

With such a carefree and careless attitude to money in his wife and with little talent for keeping any of it himself, Dylan was doomed to mounting debts and occasional expenses. Caitlin recognised that the lack of moderation and love of racketing waste in both of them was fatal. They always lived in hope of a mystical sum of money, which never came to solve all their problems. In the interim, they drank in the evenings to forget their problems, and they took out the frustrations of their lives in their attacks on each other.

This was the part of Dylan's married life which was so frequently misunderstood, and which led to the view of many of Dylan's friends that Caitlin and marriage prevented him from fulfilling himself as a poet. They often had murderous quarrels in public as well as in private. To outsiders this violence and shrewishness on the part of his wife appeared to destroy the security Dylan needed to write. In fact, the truth was the opposite. It was only because of the security provided first by his mother and then by Caitlin that Dylan managed to write at all: he was a poet of the villa and the family. The frustrations bred by this dull and simple life, the lunges away from poverty through alcohol, led to a war between the two of them that was the catharsis of all their niggling and monotonous days.

Their fights were an essential part of their daily life, 'and became fiercer and more deadly at each onslaught, so that you could have sworn no two people reviled each other more; and could never, under any fabulous change of circumstances, come together again.' Yet these fights were almost worthwhile because of the reconciliation which followed, the air clean, love assured, quarrelling indefinitely postponed until the next instalment.

Such were the excesses of Dylan's life on the home front, while the world was fighting its own battles across the globe. At only one point did the madness of the time intrude into Dylan's domestic strife. To New Quay in that summer of 1945, an exhausted commando officer returned, bringing with him his weapons. Captain Killick had not been through the reconstruction camps, set up to make ex-soldiers forget how to kill, and he found himself in a pacific town, which had ignored the hostilities and saw his courage as a form of brutalism. His wife was a neighbour of Dylan's and he was jealous of Dylan's presence near her while he had been away fighting.

He began to insult the clients of the Black Lion, and at closing time he argued with a Miss Fisher outside and slapped her face. Dylan and other pub regulars knocked him down and went home. His wife and child fled to the Majoda bungalow, and he followed her, loosing bursts of rapid-fire through plywood and asbestos walls. All crouched down, and as a witness, E.C. Jones, declared at the later trial of the deranged Captain: 'The door burst open and the accused came in looking very wild and wearing dark glasses. There was a sub-machine gun and a grenade in his hands. There were scratches and blood on his face.' Trying to calm the intruder, Dylan told him not to be a fool, while Caitlin said that there were two babies in the other room. 'He then discharged the machine gun into the ceiling and continued to mutter "Hell, hell," stating that six men had held him down and kicked him in the stomach.' They had not, outside the Black Lion, but in his confusion, the Captain saw them as enemies. Dylan, however, showed a certain courage and persuaded the Captain to hand over the sub-machine gun, although in a swing of mood, the intruder now threatened to blow everybody to kingdom come unless he got his gun back. Dylan returned to him the weapon. This pacified the raging husband, who went off with his wife and child.

This stupid, hysterical episode mirrored the madness of the end of the war. Curious, indeed, that there were so few murders or outbreaks of violence among the millions of trained killers returned home from their military jobs. There was a great unsettling into peace, and the episode confirmed Dylan in his first Llareggub of *Under Milk Wood* as a sane lazy town surrounded by a world gone insane with being at war. He had fled to Wales to secure his precarious peace. His tooth-and-clawing was reserved for his beloved enemy, his wife. He was writing his most rural and lyrical poems in denial of the times. If once the war intruded upon him, he would exclude it more thoroughly than ever. He had written again to T.W. Earp, claiming that not even Donald Taylor and films would get him out of his seaside truce:

> It's a long way from London, as the fly bombs,
> And nothing of Donald's guile can lug me
> Away from this Wales where I sit in my combs
> As safe and snug as a bugger in Rugby.
> We've got a new house and it's called Majoda.
> Majoda, Cards, on the Welsh-speaking sea.
> And we'll stay in this wood-and-asbestos pagoda
> Till the black-out's raised on London and on me.

Dylan did not stay in his Majoda by the sea. Living conditions in post-war England seemed so hard and progress so slow that Dylan kept on begging American acquaintances to help him and his family to emigrate across the Atlantic. In July 1945 he was writing to the American anthologist Oscar Williams, asking him to find a sponsor for the poet's family, whether it were Harvard, *Time* magazine or a rich man. 'A patron would do just as well, to say that he will look after me & mine in luxury, New York, or even in a kennel, Texas. I should most like to read, library or lecture at Harvard.'

Later, Dylan pleaded with his American publisher to bring him over, and then he tried for a job with the University of Virginia. These many attempts to reach the United States would be the background of his later acceptance of John Malcolm Brinnin's offer of an American lecture tour in 1949. Dylan was not seduced into first crossing the Atlantic; he had been trying to do so for five years. No victim ever went more willingly to his gregarious death by strangers.

While waiting to emigrate, Dylan made makeshift arrangements for living in England. There were small flats in London, friends' hospitality in the country, and finally an odd circular log cabin at the end of the garden of the Oxford historian, A.J.P. Taylor, and his wife Margaret, who was fond of Dylan and took him in to stay for a year. As with so many penniless writers, Dylan was still looking to a sold screenplay to solve his financial problems. At first, Donald Taylor kept him on his retainer, putting him to work on the screenplay of Maurice O'Sullivan's charming book about twenty years a-growing in the Blaskets, wild islands off the coast of Ireland. The half-finished script owed much to Dylan's perfect understanding of O'Sullivan's loved country boyhood; but as a film it was more Flaherty and documentary than feature film.

Soon, Taylor switched Dylan on to a project called *Suffer Little Children*, after trying him on a documentary on Labour, although Dylan protested he was not 'politically very acute' and would have to 'rely, as always, upon emotionalism'. *Suffer Little Children* was also never made, although some of the dialogue sequences ended in a Diana Dors vehicle called *Good Time Girl*. Dylan kept complaining to Taylor that he could not live in New Quay in 1945 on his retainer, now cut again to £8 a week; but he went on trying to complete a saleable feature script, after abortive attempts to deal with the lives of Robert Burns and Crippen.

Another subject suggested by Donald Taylor to Dylan during this period was the bodysnatching of Burke and Hare, and Dylan finished the script under the title of *The Doctor and the Devils*. Taylor was interested in the character of the historical Dr Knox, who needed the corpses supplied by the two Edinburgh resurrectionists for his studies in anatomy in the early nineteenth century. Although inspired by James Bridie's play, *The Anatomist*, Taylor and Thomas seem to have ignored the successful treatment of the subject made with Boris Karloff, *The Bodysnatchers*. The new script, however, was full of touches of the best of Dylan's conjuring prose. The opening sequences had such passages as:

The straw-strewn cobbles of the Market are crowded with stalls. Stalls that sell rags and bones, kept by rags and bones. Stalls that sell odds and ends of every odd kind, odd boots, bits of old meat, fish heads, trinkets, hats with feathers, broadsheets, hammers. Stalls with shawls. Stalls like ash bins ... There are many, many children, some very old.

Dylan used to call such passages his 'descriptive-visual' writing, and wonderfully evocative they were. To his friend Maclaren-Ross, he declared his intention of writing a 'complete scenario ready for shooting which would give the ordinary reader an absolute visual impression of the film in words and could be published as a new form of literature'.

Eisenstein had once proved that a paragraph of Dickens could be broken down, each phrase a separate shot, and it could become a perfect sequence, so immediate and apt were the succession of words and the placing of the commas. Dylan certainly had the same intentions and qualities in his powerful and just descriptions of action. His dialogue was, frankly, too literary for the medium, which was a mass art. One speech which Dylan gave to Dr Rock (Knox) in *The Doctor and the Devils* showed this elegant failure.

ROCK'S VOICE: ... When I said, cool as ice, one morning – cool as fire! – 'Elizabeth and I are married.' Oh, the shame and the horror on the faces of all the puritanical hyenas, prudery ready to pronounce and bite, snobbery braying in all the drawing-rooms and breeding-boxes, false pride and prejudice coming out of their holes, hissing and spitting because a man married for love and not for property or position nor for any of the dirty devices of the world.

With his powers of description providing only an inspiration for any director and dialogue better used on the stage, Dylan did find a competent technique of film construction which drove the story forward on Taylor's suggestion. The style was old-fashioned, in the manner of those well-made British historical dramas, long on education and short on action. Yet in its time, it seemed excessive. For fear of censorship, his script avoided violence despite the fact that sixteen murders were committed by Broom (Burke) and Fallon (Hare) to provide fresh corpses for the anatomists. The smothering of the victims was suggested, not seen. The outrage lay in the trenchant cynicism of the offensive Dr Rock. 'When *I* take up assassination,' Rock was made to say, 'I shall start with the surgeons in this city and work *up* to the gutter.' Explaining the fresh corpses brought by his bodysnatchers, Rock declared: 'They are corpse-diviners. Or, as some have green fingers for gardening, so they have black fingers for death. Do you expect the dead to walk here, Tom? They need assistance.'

Dylan had been obsessed in his pre-war days with shocking prose, and blood and guts all over the Surrealist paragraphs of *The Map of Love*. So it was curious to find him so restrained in his best screenplay, although it deals with bodysnatchers. Perhaps, as in the good films of Dylan's contemporary Val Lewton, the horror in *The Doctor and the Devils* was best suggested, not depicted. Yet Lewton dealt with psychological terror, not with a succession of murders. And Dylan's talent for prose was, at the last resort, too great for his medium.

Although Dylan begged Graham Greene early in 1947 to help him in getting the screenplay made, it would not be shot until much later, and it would not work as a film. Greene said that he liked the script and Dylan thanked him for it — 'if anyone could *like* such a nasty thing.' He begged Greene to secure him more film work from Rank to pay his bills, writing: 'I want, naturally, to write a hundred-times-better script, and I'm sure I can. I can write other than horrible stories, and I want to.'

In fact, in 1948 Dylan did get more film work. For British National Pictures, he polished the dialogue of two films directed by Dan Birt, *Three Weird Sisters* and *No Room at the Inn*. The producer Ivan Foxwell paid Dylan £500 for his labours, yet the poet cadged so many £10 notes that he had to write half a lost script of *The Little Mermaid* for free. Then he progressed to writing for Gainsborough Pictures, for which he worked on three films; all these scripts have been published. The first of them was called *The Beach at Falesá* and was taken from a story by Robert Louis Stevenson. There was little merit in this script by Dylan, nor in his extended treatment of the Welsh revolt of 1843 against toll-gates, called *Rebecca's Daughters*. This second screenplay was, actually, a ten-times-worse piece of work than *The Doctor and the Devils*, with cardboard characterisations of English gentry and cross-dressing Welsh rebels, and terrible dialogue such as 'Mayhap you stopped at the Black Lion.' Four decades after Dylan's death, the film was made and flopped on the poet's pretensions.

The other piece of Dylan's screenwriting was the first section of an original film operetta called *Me and My Bike*, which Dylan wrote for Sydney Box. Dylan boasted about his enthusiasm for this project, because Box had given him 'carte blanche as to freedom of fancy, non-naturalistic dialogue, song, music, etc . . .' But Dylan performed an incomplete and shoddy job on his final script, for he was already too busy on 'judging, my God, Poetry Festivals, and Third-Programming'. If there was a saving grace in *Me and My Bike*, it was in Thomas's idea for the film, covering the whole span of the life of a man, who 'rides penny-farthings, tandems, tricycles, racing bikes – and when he dies at the end, he rides on his bike up a sunbeam straight to heaven, where he's greeted by a heavenly chorus of bicycle bells.' The execution of the lyrics was hurried and facile, with lines reading like inferior Ogden Nash, such as:

... Man's best Friend is the horse
  Everybody agrees
 But when I say gee it whoas up
And when I say whoa it gees up, knees up;
  When I say whoa it gees.

So ended Dylan's screenwriting period which lasted for eight years. These jobs brought him a regular salary, some gain in clarity, and some waste of his poetic years. His other regular patron, which was to encourage his best work and pay him badly for it, was the British Broadcasting Corporation. Between his wars with its contracts department and His Majesty's Inspector of Taxes, who had discovered by 1948 that Dylan had never filled in a tax form, the poet spent the last five years of his life in a straitjacket of debt, with half his earnings from more than forty broadcasts deducted at source by the tax collector, as well as the most of the money from Gainsborough Pictures. The effort to solve his financial worries by film-writing had left Dylan only deeper in debt. He had already presaged his fate in his early poem, 'Our Eunuch Dreams':

... In this our age the gunman and his moll,
Two one-dimensioned ghosts, love on a reel,
Strange to our solid eye,
And speak their midnight nothings as they swell;
When cameras shut they hurry to their hole
Down in the yard of day ...

This is the world: the lying likeness of
Our strips of stuff that tatter as we move
Loving and being loth;
The dream that kicks the buried from their sack
And lets their trash be honoured as the quick.
This is the world. Have faith.

[155]

Hounded by creditors and deeply in debt, Dylan had answered a second set of questions in September 1946 in *Horizon*, 'The Cost of Letters'. The replies reflected both Dylan's sensibility towards the times – less Marxist now, more a matter of the Welfare State – and his wish to slough off his financial problems on to a patron, the government or a private Maecenas. He more strongly stressed the urge of the poet for individual freedom, and he defended the necessity of earning money for a family by taking on a second job. His regret was that he could no longer live cheaply enough to survive by his own art. Yet he advised young and hopeful writers to write. His personal disillusion had never extended to his chosen profession.

1. How much do you think a writer needs to live on?
He needs as much money as he wants to spend. It is after his housing, his feeding, his warming, his clothing, the nursing of his children, etc., have been seen to – and these should be seen to by the State – that he really needs money to spend on all the luxurious necessities. Or, it is then that he doesn't need money because he can do without those necessary luxuries. How much money depends, quite obviously, on how much he wants to buy. I *want* a lot but whether I *need* what I want is another question.

2. Do you think a serious writer can earn this sum by his writing, and if so, how?
A serious writer (I suppose by this you mean a good writer, who might be comic) can earn enough money by writing seriously, or comically, if his appetites, social and sensual, are very small. If those appetites are big or biggish, he cannot earn, by writing what he wishes to write, enough to satisfy them. So he has to earn money in another way: by writing what he doesn't want to write, or by having quite another job.

3. If not, what do you think is the suitable second occupation for him?
It's no good, I suppose, saying that I know a couple of good
writers who are happy writing, for a living, what they don't particularly want to write, and also a few good writers who are
happy (always qualified by words I'm not going to use now)
being bank clerks, Civil Servants, etc. I can't say how a writer
can make money most suitably. It depends on how much
money he wants and on how much he wants it and on what he
is willing to do to get it. I myself get about a quarter of the
money I want by writing what I don't want to write and at the
same time trying to, and often succeeding in, enjoying it. Shadily
living by one's literary wits is as good a way of making too little
money as any other, so long as, all the time you are writing BBC
and film scripts, reviews, etc, you aren't thinking, sincerely, that
this work is depriving the world of great poem or a great story.
Great, or at any rate very good, poems and stories do get
written in spite of the fact that the writers of them spend much
of their waking time doing entirely different things. And even a
poet like Yeats, who was made by patronage financially safe so
that he need not write and think nothing but poetry, *had*, voluntarily, to give himself a secondary job: that of philosopher,
mystic, crank, quack.

*4. Do you think literature suffers from the diversion of a writer's energy
into other employments or is it enriched by it?*
No, to both questions. It neither suffers nor is it enriched.
Poems, for instance, are pieces of hard craftsmanship made
interesting to craftsmen in the same job, by the work put into
them, and made interesting to everybody, which includes those
craftsmen, by divine accidents: however taut, inevitably in
order, a good poem may appear, it must be so constructed that
it is wide open, at any second, to receive the accidental miracle
which makes a work of craftsmanship a work of art.

[157]

5. Do you think the State or any other institution should do more for writers?

The State should do no more for writers than it should do for any other person who lives in it. The State should give shelter, food, warmth, etc., whether the person works for the State or not. Choice of work, and the money that comes from it, should then be free for that man; what work, what money, is his own bother.

6. Are you satisfied with your own solution of the problem and have you any specific advice to give to young people who wish to earn their living by writing?

Yes and No, or *vice versa*. My advice to young people who wish to earn their living by writing is: DO.

10

Broadcasting the Word

─────────

I do not remember – that is the point – the first impulse that pumped and shoved most of the earlier poems along, and they are still too near to me, with their vehement beat-pounding black and green rhythms like those of a very young policeman exploding, for me to see the written evidence of it. My interpretation of them – if that is not too weighty a word just for reading them aloud and trying to give some idea of their sound and shape – could only be a parroting of the say that I once had.

Dylan Thomas, 'On Reading One's Own Poems'

THE process of city deterioration and country recuperation was beginning to accelerate. The fault and the wages lay in Dylan's job. The BBC was a proud and jealous and penny-pinching organisation, which looked after its own, was clubby, and did not pay well. Dylan could broadcast about once a week, including many of the radio pieces collected in *Quite Early One Morning*. In his preface to this collection, Dylan's Welsh producer, Aneirin Talfan Davies, testified that Dylan's reading of his own poems increased his influence as a poet. The bardic tradition, by which a poet chanted his own verses, suited Dylan particularly well, as he enjoyed his rich performance, even if he knew of the pitfalls of exaggeration. He declared himself one of the dangerous group of readers-aloud of his own poems who managed 'to mawken or melodramatise them, making a single simple phrase break with the fears or throb with the terrors from which he deludes himself the phrase has been born'.

Yet such was the power of Thomas's recorded voice that it was impossible to separate the hearing of his poems from the sound of him reading them. There was a magnificence and a resonance in the voice of the man which reverberated in the memory. However well others might read the poems, Dylan's own voice seemed to superimpose itself over all, making other versions inadequate. In that way, he answered his own self-doubts about the indulgence of serving as his own bard on the most popular medium of his time. As he mused on the air:

Reading one's own poems aloud is letting the cat out of the bag. You may have always suspected bits of a poem to be overweighted, overviolent, or daft, and then, suddenly, with the poet's tongue around them, your suspicion is made certain. How he slows up a line to savour it, remembering what trouble it took, once upon a time, to make it just so, at the very moment, you may think, when the poem needs crispness and speed. Does the cat snarl or mew the better when its original owner – or father, even, the tom-poet – let it out of the bag, than when another does, who never put it in.

This tom-poet did. Certain of his readings became internationally famous. The Third Programme only gave a small audience for his poetry readings, both from his own poems and from those of other poets such as Wilfred Owen and Sir Philip Sidney and Henry Vaughan and Edward Thomas. Yet his prose pieces of reminiscence were repeated again and again, for the rich phrases and humour and joy of them, the quality of grand nostalgia for all the Christmases rolling 'down the hill towards the Welsh-speaking sea, like a snowball growing whiter and bigger and rounder, like a

The maturing poet in relaxed discussion with his Swansea friend John Ormond.

'Cheers' – Dylan and Caitlin at their most relaxed
in the bar of Browns Hotel in Laugharne – a favourite pub.

Dylan's house during his trip to Italy –
a postcard home to his folks.

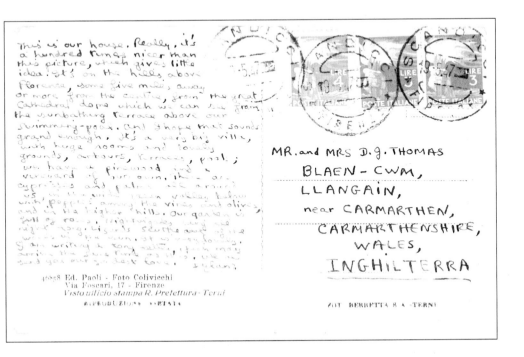

This is our house. Really, it's
a hundred times nicer than
this picture, which gives little
idea! It's on the hills above
Florence, some five miles away
or more from the centre, from the great
Cathedral dome which we can see from
the sunbathing terrace above our
swimming-pool. And I hope that sounds
grand enough. It's a very big villa,
with huge rooms and lovely
grounds, arbours, terraces, pool;
we have a vineyard of our own, there are
cypresses and palms all around
us ... and green valley below
with poppies among the vines and olives
and on the higher hills. Our garden is
full of roses, nightingales sing all
night long. Lizards scuttle out of the
walls in the sun. It is very lovely.
I am writing a long letter, which may
arrive the same time as this. We send
and you our very best love. Dylan.

46858 Ed. Paoli - Foto Colivicchi
Via Foscari, 17 - Firenze
Visto ufficio stampa R. Prefettura - Terni

MR. and MRS D. J. THOMAS
BLAEN - CWM,
LLANGAIN,
near CARMARTHEN,
CARMARTHENSHIRE,
WALES,
INGHILTERRA

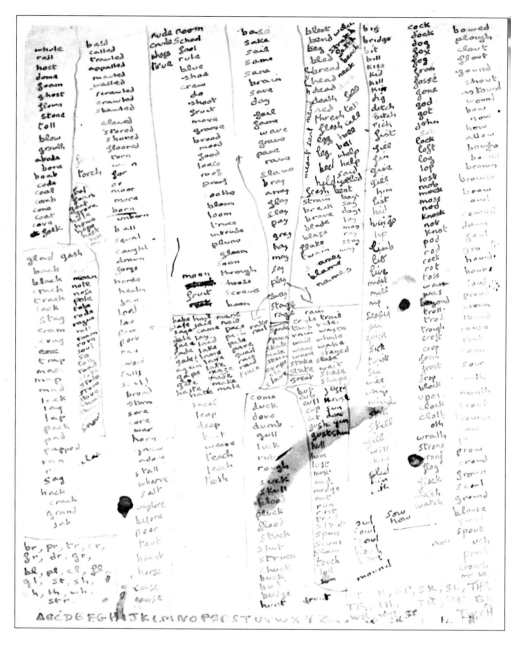

'I am an intricate painstaking craftsman in words' –
an example of one of Dylan's elaborate work-sheets.

A rare, smiling Dylan, on his first trip to New York in 1951.

Dylan's pre-lecture-tour shopping list and
personal account. Money was always a problem –
'£40, if I'm lucky'.

Coat for Cat
Boots for Cat
Coat for Dylan .

This could be   Dark Suit for Dylan
done for   Outfit for Llewelyn
£ 150   Llewelyn's School Fees
                Cash for voyage
                2 Warm Scarves

                Rates
                Savage
                Summons

£25 —— from Louis.
£60 —— 3 articles (1 I write 'em)

£40, if I'm lucky.

Dylan in the White Horse Tavern New York. Liz Reitell inscribed the original 'The last photo of Dylan' taken the day before he fell into his fatal coma.

Dylan's Grave in Laugharne.

cold and headlong moon bundling down the sky that was our street.' That large and bell-sounding voice was like the tones of the favourite uncle, who made that faraway time of long ago seem more full of plums and cackles and brandy than the nowadays.

Aneirin Talfan Davies declared that Dylan was aware of the dangers of his noble style of delivery, sometimes calling himself 'a second-rate Charles Laughton'. Yet in fact, he so enjoyed his performances that his running-down of his style appeared only to be false modesty. He was never pompous, if he was sometimes exaggerated; he was never untrue to the words, if he did sometimes inflate their emotive strength. Davies never forgot Dylan's own reading of the closing liturgical lines from 'Ceremony After A Fire Raid', when he thundered out the lines from an oversized jacket and a vast expanse of rumpled shirt:

> The masses of the sea under
> The masses of the infant-bearing sea
> Erupt, fountain, and enter to utter for ever
> Glory, glory, glory
> The sundering ultimate kingdom of genesis' thunder.

Frequent broadcasting also refined in Dylan what documentary screenwriting had begun to do, the need to be clear for a mass audience. Dylan himself declared on the radio that it was impossible to be too clear. Sensitive as he was to all criticism, accusations of wilful obscurity hurt Dylan the most, for it was his worst fault. The very complexities of his style caused it to tangle from time to time. Many private intonings and some public utterings were needed to undo the knots in some of his poems. Chanting and shouting his verses made them alive to him.

Naturally, Dylan's reputation grew slowly. In January 1947, he wrote to his parents from Oxford and mentioned a broadcast which he had delivered on 'Tonight's Talk' after the news bulletin. He declared that a lot of people had found the talk eccentric; it certainly was not what most people expected to hear after the news. He had received quite a big post from it, 'half of it enthusiastic, the other half calling me anything from obscurantist to poseur, surrealist comedian to Bedlamite.' In these salad days of his wireless work, Dylan still had to accustom a wider audience to his particularities, profound or comic though they were.

This letter also spoke of his best radio piece of the period, *Return Journey*, which was eventually first broadcast on 15 June 1947. This autobiographical coming home of the prodigal son to Swansea was produced by Philip Burton, and was Dylan's town counterpart to the later *Under Milk Wood*. For Dylan could now recognise the deep and abiding influence that the comfortable villa'd Welsh half-way town still had upon him. His return to it, though, was suffused with the notice of change and the acceptance of death. Two physical metamorphoses had taken place – the frog-goggling boy had become the heavy man, and German bombers had blitzed the heart of Swansea for three days, making rubble of many of its familiar landmarks.

So old Dylan searched for his lost youth through the ruins of his birthplace under a snow-blanket on a wild February morning, walking by the 'fish-frailed, netbagged, umbrella'd, pixie-capped, fur-shoed, blue-nosed, puce-lipped, blinkered like drayhorses, scared, mittened, galoshed, wearing everything but the cat's blanket, crushes of shopping-women crunched in the little Lapland of the once grey drab street,' only for the search to end in Cwmdonkin Park with the keeper saying that young Dylan and his friends were dead.

Warm and elegiac, yearning for the past that could never come again, Dylan found his true prose voice in the broadcasting of it. For a whole year, he hardly wrote a poem. The BBC had the most of him, certainly the best of him, and paid him too little for his labour. The files of the BBC were full of Dylan's requests for money, of his failure to produce commissioned work, of his quarrels with the accounting department. In one issue of the *Listener* after Dylan's death, Alan Rees went through the files and found a hilarious story of begging on one side and niggling on the other. The refrain was the same to the end of the final silencing of that resounding voice. '*And*, if it *is* possible to get a little money soon,' Dylan wrote pleading to one of his producers, 'could it be got, somehow, straight to me, & not through my agents, d'you think? I'm in a hell of a money mess, sued on all sides; trying to finish several things . . . but worried to death; ill with it.'

Dylan never made enough to keep himself and his family. Margaret Taylor was their great benefactor at this time and for the next four years, when she capped her charity by buying the Thomas family the Boat House at Laugharne. In 1946, she had lent them her log cabin in her Oxford garden and Dylan the use of a caravan to write in peace. Her historian husband soon grew tired of the noise of the Thomas family and of Caitlin's and Dylan's continual requests for money. Yet Margaret Taylor had money of her own, and she conceived her role as a patroness to the poet. As he usually drank away his earnings from broadcasting in London before he made his way back to Oxford, Mrs Taylor was continually helping Caitlin with the housekeeping. This added to Caitlin's resentment of the situation, to have to accept both the frequent absences of her husband and the charities of his friend. In the end, she quarrelled with Margaret Taylor, biting the hand that fed her for fear it might pat her on the head.

Dylan backed Caitlin in this quarrel throughout that bitter winter, when all was rationed, heating was unlikely, survival until spring was all. A travelling scholarship worth £150 was procured for Dylan from the Society of Authors, and he and the family were packed off to Italy. Realising that living at close quarters with the Thomases had now become impossible, Mrs Taylor bought a tumbledown farmhouse outside the village of South Leigh in Oxfordshire. This was readied against the Thomas family's return from abroad. Euphemistically, it was called the Manor House, although it was little bigger than a cottage.

There Dylan and Caitlin and their two children had a settled home for the first time in years. If it had no bath and was isolated, it became a necessity because of Dylan's sense of family duty. His schoolmaster father was now a shrunken and ailing old man; his mother broke her knee and could not look after her husband. So Dylan went to Wales and brought them back to live with him at South Leigh. The chores devolved on Caitlin, the responsibility on Dylan. He had taken his parents in before the dying of their light.

Dylan's motives in this action were obscure. He could hardly afford to add to his dependants, yet his Welsh sense of family decency made him offer the gesture and then see it through to the end. Of course, he paid less of the cost than Caitlin. He moved his caravan a little way away from the house to an orchard, after Caitlin had tried to tip him out of it. He spent more and more time in London, fleeing from family and parents; Caitlin became more vocal and violent as her cares mounted. Yet his parents were to stay near Dylan until his father's and his own death, giving him the final mothering and spoiling which he always needed.

Dylan's financial woes and worries increased. There was not only the catastrophe about his unpaid income tax, but there was also the difficulty of earning enough to pay the daily bills. Rich friends had been impoverished by the war. To John Davenport, now also down on his luck, Dylan could repay no money. He could only commiserate. 'There's nothing here to sell. My soul's sold, my wits wander, my body wobbles, Aeronwy is too young, I won't let Caitlin, the only pictures on our walls are from Picture Post, our dog is a mongrel, our cat is half a mouse. Small cheer for the needy in the old Manor House.'

In these straits, unable to reach America or to settle his debts, Dylan began yearning for the lost paradise of Laugharne again. For too long, as he said in a broadcast, he had been living among strangers in a dark and savage country, 'breathing an alien air, hearing, everywhere, the snobcalls, the prigchants, the mating cries, the tom-toms of a curious, and maybe cannibal race.' He wanted to rent the Castle at Laugharne which Richard Hughes had left.

This proved difficult, but Margaret Taylor once again came to the rescue, despite her running battles with Caitlin. She sold the Manor House at South Leigh and used the money to buy the Boat House at Laugharne as a gift for Dylan and his family, while he rented a cottage called the Pelican House for his aged mother and father. By this act of mercy and charity, Mrs Taylor brought some peace to the poet's last years, and he was grateful to her.

Dylan's family wandering was over; he had ended in a nostalgic island of a town of an old Wales that would survive only in the pages of his unwritten *Under Milk Wood*. As he wrote to Margaret Taylor in a last hopeful letter before leaving South Leigh for Laugharne:

O to sit there, lost, found, alone in the universe, at home, at last, the people all with their arms open! and then, but only through my tears, the hundreds of years of the colossal broken castle, owls asleep in the centuries, the same rooks talking as in Arthur's time which always goes on there as, unborn, you climb the stones to see river, sea, cormorants nesting like thin head-stones, the cockle-women webfoot, & the undead, round Pendine head, streaming like trippers up into seaside sky, making a noise like St Giles Fair, silent as all the electric chairs and bells of my nerves as I think, here, of the best town, the best house, the only castle, the mapped, measured, unhabited, drained, garaged, townhalled, pubbed and churched, shopped, gulled, and estuaried one state of happiness!

Once he had arrived in the Boat House, Dylan again wrote of his feelings to Margaret Taylor. He said he could never thank her enough for making a fresh beginning possible, and for all her labour and anxiety in the face of callous and ungrateful behaviour. The only way to show his deep gratitude was to be happy and to write. He was happy and writing at last – when he was not away or abroad.

For Dylan, the decadence of post-war London could at last be left behind. Soho and Fitzrovia were degenerating into areas of vice and crime. The Fitzroy Tavern changed from the beacon of Bohemia in the 'thirties to a sexual encounter parlour, mainly for gays. It was to be raided and prosecuted as a disorderly house.

The regulars hardly noticed the changes over the years. Fitzrovia had always tolerated all sorts of behaviour. Prostitution and homosexuality were nothing new under the black-out or the lamplight. What was new was their concentration in certain pubs and their overtness. In the war, open sexual behaviour had been permitted in the belief that the boys were having a good time before going back to camp or to die abroad. And there was the bombing. Danger allowed licence. In what came to be called 'The Age of Austerity' after the war, however, the parade of sex in the pubs and the clubs and the streets seemed like flaunting it unnecessarily. Although London might have become the vice capital of Europe, performances were best left behind doors.

The heart of clubland moved back to Mayfair, although the Gargoyle off Wardour Street persisted in its slow decline until sold by David Tennant to become a glorified strip club. There, in one of his last exhibitions, Dylan was lampooned by a fellow Fitzrovian in a poem, 'On Seeing a Young Dog in the Gargoyle':

I saw him sitting in the Gargoyle,
Very drunk and very ill:
Fields of Fern Hill green and golden
Deep the shadows of Bunhill.
'Double whisky! Double brandy!
Double-dyed is hard to kill.
Where is Vernon? Where is Louis?
Have I slept with you before?

Sticks or paper, match or shovel
Cannot make an old flame roar.'
Pange lingua gloriosii . . .
Pools of phlegm upon the floor.

The question of 'Where are the Peace Poets?' was not asked for five years after the end of the war. Not until 1950 did International PEN hold a publicised meeting to consider 'The Crisis in Poetry' and demand why the younger war poets had given up their craft, and why the heights of Parnassus were now occupied by aged T.S. Eliot and Edith Sitwell and Edwin Muir, or by those who had not served in uniform, such as Dylan Thomas and Norman Nicholson. Religious and metaphysical and neo-Romantic poetry in England, nationalist and regional poetry in Scotland and Wales and Ireland, these characterised the aftermath of war.

With his usual penetration, Stephen Spender summarised the mood of the young poets in his important booklet for the new British Council, 'Poetry Since 1939'. They were involved with more than the ideology of British democracy, and although they supported left-wing policies on the whole, they were not enthusiastic. 'They have abandoned the hope of an integration of their own highest interests, their own humanity, their own personalities within any politically organised society. In this, they have reacted sharply from the writers of the 'thirties. They are concerned partly

[167]

with trying to construct a vision of the time which accepts the fact of social disintegration, partly with trying to develop their own taste and talent within their own isolated conspiracy of intelligent and frustrated minds.'

With the self-imposed or induced silence of many of the younger writers, the established publishers and authors recovered their nerve and control. Literature, as Alan Ross noticed, 'took a temporary turn to the Right. The days of social realism, of prole-tarian art and documentary reporting were gone forever . . . The best writing was upper-middle class and upper-middle aged; and that too was a sign of the times.' In *Left Hand, Right Hand*, Osbert Sitwell began an autobiographical reconstruction of a past world of aristocratic excesses and eccentricities which showed that it was the privilege of the privileged, not of the Bohemians, to shock in the arts.

Edith Sitwell's literary parties became the caravanserai of the established and the tamed rebels. Eliot and Spender and MacNeice would be joined by Dylan Thomas and Roy Campbell. Critics and editors included John Lehmann and Kenneth Clark as well as Osbert and Sacheverell Sitwell. This was almost a literary establishment reminiscent of the Bloomsbury circle, against which the Sitwells had once set themselves. Such people were the ones castigated by the American critic Edmund Wilson, when he saw English culture in decline after 1945 with its labouring and shopkeeping people made more equal by restrictions, but over-shadowed by 'a fading phantom of the English public school'.

The dispersal of many of the wartime poets from London back to their outlying homes was leading to a new fashion of 'regional-ism'. Poets should stay in and hymn their native lands. Even Dylan broadcast in scathing terms on metropolitan exiles in 'Swansea and the Arts'. Welsh artists who lived permanently in London cor-seted their voices and claimed Soho was good for their gouaches. 'They set up, in grey, whining London, a little mock Wales of their own, an exile government of dispossessed intellectuals dispossessed not of their country but of their intellects.' Yet too many Welsh artists stayed at home too long, 'giants in the dark behind the parish pump, pygmies in the nationless sun, enviously sniping at the artists of other countries rather than attempting to raise the standard of art of their own country by working fervently at their own words, paint, or music.' Too many Welsh artists talked too much about their position in Wales. 'There is only one position for an artist anywhere: and that is, upright.'

His response was the same as that of Robert Lowell, lecturing at Harvard. When asked where he thought he stood or swam in the mainstream of American poetry, he rocked on his heels and replied, 'Right here.' Dylan's poetry was immortal, wherever he was or was said to be. He was merely to be killed by drink in the insatiable cities of England and the United States of America. That other genius from Fitzrovia, Francis Bacon, who failed to drink himself to death until his eighties, met Dylan in a Soho bar before the poet's death of alcoholism, but the encounter was a deadly failure to the listeners at the ringside. 'They both wanted to do the same thing – talk.'

Bacon was the antithesis of the Soho creed, a painter who survived success in a society which preferred failure. Even the art critic and jazz singer George Melly agreed that flight was the only solution to Fitzrovian life. 'In the end there comes a time when you must fight free or go under.' Most of the Fitzrovians followed the artists and dispersed after the war or worked for the state. If they wanted to live long, they went away and returned infrequently. Bacon would demonstrate that a Bohemian life might provoke an artist into fifty years of supreme creativity, while Dylan Thomas would become the testimony to its morose fatality.

11

Abroad

I think England is the very place for a fluent and fiery writer. The highest hymns of the sun are written in the dark. I like the grey country. A bucket of Greek sun would drown in one colour the crowds of colours I like trying to mix for myself out of a grey flat insular mud. If I went to the sun I'd just sit in the sun; that would be very pleasant but I'm not doing it, and the only necessary things I do are the things I am doing.

from a letter to Lawrence Durrell by Dylan Thomas,
December 1938

THE first time Dylan ever left the British Isles was in the spring of 1947 before he settled finally at Laugharne. Using the travelling scholarship from the Society of Authors, he went with his family and with Caitlin's sister, first to the Italian Riviera, and then on to a villa outside Florence. As he wrote back to his parents, 'Our garden is full of roses, nightingales sing all night long.' There, 'the pooled pondered rose goldfished arboured lizarded swinghung towelled winetabled Aeronshrill garden' led to 'a Niobe's eisteddfod of cypresses'. Despite the cries of the children, Dylan found some sort of peace and began to write the most ambitious poem of his life. 'In Country Sleep' was to have been the first of four parts of a major work; in fact, he did complete two parts more, 'Over Sir John's Hill' and 'In The White Giant's Thigh'; the final poem which was to relate all together in a great hymn to the natural universe was unwritten at the time of Dylan's death.

Dylan's intention in the poems was clear to him. All his life, religion had bothered him and the world had dumbfounded him. He could not escape God because of the beauty of His works. As Dylan wrote of the poems in 1951, they were 'poems in praise of God's world by a man who doesn't believe in God'. There again, that statement was not quite true. Dylan was unwilling to believe in God, but his very thoughts and words and rhythms were suffused with biblical themes and heavenly reverences, for a natural god or God in nature.

> . . . A hill touches an angel. Out of a saint's cell
> The nightbird lauds through nunneries and domes of leaves
> Her robin breasted tree, three Marys in the rays.
> *Sanctum sanctorum* the animal eye of the wood
> In the rain telling its beads, and the gravest ghost
> The owl at its knelling. Fox and holt kneel before blood . . .

If Dylan referred in the poem to the Bible as tales and fables, yet he praised 'The saga from mermen to seraphim leaping!' He worshipped legend and God in His legends, Celtic and Christian. He was the heir and victim to the Welsh sense of music and beauty and sin. As he wrote in 'Over Sir John's Hill' of the estuary of his loved Laugharne:

> It is the heron and I, under judging Sir John's elmed
> Hill, tell-tale the knelled
> Guilt
> Of the led-astray birds whom God, for their breast of
> whistles,
> Have mercy on,
> God in his whirlwind silence save, who marks the sparrows
> hail,
> For their souls' song.

These were not lines written by an unbeliever, but by a man slowly won over to what Dylan called in his radio talk on these last poems, 'the godhead, the author, the milky-way farmer, the first cause, architect, lamp-lighter, quintessence, the beginning Word, the anthropomorphic bowler-out and blackballer, the stuff of all men, scapegoat, martyr, maker, woe-bearer – He, on top of the hill in heaven, weeps whenever, outside that state of being called his country, one of his worlds drops dead, vanishes screaming, shrivels, explodes, murders itself. And, when he weeps, Light and His tears glide down together, hand in hand.' The poems showed how, by celestial mercy, the dead earth rose to exult. The ancient myth of the divine destroyer and redeemer was sung again.

Dylan began this 'affirmation of the beautiful and terrible worth of the Earth' when he was away from that part of his earth that spoke to him. He was homesick abroad, he travelled badly. He complained from his Italian villa to his English drinking companions: 'This pig in Italy bitterly knows – O the tears on his snub snout and the squelch in the trough as he buries his flat, Welsh head in shame, and guzzles and blows – that he should have written, three wine vats gone . . . but with a grunt in the pines, time trottered on! the spirit was willing: the ham was weak. The spirit was brandy: the ham was swilling. And oh the rasher-frying sun! What a sunpissed pig I am not to dip a bristle in Chianti, and write. I have so many excuses, and none at all.'

Dylan always did have too many and no excuses. His new reason for not writing was the shift from beer to wine, from cloud to sun, so that his face flamed scarlet from the exposure to both. He did not get on too well with the young intellectuals of Florence, finding them a damp lot. Unless he clowned more than usual, playing Tarzan, cracking nuts with his teeth and falling in the pond, he could not break through the barrier of language. He thought himself witty in Italian, but this was Italian courtesy; he thought himself violent in behaviour, but Italian descriptions of him show him morose and silent, talking little, 'preferring gestures of comprehension or dissent, remaining isolated within his own solitude'.

His bar was the Café Giubbe Rosse, where he would accept and offer drinks and have to remain largely dumb. Only Stephen Spender was in Florence to add to the British literary circle, and Dylan found his presence sad. 'He is on a lecture tour,' Dylan wrote of Spender. 'He is bringing the European intellectuals together. It is impossible. He said in a lecture I saw reported: "All poets speak the same language." It is a bloody lie: who talks Spender?'

The distance from home, however, increased Dylan's love of it. He might have been in exile, so much did he long to get back. 'In Country Sleep' sang with the nostalgia for what he remembered, while his letters complained of the bloodiness of being away. 'I am awfully sick of it here, on the beautiful hills above Florence,' he wrote to T.W. Earp, 'drinking chianti in our marble shanty, sick of vini and contadini and bambini, and sicker still when I go, bumby with mosquito bites, to Florence itself, which is a gruelling museum.' His was no Grand Tour, but a continual torment about having to be cultured and away. He could even mock at his own condition, as always:

> In a shuttered room I roast
> Like a pumpkin in a serra
> And the sun like buttered toast
> Drips upon the classic terra,
> Upon swimming pool and pillar,
> Loggia, lemon, pineclad, pico,
> And this quite enchanting villa
> That isn't worth a fico,
> Upon terrace and frutteto
> Of this almost a palazzo
> Where the people talk potato
> And the weather drives me pazzo . . .

At the end of July, Dylan absconded with his family to Elba where it was even hotter, but he was happier being at the seaside with children, no Swansea beach, but an inferno where he could hardly hold a pen for the blisters on his hands, the waterfall of sweat in his eyes and the peeling of his rainsoft skin, as he sat on his 'Sing-sing-hot-seat' in his hotel. Back he scrambled to Oxfordshire in mid-August, never to return abroad with his family again.

He did, however, go to Prague in 1949 to help inaugurate the Communist Writers' Union. Dylan was not a member of the Communist Party, although many of his Fitzrovian drinking companions had carried the card in the 1930s, before the Stalin 'purge' trial and the attack on Poland with Hitler had made orthodox Communism stink in the nostrils of many of the more literary Party members. Neither was Dylan a fellow-traveller; for he did travel badly with any formal or foreign doctrine. On the other hand, he was a sympathiser with the aims of Communism, for no contemporary political doctrine declared more principles in the struggle of humanity against the evils of industrialism and capitalism. If the practice of Communism was often shoddy, well, the spirit was willing: the ham was weak – as in the pig masters of George Orwell's *Animal Farm*.

If Dylan had any political label, he must have been classified as a romantic Socialist, entirely for his own advantage, yet with freedom for all. He wanted his basic money problems taken over by the state so that he could choose to write without financial pressure. For whatever clandestine political motive, Dylan would sign documents such as the Stockholm Peace Petition and the Rosenberg Petition, which his disillusioned ex-Communist friends would not touch. When in Prague, Dylan chose to remain in his jovial blinkers, seeing the snowy and Kafkaesque world of that city as rosy-pink in his view. He evaded the issue of the censorship of Czech writers by taking to beer and slivovitz and personal answers. When one Czech writer and translator told him that it was impossible to publish modern poetry in Prague at that time, he replied that publishing did not matter. He would take a job in Prague, if he had to, and write as he wished. 'A real poet must stand everything and it doesn't matter if he publishes or not.'

His real friend was a cheery ex-Surrealist called Vitezslav Nezval, whose boisterous jokes and drinking with Dylan were one of the causes for his political disgrace during the Official Writers' Congress, so that he was forbidden to deliver his speech at the final session. This governmental act somewhat disillusioned Dylan, but he stepped clear of the pack-ice of the Cold War. In his speech to the Congress, he merely declared that he was a Welsh poet, who had no other wish than to write poems, but who unfortunately had to work to live. Then he sincerely conveyed the genuine friendship of all English and Welsh writers to any writers' organisation that owned both a daily paper and its own magazine.

Rather like the jesting Pilate, Dylan did not stay in Prague for an answer to the only relevant questions – If there is a writers' organisation, who can belong to it, what may be published by it? Dylan had the freedom to return to Wales and that he did. His only trip to a Communist-governed state was a holiday and an irrelevance to him, proving him to be as apolitical as he sometimes claimed to be.

Whatever money Dylan earned from his film and wireless work, he wasted in pubs or taxis back to Oxford, where the infinite patience of the historian husband of Margaret Taylor was running out. Indeed, her relationship with the Welsh poet would be a cause in their separation and divorce. In his memoirs, A.J.P. Taylor claimed to have financed the house at South Leigh, not his wife, on condition that she gave no more time and subsidy to the sponging Thomas family. He would often return home to Oxford to find his own children and home deserted, because Margaret was pubbing with Caitlin and Dylan, who boasted that 'he had got the wife of a rich don hooked on him'. The relationship was not sexual, for the many women who gave money and love to Dylan appeared to want to mother him rather than bed him. His airs of lost innocence and childish genius and utter helplessness appealed to literary ladies, who felt that some of the stardust shaken from his curls would fall upon them.

Of course, Margaret did not stop aiding and abetting the Thomas family, buying them the Boat House in Laugharne and even renting for them a flat in Camden Town as well as purchasing for herself and her children two places to stay in Laugharne and in London. She would not be separated from her chosen alternates, even if her marriage had to go. She never explained to A.J.P. Taylor why the Welsh poet was more important to her than the Oxford historian and the father of her children. And so they parted.

The next person to be obsessed by Dylan and the future arbiter of his fate would be an American poet and critic, John Malcolm Brinnin, who was often published with Thomas in poetry magazines. Brinnin was both puritanical and gay, yet again in his relationship with Dylan there was no homosexuality. The Welsh poet, indeed, used to sneer at queers and pansies in bars, and yet he attracted the admiration and devotion of much of the gay world. His only conspicuous failure was with Truman Capote, who would tell Brinnin 'to quit playing wet nurse to an overgrown baby who'll destroy every last thing he can get his hands on, including himself.'

Brinnin could not manage to invite Dylan over to the United States for a lecture tour until he was appointed the director of the Poetry Center of the Young Men's and Young Women's Hebrew Association in New York. That such a body should become the sponsor of the leading Celtic poet was odd, although Brinnin declared that his only reason for accepting the job was to invite Dylan across the Atlantic. However that might be, Dylan was summoned for two well-paid poetry readings. The Welsh poet immediately accepted, for the United States remained his promised and golden land. He asked Brinnin to fix up more paid lectures for him. Brinnin now accepted, becoming Dylan's lecture agent and much more, his 'reluctant guardian angel, brother's keeper, nursemaid, amanuensis, bar companion'. In fact, Brinnin was to do none of these jobs well enough, for he himself was too involved with Dylan and certainly not strongly angelic enough to guard Dylan from his demons of drink and smothering by strangers.

Yet on that first tour, Dylan's strut into the fond and deadly embrace of the United States was begun. Brinnin's book, *Dylan Thomas in America*, was its record. All he wrote was true; what he did not say howled between the lines. Dylan was evidently devastated by Manhattan, 'this Titanic dream world, soaring Babylon, everything monstrously rich and strange'. He immediately took refuge in some of the seedier Irish bars of Third Avenue and particularly in the White Horse Tavern, 'as homely and dingy as many a London pub, and perhaps just as old'. He began to confound and alarm the inhibited Brinnin, appalled that the 'purest lyrical poet of the twentieth century' should live a discrepancy 'between the disciplines of art and the consolations of liquor, bar-room garrulity, encounters with strangers, and endless questing for meaningless experience'.

Poor Dylan. Poor Brinnin, wanting to take care of his hero and impose sanity upon him, also wanting to get rid of him and his self-devouring miseries. Brinnin was no Caitlin, to bluff out Dylan and control him. For Brinnin was a prissy and exact man, who could not understand or command a Dylan, still playing at Sam Bennet in this cornucopia of free liquor from the easily impressed, still playing the Swansea hard innocent with an 'ability neither to reject nor to accept, neither wholly to go nor to stay'. As Caitlin knew, if Dylan could get away with the responsibility for his excesses by appearing to have them put upon him, he would do so. For then he could excuse his Welsh conscience and sense of sin; it was not him, it was the others. Some are born drunks, some achieve drunkenness, but Dylan liked to have drunkenness thrust upon him. This America liked to do, and Brinnin could not stop it.

The result was that this first lecture tour of three months was a roaring success, or roaring and a success. Dylan lived up to his roistering and shocking reputation, while turning in some of his greater performances as a lecturer. Brinnin described him before his first appearance, when Dylan was sick and vomiting blood. Yet at the right time he walked on the stage, 'shoulders straight, chest out in his staunch and pouter-pigeon advance', and proceeded to give the first of those shows which Brinnin thought were to bring to America a whole new conception of poetry readings. Yeats, Hardy, Auden, Lawrence, NacNeice, Alun Lewis, Edith Sitwell, and finally his own poems were Dylan's usual repertoire, and he received ovations from the people who packed the auditorium. He did seem that fat Rimbaud come again, Villon and more, the romantic poet in his ecstasy and agony. And his poems were those of genius, too.

Karl Shapiro wrote of Dylan's presence creating an impossible gathering, 'a general audience for a barely understandable poet'. To express his poems, Dylan did not have to clarify them. He became a producer of himself, a clown at his own tragedy, the dramatist of himself as a poet. For his audience understood him as a mob understands its leader without necessarily taking in his words. His listeners were probably 'the first nonfunereal poetry audience in fifty years, an audience that had been deprived of poetry by fiat'. Dylan set them alive by his voice of elation and anguish ringing over their heads. 'They know it is acting. They know this is poetry and they know it is for them.'

Although he would suffer from agonising stage-fright before

every appearance, Dylan certainly knew of his power over his hearers. After one early lecture in London he complained of his own character as a performer. 'I detest the humility I should have, and am angry when I am humble. I appreciate the social arrogance I have in the face of my humility.' Dylan felt he had to be peacock-proud in his public character, while wanting to have the attractive modesty of the confident and the famous. He could never forget how hardly he had made his way; he wanted to hide his lack of knowledge of the world by flaunting his power of words and cocksure attack on anything superior. Even more brash than the poor boy made good was the suburban poet notorious outside his own town. If prophets and poets were without honour in their own country, they were stuffed with it abroad.

In a sense, poets only write for their peers. The way to be appreciated is to earn the respect of fellows in the same craft. Dylan hated the atmosphere of the American campus with its nitpicking academics. Of course, he ran down those who had doctorates because he was afraid of intellectuals: he had never had a university education. Yet he was proud to take over one of Robert Lowell's classes at the Writers' Workshop of the State University of Iowa. His moods varied, given his intake of alcohol, from depression to a public celebration of his art. To the Scottish critic David Daiches at Cornell University, Dylan said that he was finished as a poet and did not want to go 'westward into the night'. To Caitlin in a letter, he confessed his fear of 'the kind of dreadful, unknown space I am just going to enter'. Yet he coped well, turning up somehow on time for seventeen shows in twenty-nine days, usually in a shirt and shoes stolen from his hosts, although he was still immersed in his baggy brown tweed suit, which seemed to be lifted from some dustbin.

Dylan was always an anarchist about other people's possessions. Property was a sort of theft, so there was nothing wrong in the theft of property. He had stolen from his sister's purse in his

Swansea youth, and clothes were a toll that he exacted from his friends and anyone kind enough to put him up. Money was minted to be cadged as well as earned. Borrowing was the right of the poet, and there was never repayment, except by the wealth of words which Dylan spilled as he sang for his beer and bourbon and martinis.

To his tour guide Brinnin, Dylan boasted of affairs with three women, including a boyish poet. Two of these claims were part of his usual exaggeration, for he was bloated now and unattractive, but his relationship with a New York magazine executive called 'Sarah' appeared to be real: her true name was Pearl Kazin. Brinnin asserted that Dylan told him he was in love with both Pearl and his wife. And the cat was let out of the bag, when after Dylan's return from the United States, the jealous Margaret Taylor would arrive back at Laugharne from a visit to London, only to inform Caitlin that Dylan had been parading Pearl round all their usual pubs and haunts in Soho and Chelsea. Dylan would, however, manage to convince his wife that his benefactress Margaret was a 'grey friend' who had been spewing out lies and poison. Even so, Caitlin would insist on accompanying her husband for his next lecture tour over the water.

Dylan was more interested in his shock value with women than in actually having sex with them. In her memoirs, Shelley Winters described how she outdid Dylan in his urge to act badly. Meeting him at dinner with Christopher Isherwood, she asked him why he had come to Hollywood. 'To touch the titties of a beautiful blonde starlet,' he replied, 'and to meet Charlie Chaplin.' Shelley granted both his wishes, allowing him to sterilise one finger in champagne and brush each of her breasts with its tip, and then taking him and her flat-mate Marilyn Monroe to dinner with Chaplin. Alas, Dylan had drunk most of a liquor cabinet before their arrival, and Chaplin soon threw out the Welshman, saying that great poetry could not excuse such drunken behaviour. Dylan's riposte was to

piss on the large plant in Chaplin's porch, although he returned on
the following morning to make some amends.

In a privately printed punning poem of his American tour,
written to his New York friend Loren MacIver, Dylan talked of
Hollywood and the Ivy League and his behaviour:

> . . . b. grable's pylons,
> is m. west a lesbian, does bette d. hustle
> in parties out there do the stars wear dishever
>   ly? Did ever poor dȳlan's
> onslaught on silence throughout his so clever
> ly agented oddyssey raise any bustle . . .
> in the chromium homes on the hills of bever
> ly, hashish, hot splashes, nipple nibble and nuzzle.
>
> Did you paint yale and harvard o'hara scarlet?
> have a bash at the deans? did you maestro their broad
>   s with a flash of cold mutton?

Of course, Dylan knew of his deliberate degradation of
himself and his talents, once he was sent back home, sodden with
liquor and with very little profit in his pocket. His judgement on
this killing process across the Atlantic was made on the BBC just
before his death from it, willy and nilly as it was. Because Dylan
voluntarily accepted to go, he would never condemn his welcome
as his assassin. For he was the swilling victim, the jester at the massacre of his own self. He laughed at the little English writers of
tiny reputation at home, suddenly become gods in Manhattan and
beyond, but he would not bite the hand that filled his glass. He was
too generous for that pub blasphemy.

See the garrulous others, also, gabbing and garlanding from one
next of culture-vultures to another: people selling the English

way of life and condemning the American way as they swig and guzzle through it; people resurrecting the theories of surrealism for the benefit of remote parochial female audiences who did not know it was dead, not having ever known it had been alive; people talking about Etruscan pots and pans to a bunch of dead pans and wealthy pots in Boston. And there, too, in the sticky thick of lecturers moving across the continent black with clubs, go the foreign poets, catarrhal troubadours, lyrical one-night-standers, dollar-mad nightingales, remittance-bards from at home, myself among them booming with the worst.

Dylan mocked at his own slow wasting, quickening in America. He was only at home at home, yet his restless years drove him abroad, as if he knew he would rather finish himself than his greatest poem. As Samuel Beckett once wrote, sometimes the only thing is to be done, to have done.

12

Laugharne and Away

And now that I am back in Wales, am I the same person, sadly staring over the flat, sad, estuary sands, watching the herons walk like women poets, hearing the gab of gulls, alone and lost in a soft kangaroo pocket of the sad, salt West, who once, so very little time ago, trundled under the blaring lights, to the tune of cabhorns, his beautiful barrow of raspberries . . . I know that I am home again because I feel just as I felt when I was not at home, only more so.

from 'Living in Wales', a broadcast by Dylan Thomas,
on 23 June 1949

AT low tide, the waters of the River Taf became a slick sheet of mud and far sand, where the fishing boats squatted as dead ducks. Yet when the tide rose, the little craft would rock and ride in front of the Boat House at Laugharne, a cottage built into the cliff, a single storey toward the street and two at the back towards the sea. A shed in a nearby garden became Dylan's 'log cabin', where he would work on his poems on a table in the long afternoons, beside a stove and a bookcase and pictures clipped from magazines of Edith Sitwell and Marianne Moore and D.H. Lawrence. The floor was littered as a flock of gulls with twisted scraps of paper from his discarded drafts of poems. There he was working intermittently on his new verse, 'Poem On His Birthday', and 'Lament' and

'Do Not Go Gentle Into That Good Night', a cry of despair for his dying father, who lived nearby in his wasting away.

The nightly activity took place in Brown's Hotel, where he and Caitlin slowly drained pint after pint of beer and whiled the hours away. Often, the booze brought out the fight in them, and Caitlin would end with a black eye or Dylan with a cut forehead. She lamented what the necessary alcohol did to both of their characters, but they could not do without it. She confessed that the booze ate up all their money and all their lives. Yet she found herself unable to snatch the pints of stout away from him, even though she spent 'agonizing hours of unadulterated boredom . . . in dull as ditchwater pubs with Dylan to preserve his sacred drinking myth'.

Yet Laugharne and family life enabled Dylan to write poetry. A second son Colm was born, even as Dylan had put the first real strain on his relationship with Caitlin, who never quite believed his explanations of the affair with Pearl. She returned to London in pursuit of her poet, only to find him unavailable. In this miserable confrontation of loves and loyalties, Caitlin won a slow and grudged and bitter victory, while the American woman accepted the end of the affair a year later, 'with all its soap-opera bubbles broken, finally'.

Caitlin insisted upon it. When the choice came, Dylan knew where his strength and the source of his poetry lay, his only stability in the racketing waste of his life. Briefly he went to Iran to work on a documentary about the oil business, and from the lonely and dry hotels there, he wrote love-letters to his Caitlin, his Cattleanchor, his dear, without whom he could not live. In the accelerating process of his rush from health to ruin, Dylan knew that he could not sever his only rope that tied him to his true craft. Without her, 'the bloody animal' did always go on. Yet with her at Laugharne, the poet could work.

The trip to the Persian Gulf for the later British Petroleum Company was to write a company documentary and showed how far Dylan would go in his quest for money – in this case, only £250 with expenses. As with so many of Dylan's other scripts, this one was never made, particularly as Iran nationalised the industry soon afterwards. Finding the obvious joke irresistible, Dylan wrote that he had tried 'to help pour water on troubled oil'. Otherwise, his money problems continued, although he was always finding new benefactors, the bookseller Bertram Rota, the American anthologist Oscar Williams, and the Princess Marguerite Caetani, who was constantly being pressed by the Welsh poet for advances on stories and poems, which he rarely finished for her magazine *Botteghe Oscure*. The tax people were attaching his broadcasting money, for he was years in arrears, and he even thought of selling the Boat House, he was 'in such a state of debt and brokeness'.

Yet the worry over the money and being unable to provide for his family and his parents did make Dylan face up to his own being. His father was reduced to six stone, and Dylan was shocked into his last fertile period of writing poetry whenever he was free from the nervous hag that rode him 'biting and scratching into insomnia, nightmare, and the long anxious daylight'. Dylan's poem on his father's dying was his own valedictory; it spoke of his own refusal to give way to his deteriorating health and abuse of his peace of mind. As much as he was his father's son, he would rage, rage against the dying of the light.

> Wild men who caught and sang the sun in flight,
> And learn, too late, they grieved it on its way,
> Do not go gentle into that good night . . .

He could not yet show his father this poem about the old man's dying, but he could write both his own celebration of his own birthday, 'his driftwood thirty-fifth wind turned age', and his own 'Lament' for the repetitive contrasts of his life, which he knew were killing him and which he could not stop. The old ram rod of the five verses of the poem was dying of women, dying of bitches, dying of welcome, dying of downfall, and finally dying of strangers. Dylan knew the causes of his unease and his chosen way of mortality.

Brinnin came to Laugharne to tempt Dylan back to America again. Caitlin did not want him to go, but, in the end, she accepted on condition that she could go as well. In the interval before leaving, she moved with Dylan to London briefly, so that he could make some money from broadcasting there. This was a trough in his fame and life, the year before his *Collected Poems* and later *Under Milk Wood* were to make him an international success, acknowledged as the leading British poet of his generation. His old drinking companions found him sad now, restless, more morose and sullen in his thorough intake. To one hearer, he looked 'like a transcendental tinplate worker', but to himself, his old tough façade was cracking. As he told an American critic, he should have been what he was over twenty years before, 'arrogant and lost. Now I am humble and found. I prefer the other.'

That second running away from Laugharne to the lecture circuit masterminded by Brinnin was even more outrageous and self-destroying than the first tour. Dylan was hardly loath to go and squander himself, prodding Brinnin to 'put out feelers, spin wheels, grow wings' for him. Brinnin duly did, meeting Caitlin and Dylan off the *Queen Mary* on 20 January 1952 with a square of red carpet in his hand. It was the best welcome that Dylan had. For Caitlin proved an impossible companion on the lecture tour, merely adding to the strain of the lionising of Dylan by making scandals in order to bring herself to his notice. To Brinnin, the loud and stormy scenes at parties proved that their marriage was essentially a state of rivalry; they had each other in a death-grip; Dylan's success in American was yet more weight on the cross that Caitlin had to bear. She could not stand being his camp-follower in America, where she was even more estranged from that private inclusive life with him, for which she fought for both of their sakes.

Caitlin's version of the trip was hardly the same. She said that she did not resent for a minute Dylan's success. She admitted the impossibility of not being won over by the adulation poured like hot fudge on Dylan and on her, by extension. She confessed herself overwhelmed by its sticky syrup, until she was left a soulless lump of inarticulate meat. 'So what can Dylan have felt like, in spite of his incredible resistance, and amazingly quick recovery powers? One moment he was flat out, in utter self-abandonment, coughing and heaving up his heart, down to the soles of his boots; the next, dolled up, like a puppy's supper, dapper and spruce, or as near as he could get to it.'

There was, however, always a grotesque flaw in Dylan dressed as a tailor's dummy. If Caitlin mentioned it, she was slaughtered. If she did not, she was accused of not being interested. 'Jocularly joking, as though that other prostrate negation, parody of romantic poet in tubercular convulsions, had no connection with the narrow world, with him. Then nervously twitching and acrimoniously nagging me, about tiny petty things, which neither of us took seriously; but which outsiders were alarmed into thinking was at least the breaking up of our marriage. But our marriage was not a cobweb house drifting on sand; and we enjoyed the back chat, if nobody else did.' The scenes were mainly the product of sexual jealousy, he of her, she of him. Thus, in a way, the scandals were proof of their love, although they got dangerously near to the killing of one another in those bloodthirsty vengeances.

The public readings of Dylan, however, merely inflated his reputation, while the whispers of scandal made faculty after literary club ready to endure a Thomas private quarrel in order to feed on the gossip for years afterwards. The only way out of a succession of dull hotel bedrooms and interminable journeys from lecture to lecture lay in the bottle for both of them. America seemed a vast continental party in a lost alien city; there was no relief from the strain. At last, in Arizona, Dylan sent a postcard to Dan Jones from the Tuzigoot stone, one of America's minor ancient monuments. On it, he wrote an epitaph of Caitlin and himself:

We were killed in action, Manhattan Island, Spring, 1952,
in a gallant battle against American generosity.
An American called Double Rye shot Caitlin to death.
I was scalped by a Bourbon.
Posthumous love to you . . .

When they arrived home, the familiar round of working and scrounging continued. Dylan had managed to glean £100 from Marguerite Caetani by sending her half of a play for voices called *Llareggub*, which had also been commissioned by the BBC under the title of *The Town That Was Mad*. He apologised for being unable to finish the work and blamed his excursion over the Atlantic, which he had flown over 'like a damp, ranting bird; boomed and fiddled while home was burning; carried with me all the time, my unfinished letters, my dying explanations and self accusations . . . with my luggage of dismays and was loudly lost for months, peddling and bawling to adolescents the romantic agonies of the dead. I made money, and it went, and I returned with none . . . and once more . . . reviewed, begged, lectured, broadcast.'

Neither Dylan nor Caitlin could ever keep any money in their hands. They were too concerned with saving themselves to save any cash. And back at Laugharne, they found their debts greater, the income tax men pressing, Llewelyn turned away from Magdalen College boarding school for failure to pay the fees. Dylan, too, had a succession of illnesses, pleurisy, bronchitis, and gout. Still, he managed to finish the final draft of the 'Prologue' for his *Collected Poems*, the most intricate of all his verses. For the first line rhymed with the last, which was also the 102nd line; the second line rhymed with the 101st, while the middle two lines rhymed with each other. Its labyrinth of perfection was so complex and wrought that Dylan seemed to be proving that he still had complete mastery over his art, however much he was putting out the embers of his life.

In fact, even his drinking in pubs was part of his working method at Laugharne. He would suddenly stop his gab for long enough to tear off the end of a cigarette packet, jot down a phrase and stuff the piece of paper in his pocket for later use, if he could find it again in the jumble of his trousers. After a heavy lunch of stew, he would retire to his shed over the estuary. Discarded lines and verses and phrases littered the floor about his feet. Once, just before his last trip to America, a neighbour found scraps of a poem torn into little pieces and lying in the lane. She tried to put the scraps together and failed. It was probably a draft for his final unfinished poem on the death of his father.

At the end of the year, just after the publication of Dylan's *Collected Poems* when the son had finally proved himself to be the great poet the father had always wanted to be, D.J. Thomas died on the words, 'It's full circle now.' In his final years, he had come close to Dylan and had learned to admire his son. They would do crosswords and drink an evening pint together in Brown's Hotel. At his father's cremation, Dylan vomited. His last unfinished poem was to the old man's memory and was discovered by Vernon Watkins. It contained the lines about God and Dylan's father:

> I am not too proud to cry that He and he
> Will never never go out of my mind.
> All his bones crying, and poor in all but pain,
>
> Being innocent, he dreaded that he died
> Hating his God, but what he was was plain:
> An old kind man brave in his burning pride.

[189]

The sticks of the house were his; his books he owned.
Even as a baby he had never cried;
Nor did he now, save to his secret wound . . .

With the death of his father, Dylan began more and more to become reckless about his own dying. His sister, too, died the next spring. Only his mother was left now, and his wife and three children at Laugharne. His own health was deteriorating more and more, his powers of recovery lessening. He began to suffer from black-outs. Once he fell down unconscious at the bar at Brown's Hotel. The proprietor picked him up. When he came round, he asked how long he had been out. 'Two minutes', was the reply. 'Oh, it wasn't long that time,' he said and ordered another drink as though nothing had happened.

He was more afraid than he appeared to be, and his fears were growing. Again he wrote to the Princess Caetani of his terrors and his self-awareness of his own psychology, both too cowardly and too brash by turns.

When I try to explain my fear, the confused symbols grow leaden and a woolly rust creeps over the words. How can I say it? I can't. I can say: One instinct of fear is to try to make oneself as little, as unnoticeable, as possible, to cower, as one thinks, unseen and anonymous until the hunt is past. My fearful instinct is to bloat myself like a frog, to magnify my unimportance, to ring a bell for a name, so that, as I bluster and loom twice my size, the hunt, seeing me monstrous, bays by after different & humbler prey. But that is not what I mean: the symbols have wet-brain, the words have swallowed their tongues.

Money matters still pressed. Debts grew. Children demanded. A wife and a mother had to be fed. Bailiffs threatened. Only another American tour seemed to offer any way out, even if it might prove fatal. Although Dylan knew he could merely play the poet there and not make poetry, yet he could live for free and send a little money home. He hated his continual begging for aid and his passion for self-glorification; 'alms, for the love of writing'. He would have to go to America again, not for what Caitlin declared was merely flattery and idleness and infidelity, but for what he called appreciation and dramatic work and friends. He had no choice, or else he did not choose to have a choice. He would leave Laugharne.

Ironically, Dylan's appreciation of Laugharne for the BBC would be broadcast at the time that he was lying dangerously ill in an American hospital at the point of death. Still more ironically, it had been recorded by him at the Swansea studios on the same day as his other final radio piece, 'A Visit to America', which he had ended with a vision of New York as 'a haven cosy as toast, cool as an icebox, and safe as skyscrapers'.

However that might have been in memory, this talk was no good prophecy for a Welsh bard. Better his nostalgia for that other axis of his life, that interminably dull estuary at Laugharne as opposed to the fatal megalopolis, a Welsh town so set that longish journeys, of a few hundred yards, were often undertaken only on bicycles, while privacy was all. Laugharne was enviable for 'its minding of its own, strange, business; its sane disregard for haste; its generous acceptance of the follies of others, having so many, ripe and piping, of its own; its insular, feather-bed air; its philosophy of "It will all be the same in a hundred years' time".' Faced with the prospect of that magical penny-pinching security and backed by the hope of returning to it, Dylan had to set out for the terminal city.

A research student asked Dylan Thomas the answers to five questions on one of the American lecture tours. The replies were recorded and eventually published in the *Texas Quarterly* in 1961, under the heading of 'Poetic Manifesto'. Dylan testified to the influence of *sound* on his poetry, to the noises and voices of childhood, to the sensuous nuances of words before they had meanings for him, to the rhythms of spoken Welsh and biblical language. Out of this jumble of reasoned nonsense came the expressed depths and passions and humour of living.

Among the tally of his influences, those of his childhood listed in his answer to the first question were certainly true, but in the second answer, he downgraded the influence of Joyce on himself for fear of being thought somewhat a plagiarist of *Portrait of the Artist as a Young Man* in his own sketches of autobiographical youth, and of many sequences of *Ulysses* which seemed to serve as the inspiration of passages in his last masterpiece, *Under Milk Wood*. Dylan was honest now about the second-hand influence of Freud on his work – an unconscious, although real, influence on his own Unconscious. He again emphasised his work at poetry, and he now delivered a swingeing and open attack on the Surrealists – too fashionable in 1934 for such a frontal assault. He concluded with an exhortation which showed his true unselfishness, his urge to communicate the love of poetry to everybody who would hear him, and his final understanding of the need to celebrate God.

THE ANSWERS CALLED 'POETIC MANIFESTO'

You want to know why and how I first began to write poetry, and which poets or kind of poetry I was first moved and influenced by.

To answer the first part of this question, I should say I wanted to write poetry in the beginning because I had fallen in love with words. The first poems I knew were nursery rhymes, and before I could read them for myself I had come to love just the words of them, the words alone. What the words stood for, symbolised, or meant, was of very secondary importance; what mattered was the *sound* of them as I heard them for the first time on the lips of the remote and incomprehensible grown-ups who seemed, for some reason, to be living in my world. And these words were, to me, as the notes of bells, the sounds of musical instruments, the noises of wind, sea, and rain, the rattle of milkcarts, the clopping of hooves on cobbles, the fingering of branches on a window pane, might be to someone, deaf from birth, who has miraculously found his hearing. I did not care what the words said, overmuch, nor what happened to Jack & Jill & the Mother Goose rest of them; I cared for the shapes of sound that their names, and the words describing their actions, made in my ears; I cared for the colours the words cast on my eyes. I realise that I may be, as I think back all that way, romanticising my reactions to the simple and beautiful words of those pure poems; but that is all I can honestly remember, however much time might have falsified my memory. I fell in love – that is the only expression I can think of – at once, and am still at the mercy of words, though sometimes now, knowing a little of their behaviour very well, I think I can influence them slightly and have even learned to beat them now and then, which they appear to enjoy. I tumbled for words at once. And, when I began to read the nursery rhymes for myself, and, later, to read other verse and ballads, I knew that I had discovered the most important things, to me, that could be ever. There they were, seemingly lifeless, made only of black and white, but out of them, out of their own being, came love and terror and pity and pain and wonder and all the other vague abstractions that make our ephemeral lives dangerous, great, and bearable. Out of them came the gusts and grunts and hiccups and heehaws of the common fun of the earth; and though what the words meant was, in its own way, often deliciously funny enough, so much

[193]

funnier seemed to me, at that almost forgotten time, the shape and shade and size and noise of the words as they hummed, strummed, jigged and galloped along. That was the time of innocence; words burst upon me, unencumbered by trivial or portentious assocation; words were their spring-like selves, fresh with Eden's dew, as they flew out of the air. They made their own original associations as they sprang and shone. The words, 'Ride a cock-horse to Banbury Cross', were as haunting to me, who did not know then what a cock-horse was nor cared a damn where Banbury Cross might be, as, much later, were such lines as John Donne's, 'Go and catch a falling star, Get with child a mandrake root', which also I could not understand when I first read them. And as I read more and more, and it was not all verse, by any means, my love for the real life of words increased until I knew that I must live *with* them and *in* them, always. I knew, in fact, that I must be a writer of words, and nothing else. The first thing was to feel and know their sound and substance; what I was going to do with those words, what use I was going to make of them, what I was going to *say* through them, would come later. I knew I had to know them most intimately in all their forms and moods, their ups and downs, their chops and changes, their needs and demands. (Here, I am afraid, I am beginning to talk too vaguely. I do not like writing *about* words, because then I often use bad and wrong and stale and woolly words. What I like to do is to treat words as a craftsman does his wood or stone or what-have-you, to hew, carve, mould, coil, polish and plane them into patterns, sequences, sculptures, fugues of sound expressing some lyrical impulse, some spiritual doubt or conviction, some dimly-realised truth I must try to reach and realise.) It was when I was very young, and just at school, that, in my father's study, before homework that was never done, I began to know one kind of writing from another, one kind of goodness, one kind of badness. My first, and greatest, liberty was that of being able to read everything and anything I cared to. I read indiscriminately, and with my eyes hanging out. I could never have dreamt that there were such goings-on in the world between the covers of books, such sand-storms and ice-blasts of words, such slashing of humbug, and humbug too, such staggering peace, such enormous laughter, such and so many blinding bright lights breaking across the just-awaking wits and splashing all over the pages in a million bits and pieces all of which were words, words, words, and each of which was alive forever in its own delight and glory and oddity and light. (I must try not to make these supposedly helpful notes as confusing as my poems themselves.) I wrote endless imitations, though I never thought them to be imitations but, rather, wonderfully original things, like eggs laid by tigers. They were imitations of anything I happened to be reading at the time: Sir Thomas Browne, de Quincey, Henry Newbolt, the Ballads, Blake, Baroness Orczy, Marlowe, Chums, the Imagists, the Bible, Poe, Keats, Lawrence, Anon., and Shakespeare. A mixed lot, as you see, and randomly remembered. I tried my callow hand at almost every poetical form. How could I learn the tricks of a trade unless I tried to do them myself? I learned that the bad tricks come easily; and the good ones, which help you say what you think you wish to say in the most meaningful, moving way, I am still learning. (But in earnest company you must call these tricks by other names, such as technical devices, prosodic experiments, etc.)

The writers, then, who influenced my earliest poems and stories were, quite simply and truthfully, all the writers I was reading at the time, and, as you see from a specimen list higher up the page, they ranged from writers of school-boy adventure yarns to incomparable and inimitable masters like Blake. That is, when I began, bad writing had as much influence on my stuff as good. The bad influences I tried to remove and renounce bit by bit, shadow by shadow, echo by echo, through trial and error, through delight and disgust and misgiving, as I came to love words more and to hate the heavy hands that knocked them about, the thick tongues that had no feel for their multitudinous tastes, the dull and botching hacks who flattened them out into a colourless and insipid paste, the pedants who made them moribund and pompous as themselves. Let me say that the things that first made me love language and want to work *in* it and *for* it were nursery rhymes and folk tales, the Scottish Ballads, a few lines of hymns, the most famous Bible stories and the rhythms of the Bible, Blake's *Songs of Innocence*, and the quite incomprehensible magical majesty and nonsense of Shakespeare heard, read, and near-murdered in the first forms of my school.

You ask me, next, if it is true that three of the dominant influences on my published prose and poetry are Joyce, the Bible, and Freud. (I purposely say my 'published' prose and poetry, as in the preceding pages I have been talking about the primary influences upon my very first and forever unpublishable juvenilia.) I cannot say that I have been 'influenced' by Joyce, whom I enormously admire and whose *Ulysses*, and earlier stories I have read a great deal. I think this Joyce question arose because somebody once, in print, remarked on the closeness of the title of my book of short stories, *Portrait of the Artist as a Young Dog* to Joyce's title *Portrait of the Artist as a Young Man*. As you know, the name given to innumerable portrait paintings by their artists is, 'Portrait of the Artist as a Young Man' – a perfectly straightforward title. Joyce used the painting title for the first time as the title of a literary work. I myself made a bit of doggish fun of the *painting*-title and, of course, intended no possible reference to Joyce. I do not think that Joyce has had any hand at all in my writing; certainly his *Ulysses* has not. On the other hand, I cannot deny that the shaping of some of my *Portrait* stories might owe something to Joyce's stories in the volume, *Dubliners*. But then *Dubliners* was a pioneering work in the world of the short story, and no good storywriter since can have failed, in some way, however little, to have benefited by it.

The Bible, I have referred to in attempting to answer your first question. Its great stories of Noah, Jonah, Lot, Moses, Jacob, David, Solomon and a thousand more, I had, of course, known from very early youth; the great rhythms had rolled over me from the Welsh pulpits; and I read, for myself, from Job and Ecclesiastes; and the story of the New Testament is part of my life. But I have never sat down and studied the Bible, never consciously echoed its language, and am, in reality, as ignorant of it as most brought-up Christians. All of the Bible that I use in my work is remembered from childhood, and is the common property of all who were brought up in English-speaking communities. Nowhere, indeed, in all my writing, do I use any knowledge which is not commonplace to any literate person. I *have* used a few difficult words in early poems, but they are easily looked-up and were, in any case, thrown into the poems in a kind of adolescent showing-off which I hope I have now discarded.

And that leads me to the third 'dominant influence': Sigmund Freud. My only acquaintance with the theories and discoveries of Dr Freud has been through the work of novelists who have been excited by his case-book histories, of popular newspaper scientific-potboilers who have, I imagine, vulgarised his work beyond recognition, and of a few modern poets, including Auden, who have attempted to use psycho-analytical phraseology and theory in some of their poems. I have read only one book of Freud's, *The Interpretation of Dreams*, and do not recall having been influenced by it in any way. Again, no honest writer today can possibly avoid being influenced by Freud through his pioneering work into the Unconscious and the influence of those discoveries on the scientific, philosophic, and artistic work of his contemporaries: but not, by any means, necessarily through Freud's own writing.

To your third question – Do I deliberately utilise devices of rhyme, rhythm, and word-formation in my writing – I must, of course, answer with an immediate, Yes. I am a painstaking, conscientious, involved and devious craftsman in all words, however unsuccessful the result so often appears, and to whatever wrong uses I may apply my technical paraphernalia, I use everything and anything to make my poems work and move in the directions I want them to: old tricks, new tricks, puns, portmanteau-words, paradox, allusion, paranomasia, paragram, catachresis, slang, assonantal rhymes, vowel rhymes, sprung rhythm. Every device there is in language is there to be used if you will. Poets have got to enjoy themselves sometimes, and the twistings and convolutions of words, the inventions and contrivances, are all part of the joy that is part of the painful, voluntary work.

Your next question asks whether my use of combinations of words to create something new, 'in the Surrealist way', is according to a set formula or is spontaneous.

There is a confusion here, for the Surrealists' set formula was to juxtapose the unpremeditated.

Let me make it clearer if I can. The Surrealists – (that is, super-realists, or those who work *above* realism) – were a coterie of painters and writers in Paris, in the nineteen twenties, who did not believe in the conscious selection of images. To put it another way: They were artists who were dissatisfied with both the realists – (roughly speaking, those who tried to put down in paint and words an actual representation of what they imagined to be the real world in which they lived) – and the impressionists who, roughly speaking again, were those who tried to give an impression of what they imagined to be the real world. The Surrealists wanted to dive into the subconscious mind, the mind below the conscious surface, and dig up their images from there without the aid of logic or reason, and put them down, illogically and unreasonably, in paint and words. The Surrealists affirmed that, as three-quarters of the mind was submerged, it was the function of the artist to gather his material from the greatest, submerged mass of the mind rather than from that quarter of the mind which, like the tip of an iceberg, protruded from the subconscious sea. One method the Surrealists used in their poetry was to juxtapose words and images that had no rational relationship; and out of this they hoped to achieve a kind of subconscious, or dream, poetry that would be truer to the real, imaginative world of the mind, mostly submerged, than is the poetry of the conscious mind that relies upon the rational and logical relationship of ideas, objects, and images.

This is, very crudely, the credo of the Surrealists, and one with which I profoundly disagree. I do not mind from where the images of a poem are dragged up: drag them up, if you like, from the nethermost sea of the hidden self; but before they reach paper, they must go through all the rational processes of the intellect. The Surrealists, on the other hand, put their words down together on paper exactly as they emerge from chaos; they do not shape these words or put them in order; to them, chaos is the shape and order. This seems to me to be exceedingly presumptuous; the Surrealists imagine that whatever they dredge from their subconscious selves and put down in paint or in words must, essentially, be of some interest or value. I deny this. One of the arts of the poet is to make comprehensible and articulate what might emerge from subconscious sources; one of the great main uses of the intellect is to *select*, from the amorphous mass of subconscious images, those that will best further his imaginative purpose, which is to write the best poem he can.

And question five is, God help us, what is my definition of Poetry?

I, myself, do not read poetry for anything but pleasure. I read only the poems I like. This means, of course, that I have to read a lot of poems I don't like before I find the ones I do, but, when I *do* find the ones I do, then all I can say is, 'Here they are', and read them to myself for pleasure.

Read the poems you like reading. Don't bother whether they're 'important' or if they'll live. What does it matter what poetry *is*, after all? If you want a definition of poetry, say: 'Poetry is what makes me laugh or cry or yawn, what makes my toenails twinkle, what makes me want to do this or that or nothing', and let it go at that. All that matters about poetry is the enjoyment of it, however tragic it may be. All that matters is the eternal movement behind it, the vast undercurrent of human grief, folly, pretension, exaltation, or ignorance, however unlofty the intention of the poem.

You can tear a poem apart to see what makes it technically tick, and say to yourself, when the works are laid out before you, the vowels, the consonants, the rhymes or rhythms, 'Yes, this is *it*. This is why the poem moves me so. It is because of the craftsmanship.' But you're back again where you began.

You're back with the mystery of having been moved by words. The best craftsmanship always leaves holes and gaps in the works of the poem so that something that is *not* in the poem can creep, crawl, flash, or thunder in.

The joy and function of poetry is, and was, the celebration of man, which is also the celebration of God.

13

Destroyer and Preserver

The briefest review of Dylan's emotional life would suggest that no man was ever more adept in killing what he loved, or suffered more in the consequence.

John Malcolm Brinnin

Now that I am a man no more
And a black reward for a roaring life,
(Sighed the old ram rod, dying of strangers) . . .

Dylan Thomas, 'Lament'

ONE of the signs of a species about to become extinct is that it fouls its own nest. It is also the sign of a man who has no will to live. Dylan, on the other hand, never fouled his own nest at home in Laugharne, where he did want to live. Testimony is still unanimous there. Although many of the townspeople felt after his death he had ridiculed them in *Under Milk Wood*, none thought of him as rather more than one of them. In fact, they seemed to put him much on the level of a workman, for he dressed and behaved like one and drank in the pub with other workmen. He stuck to beer, he never caused a scandal, he was faithful to Caitlin, he paid his bills in the end, he was a good neighbour in house and pub in a most conservative town – 'true bloody blue to the core,' as Dylan called it, 'even the workers vote Liberal and as for listening to a word against *dear* Winston . . .'

Even drink was no problem to Dylan when he felt secure and at home. He was very specific about this to his patroness, the Princess Caetani, who kept on sending him money for the first draft of *Under Milk Wood*. Dylan wrote from Laugharne that he was frightened of drink too, but only when he was whirlingly perplexed and magnified his ordinary troubles into monsters:

When I am here, or anywhere I like, and am busy, then drink's no fear at all and I'm well, terribly well, and gay, and unafraid and full of other nicer nonsenses, and altogether a dull, happy fellow only wanting to put into words, never into useless, haphazard, ugly, unhappy action, the ordered turbulence, the ubiquitous and rinsing grief, the unreasonable glory, of the world I know and don't know.

If, then, Dylan was so frightened of drink and self-destruction when he was away from home, why did he go on the four successive lecture tours of America that were to culminate in his death? An answer seemed to lie in his quick powers of recovery, once he reached anchor and Caitlin at Laugharne again, a feeling that he would always be able to recuperate in Wales, however unsteady his progress abroad. In one letter to American friends, he begged to be remembered, 'round, red, robustly raddled, a bulging Apple among poets, hard as nails made of cream cheese, gap-toothed, balding, noisome, a great collector of dust and a magnet for moths, mad for beer, frightened of priests, women, Chicago, writers, distance, time, children, geese, death, in love, frightened of love, liable to drip.' He went on fondly about a final liquid, libidinous fortnight in New York, and he declared that, as a result, he had never felt physically better in his life with a spring in his step and a song in his gut 'and poems to write and no need to hurry to write them'. He wrote that he had to ruin his health again because he felt so preposterously well.

Dylan had always lived under Milk Wood. Wales was a country of recent cities, and in every suburban Welsh boy hid a nostalgia for a 'timeless, mild, beguiling island of a town', which his grandmother still remembered like Mary Ann Sailors as the Chosen Land, and where life was still simple and peaceful and direct. For the boy Dylan, Cwmdonkin Park had been a shadow on the green liberty of Mumbles. For the young Dylan, Swansea had been neither London nor Laugharne, but a dirty town of a place where small and hardly-known and never-to-be-forgotten people lived and always lost.

He had not intended to lose there, so he had left, first for London and the seven deadly sins suggested in the incomplete *Adventures in the Skin Trade*, and afterwards, dying of strangers, he had returned to New Quay and Laugharne and all the deadly virtues of small-town Wales that plagued him into escaping once more. Yet he had always carried with him an idea which he had mentioned to Bert Trick in his Swansea days as a reporter, the story of a row of terrace houses at a place called Llareggub, where all the inhabitants came out to blab their dreams and hidden desires.

This idea had grown in Dylan's mind in London and in Laugharne, both of which in 1934 he had first visited. A year later, he had written of 'the stories of the reverend madmen in the Black Book of Llareggub' in his Surrealist story called 'The Orchards'. And just after the outbreak of the war, when he and Caitlin had been staying with Richard Hughes in Laugharne Castle, he had acted in a local one-act farce called *The Devil among the Skins*. Afterwards, as Richard Hughes recalled in a broadcast on the Third Programme, 'we all agreed it was absurd to perform such utter rubbish to so noble an audience as the burgesses of

Laugharne. Then Dylan had an idea: "What Laugharne really needs is a play about well-known Laugharne characters – and get them all to play themselves."'

The war had intervened and Dylan had gone to live in a bungalow in New Quay during the fall of Germany. Here he had written *Quite Early One Morning*, a sketch of life in a seaside town suspiciously like New Quay, for Aneirin Talfan Davies, his BBC talks producer. Dylan had recorded the programme in his rich rhetoric and the broadcast was successful, despite some adverse comments from the Head of Talks that surfaced many years later, criticising Dylan's 'breathless, poetic voice', for the words had not seemed to carry its sense.

However that was, Dylan's words were a foretaste of *Under Milk Wood*. He spoke of a sunlit sea-town with the sea 'lying down still and green as grass after a night of tar-black howling and rolling'. The town was not yet awake, while babies cried in the upper bedrooms of salt-white houses dangling over water, and 'miscellaneous retired sea captains emerged for a second from deeper waves than ever tossed their boats, then drowned again' in the big seas of their dreams. Landladies in the 'bombasined black of their once spare rooms' remembered 'their loves, their bills, their visitors'. The town was not yet awake, while the narrator 'walked through the streets like a stranger come out of the sea', hearing the terrible and violent dreams of the mild-mannered men and women. Cockcrow and larks called the town awake slowly, and some of the voices began to sound, including:

. . . I am Mrs Ogmore-Pritchard and I want another snooze.
Dust the china, feed the canary, sweep the drawing-room floor;
And before you let the sun in, mind he wipes his shoes.

This prelude to *Under Milk Wood* echoed Edgar Lee Masters's *The Spoon River Anthology* with its ideas of dead and living people speaking out their dreams and doings in simple poetry, and in fact one of the last programmes Dylan did for the BBC was on the American poet's work. Then again, Dylan was influenced by Thornton Wilder's *Our Town*, a debt which he hardly acknowledged. Yet he discarded his own first structure for his long radio play, as outlined to Richard Hughes and Constantine Fitzgibbon during the war, and to his Welsh wireless producer Philip Burton in 1947 in the Café Royal. Then he had wished to write something called *The Village of the Mad*, in which Llareggub would be put on trial for insanity by an official inspector from the war government. In the course of the trial, the villagers would prove themselves free and feckless and sane in a world gone mad with fighting and regulations, greed and regimentation. Llareggub would end by asking for barbed wire round it to save its dangerous and infectious happiness from contamination by the rest of the crazy human race.

This plot derived from the war and possibly from the fact that a secret weapons establishment was built with its barbed wire and sentries just down the coast from Laugharne on the Pendine Sands, within earshot of Dylan's Boat House. Dylan might have escaped the war physically, but his mind rebelled against his cowardice until he seemed to have erected an anarchic love of life into a more human cause than patriotism. As the war's influence ebbed into the slow peace of the early 1950s, so Dylan dropped the structure of *The Village of the Mad* into something similar to his only other long radio play, *Return Journey*.

In that, a narrator, who was himself, came back to Swansea and heard in the voices of his memory and of the living and the dead, the accounts of his own past life and adolescent dreams. The narrator tacked up 'the snowblind hill, a cat-o'-nine-gales whipping from the sea,' to Cwmdonkin Park where dusk was folding it around 'like another, darker snow'. There the park-keeper remembered the little Thomases by their thousands, just as Captain Cat

[205]

was to remember his sailors under the waves. They were all 'dead . . . dead . . . dead.'

So a freer form of *Under Milk Wood* suggested itself to Dylan as he began to work on it after 1949 in Laugharne. Within two years, he confessed to the Princess Caetani of his changed intentions, that he wanted 'a piece, a play, an impression for voices, an entertainment out of the darkness of the town I live in'. Jobs for quick cash got in the way of Dylan finishing the radio play. Even at its first stage performance in the Young Men's and Young Women's Hebrew Association in New York in 1953, Dylan was said to be still drafting the last revisions to it as he and the other actors went on the stage.

A shorter version, however, in 1952 called *Llareggub, a Piece for Radio Perhaps*, had already appeared in the Princess Caetani's *Botteghe Oscure*. This unfinished script had reached the publisher with the declaration that only very special circumstances were preventing Dylan from carrying on with the work every minute of the day. These very special circumstances were, naturally, a shortage of money – Dylan wanted £100 for the fragment, which was basically half the length of the final play, ending on Captain Cat's line, 'Organ Morgan's at it early. You can tell it's spring.' Douglas Cleverdon fully explained the various manuscripts of *Under Milk Wood* up to the final version given to him for performance by the BBC. After Dylan's death his widow Caitlin sued Cleverdon unsuccessfully for the return of the manuscript, which had been sold; but she lost the case. Cleverdon claimed that he had been given it by Dylan, who had left it in a pub, rather as Lawrence of Arabia had left his draft of *The Seven Pillars of Wisdom* in a bag at Reading station. Certainly, Dylan never received from his play in his lifetime what the manuscript fetched after his burial. Yet it was broadcast practically without cuts on the Third Programme two months after the poet's death – thirteen words in all were omitted according to Cleverdon, 'two tits and a bum'.

In a way, the finishing of *Under Milk Wood* was the finishing of
Dylan Thomas. He paid for his spoken masterpiece with the still-
ing of his voice. From its solo performance by Dylan in the Fogg
Museum at Harvard on 3 May 1953 to its fourth stage performance for the Young Men's and Young Women's Hebrew
Association on 25 October of that year, just before his death on 9
November, Dylan was made a lion and made drunk to delirium by
his American friends and spongers. 'He succumbed', as Caitlin
later wrote, 'like a mesmerized bait, only in this case a short-legged
one, to the multitudinous, scavenging, spawn of America.'

Only the brief interval of his return to Laugharne from his
third American tour for the summer of that last year and only the
restraints of home life made Dylan begin to recover from the
temptations of 'unflagging, disarming American charm'. Yet even
ill health and Caitlin's fear could not stop him from going back to
the success of *Under Milk Wood* and to his final dying of strangers
in that concrete world of the mad that the villagers of Llareggub
had always wanted to keep to the far side of the barbed wire.

Richard Burton, who was Dylan's friend and drinking companion, played Dylan's role of the First Voice in the BBC recording,
the Argo record of it, and finally in 1971 in the film version. He
told me that he had spoken the words over a thousand times
waking and sleeping, and that to him the whole play was about
religion, sex and death. He had on his conscience that Dylan had
begged him for a few hundred pounds, so that he would not have
to go again to America to die on his last tour there; but the actor
at the time was earning less money than the wastrel poet, as were
many of the writers whom Dylan never stopped dunning.

Dylan had always seen himself in the role of the tubercular
poet; one of his favourite tricks was coughing into his handkerchief because of too many cigarettes, then pretending he was a
lunger and that he had brought up blood. Yet both of his wireless
plays echoed with prophecies of his early death. As Caitlin wrote,

'Dylan and dying, Dylan and dying, they don't go together; or is it that they were bound to go together; he said so often enough, but I did not heed him.'

Under Milk Wood opened with two unexplained voices commenting on the seaside night town of Llareggyb, politer now in its revised spelling. These voices were not explained, their connection with the character of the town unknown. They seemed like natural spirits of the place, taking the hearers through night and dawn and day and dusk back to the final ambiguous description of Milk Wood itself, no longer as in its first mention a place of wedding dreams, where young girls were 'bridesmaided by glow-worms down the aisles of the organ-playing wood', but finally a place of Satan and Eden, lust and innocence, 'whose every tree-foot's cloven in the black glad sight of the hunter of lovers', with Polly Garter's voice sounding last of all for the townsfolk:

> But I always think as we tumble into bed
> Of little Willy Wee who is dead, dead, dead.

Dylan had always been accused of being a destroyer of others as well as of himself, while Caitlin was given the role of his preserver or his destroyer, depending on the point of view. Dylan certainly viewed Caitlin as his preserver, his Sunday wife who bore him angels – 'Harpies around me out of her womb!' She knew how to provide the opposition he needed, 'gentle, but firm, constant curbing, and a steady, dull, homely bed of straw to breed his fantasies in'. Playing the *enfant terrible* killed him, the urge to shock, to amuse, to drink to the last round and the last crowd. Already on the verge of delirium tremens during those last days in New York, he still had to go on what Scott Fitzgerald called a collegiate drunk, to return to his hotel room with the boast, 'I've had eighteen straight whiskies. I think that's the record.'

Brinnin's *Dylan Thomas in America* told of Dylan's dying in harrowing detail without ever telling the root cause of it. To Brinnin, Dylan wanted to destroy himself. America was only the excuse for self-sacrifice. Dylan was deliberately intimate with anybody who approached him. He was on a perpetual drunken spree even without alcohol. His gaiety was not so much spontaneous as premeditated – at first chosen, then a matter of abandon. Actually, estranged from Dylan, Brinnin had handed over the management of the poet to his twice-married assistant, Liz Reitell, who was herself attached to Dylan, but unable to save him.

Dylan's caricature of himself as 'the dollar-mad nightingale' in search of 'naked women in wet mackintoshes' was a flight from having to write, from having to earn money for his family, a deliberate suicide of genius for which no other person could be blamed. Now he began another affair with Liz Reitell, almost a more competent minder than Caitlin at Laugharne, though incapable of controlling him. Even in the love affair with the New York magazine executive Pearl, Dylan had presented himself jeeringly as a 'beer-cheapened hoddy-noddy' with 'his sodden bounce, his mis-theatrical-demeanour, the boastful tuppence!'

In his careful examinations of Dylan's death, George Tremlett doubted Brinnin's accounts, which veered from one emotional extreme to another, witnessed by Liz Reitell, who was detaching Dylan from the absent Brinnin. In fact, she arranged for Dylan to sign a contract with a rival lecture tour operator, Felix G. Gerstman, on 30 October 1953, for a punishing schedule. 'It is agreed that you also have the right to cancel performances contracted for if the gross income of bookings does not reach the amount of a weekly average of $1,000.' More of Dylan's plans included travelling to Hollywood to write a libretto for Stravinsky on a second Garden of Eden which grew after a nuclear holocaust; also writing the screenplay of *Ulysses* for Michael Powell, as well as working with the wireless producer Philip Burton on a stage play, *Two Streets*, an antiphonal drama about two young lovers who only met in a dance hall too late.

Dylan had everything to live for, while Brinnin had lost him and Reitell was fighting to keep him in America. In Caitlin's opinion, both of them were in love with her husband. They exaggerated his responsibility for his own dying in order to excuse their own limp connivance in it. Caitlin actually wrote to Liz Reitell, accusing her of stealing the greatest poet in the world. The New Yorker had no right to any part of him. For Dylan did seem smitten, writing in an unpublished letter to the American woman of his love and financial dependence on her. 'What a money letter, when all I want to say is I love you & miss you very very very much. Dylan.'

Unfortunately, Dylan had also fallen into the American habit of popping pills along with his alcohol, a deadly mixture. This was the beginning of the drug culture of Greenwich Village, the uppers and downers that were to develop into the quick fixes of cocaine and heroin and the play *Waiting for Cowboy* rather than *Godot*. To keep himself performing, Dylan was taking benzedrine and sleeping-pills, phenobarbitone and atropine. He was suffering from occasional black-outs and Liz Reitell called on a Dr Feltenstein to give him large amounts of cortisone and morphine. After a last successful reading of *Under Milk Wood* and a poetry reading and symposium at the City College of New York, Dylan collapsed at the Chelsea Hotel, vomiting. He turned blue and went into a coma and was transferred to St Vincent's Hospital, where he died after several days, apparently of pneumonia, while a nurse was bathing his body. The alcoholic poet John Berryman was a witness and wrote back to Vernon Watkins that Dylan's body was 'utterly quiet'. He looked so tired 'you might once more have burst into tears'.

The most reliable witness of Dylan's dying was his fellow Fitzrovian poet, Ruthven Todd. He wrote from New York on 23 November a round-robin letter, accounting for Dylan's last days to Louis MacNeice and his friends. He saw Dylan on 3 November in his room in the Chelsea Hotel with two other people. Dylan was 'vastly amusing, busily inventing a schizoid bar in which one was one's only customer'. On the Wednesday of his collapse, Dylan had only had two beers with Liz Reitell at the White Horse Tavern before going down in the Chelsea, apparently of alcohol poisoning. He was given a quarter of a grain of phenobarbitone, which he sicked up, before the morphine shots. Liz Reitell remained with him: 'looking after Dylan was no part-time job'.

According to Todd, almost the last words of Dylan were: 'What an undistinguished way to reach one's thirty-ninth year.' He had the dates wrong, but Liz Reitell 'spoke to Dylan who was murmuring drowsily and assured him that his horrors would pass.' When his face turned blue and he was transferred to St Vincent's Hospital and went into a coma, the doctors there performed a tracheotomy to enable Dylan to breathe better. Todd visited his friend early on the Saturday morning before he was put into an oxygen tent, 'from which he was not to emerge again'. Brinnin flew down to confer with Reitell and Todd, who had all of Dylan's effects packed and put in storage in the Chelsea. This group of the dying poet's friends were joined by Dave Slivka, who would make the death mask of Dylan. A rival group disapproved of what they were doing, led by the anthologist Oscar Williams – often mocked by Dylan – and the publishers George Reavey and James Laughlin of the New Directions Press.

Dylan loved to shock, to wound, to strike out, but he found himself in the end an inward man, maimed in the gut, killed by his own boozing and indiscretions. Brinnin and his friends even had Caitlin confined in an expensive psychiatric home for her own good as Dylan was dying, because of her wild outbursts and hysteria. Even while he was dying, she had lambasted her husband in a letter, begging for money to avoid summonses, or else she would go on the streets to feed the children, and he would be unreservedly the cause of it, 'by having a lump of iron slop, instead of a man's heart in your flabby breast'. As Caitlin came home on a boat with Dylan in his box, she asked herself who was so desirous of having her out of the way. She had left New York with her husband's embalmed body, 'sodden, limp from indistinguishable hangovers', half killed by the care of his friends.

Such destroying kindness, such indulgence of self-destruction, such yielding to the excesses of genius for the pleasure of observing them, while privately condemning the same excesses for the preservation of one's own distance and conscience, this was what Caitlin could never forget. She did not try to preserve herself after Dylan's death, she plunged into his riotings and failed at them, not forgiving the meticulous Brinnin for his accounts of the money earned, his wariness of the laws of libel, his implication that his behaviour was beyond reproach, while only the poet's was bad.

To Caitlin, Brinnin was so visibly sensitive that he made her feel like a rhinoceros rooting in an exquisite bed of flowers. She herself tried to join Dylan in his dying. 'Whenever I was being extra bad, I said to myself: if it had been the other way round, Dylan would have been twice as bad. But of course it could not have been the other way round; it was one of those ugly preordained things that *had* to happen this way round. More than that I do not know; but there is no doubt Dylan would have made a better job than me of killing himself: for damnation he has done it has he not?'

Wynford Vaughan-Thomas and other friends and trustees told of Dylan's funeral, which seemed a wake as full of mythology as the tales of his exploits in bars and beds. There was the story of the friend in the funeral parlour, who looked down at the poet's painted face, loud suit and carnation in his buttonhole, only to declare, 'He would never have been seen dead in it.' There was the story of the coffin being met at Southampton Dock by the local undertaker, who took the wrong western road back to Wales and was discovered by the police heading towards Cornwall; told of his mistake, he declared, 'Nobody said to me this blood country was forked.' Then there was the undignified sight of one or two of Dylan's hangers-on slipping away from the beautiful simple burial ceremony at Laugharne to get back to the Boat House and rifle through the poet's manuscripts before the rest of the mourners returned; luckily one of the trustees of the estate got there first.

In his going as in his living, Dylan was bled dry by interested strangers, even at that final 'tame, cup of tea, whisky-nipping, saucepan-domesticated, mingling of the original black beetles, raffish Londoners, and Swansea boys in their best provincial suits . . . all caring according to their means, and class. But caring', as Caitlin wrote, 'more than anybody had cared at a funeral since.' If that last wake was a boozing affair, it was because Dylan had asked that people should get drunk when he was laid in the Green Banks. A tradition in Wales and at Laugharne also held that nothing became a man so in life as the size of his death. A small funeral meant a small life, a large funeral bore testimony to fame. As Edward Vale once wrote, 'No matter how shabbily you have lived, you will be respected in Wales when you have become a corpse.'

After he had outlived his adolescent preoccupation with an early and Keatsian death, Dylan did not want to commit suicide, by drink or anything else. Brinnin claimed that in New York Dylan said that he wanted to die. Yet this was spoken in broken health and alcoholic melancholy. He only sought relief from the crack-up of his pouchy deteriorating body. In his last agony, there was nobody who could restrain him or help him, and nobody to admit responsibility for not being able to do so. If the Americans loved him, they washed their hands of his ending as carefully as the cousins of Pontius Pilate.

Had Dylan only lived latterly like the parody of a poet on the spree, he would have been forgotten. Yet these last years produced *Under Milk Wood*, a hymn to family and children and Laugharne, the sweetest of elegies for those he loved. Some criticised him later for deriving the ideas and images from the Circe episode in Joyce's *Ulysses*; but Dylan's play was no plagiarism. This was a metamorphosis of his Welsh experience. So was the dying fall of his last supreme poems of self-awareness, his 'Lament' for himself, his rage against dying on his father's behalf, and his own 'Poem On His Birthday', full of the joy of the mustardseed sun and the switchback sea, and the knowing that he would not reach forty years of age.

> . . . Oh, let me midlife mourn by the shined
>   And druid herons' vows
> The voyage to ruin I must run,
>   Dawn ships clouted aground,
> Yet, though I cry with tumbledown tongue,
>   Count my blessings aloud . . .
> And this last blessing most,
>   That the closer I move
> To death, one man through his sundered hulks,
>   The louder the sun blooms
> And the tusked, ramshackling sea exults . . .

14

Heritage and Legacy

———————

Too many of the artists of Wales spend too much time talking about
the position of the artists of Wales.
There is only one position for an artist anywhere: and that is, upright.

from 'Wales and the Artist', a broadcast by Dylan Thomas
24 October, 1949

JUST as there were horses for courses, there were drinkers for
Soho, which was, after all, originally a call to the hunting dogs pur-
suing a hare to the kill. The post-war Fitzrovia of Dylan Thomas
was wasted in plunges from the bottle or a flight to the provinces.
Many of the painters and composers and poets were hounded to
their deaths, the victims of alcoholic excesses in the decades after
the 'forties – Nina Hamnett and John Minton, the two Roberts,
Colquhoun and MacBryde, the composer Constant Lambert and
Dylan Thomas, who had already foreseen his end almost since his
beginning. His actual death in 1953 after a drinking bout in New
York signalled the destructive powers of too many pints and
chasers in too many pubs full of artists and their acolytes. The life
that Fitzrovia gave it also took away. In his poem, 'At the Wake of
Dylan Thomas', George Barker told of the example of his fellow
poet's burial:

... Simply by dying we add to the manic chorus
And put the fear of God up all surviving.

And now he's gotten, first of all and foremost,
You, Dylan, too, the one undoubting Thomas,
The whistler in the dark he's taken from us.

'It was a shock to hear about Dylan Thomas,' one of his Soho acquaintances, Mary Sarton wrote. 'I shall always remember the flood of relief I felt when I first read "October Morning" and "Fern Hill" and "Do Not Go Gentle into that Good Night", as if a long starvation were at an end. It is cruel that he should go, but it is, I suspect, the Dionysian fate, the exalted feverish climb.' Such a death made her feel responsible for her own poetic future. 'To use it well, to keep growing, to be implacably self-demanding and self-critical.' She wondered what would have been the consequences of Yeats or Marianne Moore dying at forty. Poets should have long lives with the best at the end.

Dylan's memorial plaque in the Poets' Corner of Westminster Abbey was to be the result of a Christian believer, who did not doubt his Thomas. President Jimmy Carter of the United States had been inspired by the works of the Welsh poet. On a state visit to Westminster Abbey, he would notice that there was no acknowledgement of Dylan; at that time, Shelley and Byron, too, were not commemorated there, because of their immoral lives. The American President would put the question to the Dean of Westminster: 'Why is Dylan Thomas not in Poets' Corner?' The misspent life would be quoted, to which the born-again and forgiving Carter would reply: 'You put him in here. And I will pray for him.' And so it would be done.

Both London and New York had betrayed Dylan, and that betrayal was something that Caitlin could neither accept nor forget. In an anguished letter to George Reavey and his wife on 16 December 1953, she stated her grief: 'though it all seems so far away and becoming less now; against the inescapable fact of Dylan lying so close – rotting, under a pile of wet Welsh earth and worms, with a mound of rainsoaked, weeping, dishevelled flowers on top.' She could not forget it, she never would. 'Better to be further away, far as possible, all the way to the Antipodes but even then, I will be there too, so it won't be much better.' As for the Reaveys' accounts of treachery in New York, Caitlin found the news a 'tinted up nightmare'. She still could not believe 'that the people who were round me, and I swear before God I can recognise love, were deliberately betraying me and Dylan, behind my back.'

Such had been the case and had always been the case. Dylan was betrayed by those who indulged his weaknesses. He himself was held to be a traitor by Welsh-speaking nationalists. He had never spoken the native tongue, given the split in his education, reared by a schoolmaster father who taught English in a seaside southern town which denied by speech and habit the hard national heritage of the mountain valleys to the north. Yet Dylan had called the problem of his divided inheritance unnecessarily, and trivially, difficult:

There is a number of young Welshmen writing poems in English, who, insisting passionately that they are Welshmen, should by rights be writing in Welsh, but who, unable to write in Welsh or reluctant to do so because of the uncommercial nature of the language, often given the impression that their writing in English is only a condescension to the influence and ubiquity of a tyrannous foreign tongue. I do not belong to that number ... It's the poetry, written in the language which is most natural to the poet, that counts, not his continent, country, island, race, class, or political persuasion.

The true question was, what was the language most natural to Dylan, what rhythm and structure of English? Dylan used to scoff at reviewers and critics who talked about the Welshness of his poetry, claiming in 1938 that he 'never understood this racial talk, "his Irish talent", "undoubtedly Scotch inspiration", apart from whiskey'. Yet, in fact, his ear for the rises and falls, stresses and syntaxes of local speech made him the heir of the bardic tradition in Wales, of the preacher and the poet of the people.

He was known to admit to the debt that all contemporary Anglo-Welsh writers had to the fierce Caradoc Evans, who had fought the first war of liberation against the philistinism and provincialism and chapel-strict standards of the pawky local literature before the time of Dylan, and who had attacked the Bible-black primness and hypocrisy of Welsh society and nonconformity with the unadmitted biblical fervour of a true nonconformist. The young Dylan had visited him once at Aberystwyth with another Welsh writer, Glyn Jones. 'We made a tour of the pubs in the evening, drinking to the eternal damnation of the Almighty and the soon-to-be-hoped-for destruction of the Tin Bethels. The university students love Caradoc, & pelt him with stones whenever he goes out.'

Like the heretic, Dylan himself was indebted to the religion and history which he often seemed to attack. If he fled from the strictures of the chapels into the rich and sensuous world of the body, making the profane holy, he did it in the language of King James's Bible, an influence he never denied. 'Its great stories of Noah, Jonah, Lot, Moses, Jacob, David, Solomon, and a thousand more, I had, of course, known from very early youth; the great rhythms had rolled over me from the Welsh pulpits; and I read, for myself, from Job and Ecclesiastes; and the story of the New Testament is part of my life.' If he had never sat down and studied the Bible or 'consciously echoed its language', yet his childhood memories worked on that common property and quarry of all those who work in the English tongue.

In his piercing look at *The World of Dylan Thomas*, Clark Emery scrutinised the vocabulary of the collected poems, to discover that, after the paramount word 'I', the most frequent words were 'sea, man, love, like, sun, eye, as, time, lie, night, wind, water, light, sleep, over, green, moon, house, sky, turn, ghost, fire, grave, star, tree, white, world, stone, tongue, wound, see, sing, tell, still, summer, walk, word, seed, weather, voice, year, lover.' Most of these terms were Anglo-Saxon monosyllables; they usually dealt with the actual and sensuous experience of a child. 'Considered together, they have a pastoral quality somewhere between that of the Twenty-third Psalm and that of "Anyone lived in a pretty how town".' The language was that of the seaside child, surrounded by his family, intrigued by his body, protected by his home, rung awake by church bells. In the centre of it all, the selfish body, sucking in all experience from Bible to back-chat, the 'commoner than water' vocabulary of Swansea and Wales.

No more than he formally studied the Bible nor sorted out his experiences academically did Dylan consciously assimilate the traditions of the eisteddfods and the Welsh bards. These depended on a technical discipline controlling sound and rhythm, an internal repetition, and a successive use of parallel constructions. The *cynghanedd* or harmony of the formal poem was achieved by the sounds of multiple alliteration and internal rhymes. As Matthew Arnold noted in his criticism of Welsh literature, the Celtic poet employed the utmost elaboration and often attained astounding skill in his work; but his content was rather short in interpretation of the world and long on sentiment, full of style and intensity, signifying not too much.

Dylan took over, perhaps uncannily, the marvellous intricacy of the labours of the bards without losing a lyric frenzy and even a whole cosmogony. His last poems were his most elaborate, wrought in Laugharne according to the traditions of the unacknowledged land of his fathers. Gwyn Jones was correct when he wrote that Dylan was 'Welsh in the cunning complexity of his metres, not only in the loose *cynghanedd*, the chime of consonants and pealing vowels, but in the relentless discipline of his verse, the hierarchic devotion to the poet's craft, the intellectual exactitude and emotional compression of word and phrase and stave and poem.'

Read and listen to the care of it all, the lilt of letters, the sounds that soothed and words that awakened the ending lines of his last finished lyric poem, 'Prologue':

> We will ride out alone, and then,
> Under the stars of Wales,
> Cry, Multitudes of arks! Across
> The water lidded lands,
> Manned with their loves they'll move,
> Like wooden islands, hill to hill.
> Huloo, my proud dove with a flute!
> Ahoy, old, sea-legged fox,
> Tom tit and Dai mouse!
> My ark sings in the sun
> At God speeded summer's end
> And the flood flowers now.

Willy-nilly, Dylan was a bard and a minstrel and a Welshman. Even if he worked in an alien tongue, it was his natural tongue; he knew no other. As the critic and writer John Wain pointed out, a Welsh poet, even an English monoglot, still did not feel, think or write like an English poet. Part of the explanation was to be found in the importance given to the *spoken* word in Wales, the tradition of the *hwyl* and the *hiraeth*. The *hwyl* was the chanting sermon, the eloquent and intense and musical preaching that was the Welsh version of the gift of tongues. The *hiraeth* was the quality found in the mass singing of Welsh hymns, the spiritual force and longing of an ancient people, as expressed in a moving tribute to Dylan composed by the First Narrator in *Under Milk Wood*, the first time it was put on in Laugharne after the poet's death:

> I tarry in this cemetery of *hiraeth*
> Not because he knew and loved his mother-tongue
> Nor because he sang a selfless psalm in Salem.
> He sought his bible in an English pub in English Laugharne
> Playing a waiting game with words and gods . . .

Dylan himself always intoned and shouted, sang and mumbled his poems in English, before audiences and in the bath, boisterously and most privately in the toils of composition. His daughter Aeron remembered her mother surrounding his tub with sweets, which he sucked during the hot suds of his performances. 'I shall never forget those times when my father used to read to me. With Grimm's fairy tales he'd do all the voices . . . He loved to act the parts and I loved to listen.' The echo of the old preacher Marlais chanted in the voice of the poet bellowing against preachers, but in praise of his own special God. The bard worked on the hundreds of intricate drafts of the religious poems that looked to Blake and Donne rather than to ape Gwilym and his native lot.

Dylan could not really understand the narrow and restricted output of either the 'court' bards who wrote in Welsh for the eisteddfods or the petty, although pretty, vision of local poets. When the young Dylan wrote his newspaper pieces on 'The Poets of Swansea' for the *Herald of Wales*, he called W.H. Davies the most gifted Welsh poet then writing in English, but he wondered why Davies had neglected the legends of his own country.

'He could have recreated the fantastic world of the *Mabinogion*, surrounded the folk lore with his own fancies, and made his poetry a stepping place for the poor children of darkness to reach a saner world . . .' Instead, Davies chose to be a hedgerow poet, describing the brevity of life, the green of the grass, and the inanity of personal expression. Although the older Dylan was to speak more kindly of Davies, praising the inevitability in his slightest verses and the unique observations in his tiniest reflections on the natural world, he never really approved of a poet who chose to be a miniaturist and refused to strike out for the wilder shores of creation.

By his work and refusal to restrict himself to being a Welsh poet with a local reputation, Dylan advanced and popularised the writings of a whole group of his Anglo-Welsh contemporaries, particularly his friend Vernon Watkins, and Gwyn Jones, Glyn Jones, R.S. Thomas, Gwyn Thomas and Alun Lewis. If Caradoc Evans fought a local war of liberation, Dylan Thomas led an international guerrilla attack on the classicism of Eliot and Auden and on the intellectual and critical dominance of London, Oxford, Cambridge, and Harvard. His romantic revolt unleashed a certain coarseness and richness of language, a revelling in comedy and bawdry, an affirmation of the holy myths rather than a snivelling at God, an orgy of the irrational as opposed to the careful classification of what was meaningful or significant.

Glyn Jones described the contemporaries and followers of Dylan. 'Bible-blest and chapel-haunted, wrestle hard as we can, we stand confessed the last, lost nonconformists of an Age.' Dylan helped them to make their way as men of letters, since his revolt was the most extreme and original of them all. Yet he, too, never escaped that first puritan training, that sense of sin, that holy infusion of childhood. He was more at home with Vaughan and Blake than with Marx and Proust. As that perceptive commentator on Dylan, John Ackerman, has stressed continually, Dylan's bardic qualities, prophetic and intuitive, eloquent and religious, rhetorical and intricate, made him grow in Gwyn Jones's words 'from dragon's tooth to druid in his own land'.

Yet some elements in modern Wales and some critics continued to dislike him for his Englishness and his sensuousness. Bourgeois and chapel society found him shocking and irreverent, while the stricter Welsh nationalists found him an Uncle Tom in *Under Milk Wood*, feeding the BBC with the fond pap and sentimental follies so dear to foreign gawpers in search of Welsh antics. This attack was joined by such moralistic and uncomprehending critics as David Holbrook, who considered Dylan's attitude to the people of Llareggub that 'of the week-ender from sophisticated London, his country people toys in a model farmyard'.

Such profound misunderstanding of Dylan's aims and purposes often hid its righteousness under an assault on his unreality, when his purpose was to conjure up the irrational forces of nostalgia and dream and pastoral, the human joy in the sensual base of love, and the human grief at the death which must come. Other critics condemned Dylan for writing with a perverse brilliance in a stepmother tongue, 'the *revenge* taken by a conquered race on the self-satisfied culture of its conquerors'. Dylan's efforts to introduce some bardic discipline and internal rhyming and alliteration, especially in poems such as 'The Conversation Of Prayer', were a dead end rather than a new influence.

Dylan had, indeed, condemned over-indulgence in strict bardic forms, stating that it succeeded only 'in warping, crabbing and obscuring the natural genius of the English language'. Yet the interplay between form and rhythm, strictness and looseness, the use of every trick of language in the poet's box, was the very strength and tension of Dylan's poetry. There never was a total surrender to sound as in the flow of Swinburne, never to straitjacket of metre as in the corset of Auden or Graves.

Dylan loved Wales and sang its countryside more clearly than any other bard or minstrel had done. He also loved its towns and the little city of Swansea, and he wrote comic and sad plays and stories about them that seemed to catch their essence in the opinions of most people who lived there or visited there. Yet Dylan's very ease of final style after his labours, his success with a mass audience as well as on the Third Programme, seemed to attract envy like flies round a melting ice-cream cornet on Swansea beach.

He never had any time for academic critics when he was alive, not only from fear of seeming ignorant to them, but also from boredom at their niggling. As Caitlin knew, he hated pretension as well as 'every type of flowery excursion into intellectualism . . . he had the same dislike, amounting to superstitious horror, of philosophy, psychology, analysis, criticism; all those vaguely termed ponderous tomes; but most of all, of the gentle art of discussing poetry . . .'

An unkind critic himself, Dylan only liked the intellectual company of working poets of the better sort, who managed to write criticism now and again. He grew out of his early lack of generosity towards his peers. That had been very much a defence of his Swansea youth, mere provincial bravado, as was the unreal destruction of his family's home by his alter ego, Samuel Bennett, in *Adventures in the Skin Trade*. In a perceptive essay, Walford Davies restated what Dylan always knew, that Cwmdonkin Drive was a refuge and an escape for him from the world as Laugharne was to be later. 'The street was a safe hole in a wall behind the wind in another country.' The young dog and the old dog remained convention-bound and convention-ridden, however much they railed against convention. As Caitlin also wrote, 'though Dylan imagined himself to be completely emancipated from his family background, there was a very strong puritanical streak in him, that his friends never suspected; but of which I got the disapproving benefit.' On one occasion in Soho, he literally tore the flesh off his hands with his nails, crying, 'To get at the bone, and then to get rid of that! What a wonderful thing!' Calvin and Wesley would have understood his action.

Suburban and sick of it, he needed a retreat from the city. Puritan and rebellious in the stewpots, he needed to retire and recuperate. Dylan was not prim outside and lecherous within, chapel to his world and brothel to his dream. He flaunted his revolt and hid his strict decencies. 'One: I am a Welshman,' he boasted in Rome in 1947, 'two: I am a drunkard; three: I am a lover of the human race, especially of women.' In fact, one: he was a poet; but the other priorities followed in that order, Welshness at the fore.

This appreciation of Dylan Thomas has tried to show that he was born to a divided bardic tradition, a bilingual speech, a split-minded people, a provincial bias; only his home was safe, first with his parents, finally with Caitlin, the womb with a view. Once secure in the Welsh suburb or country, he longed for the city; once disgusted by the city or foreign parts, he yearned for the deathful peace of Wales.

Two letters, one to Bert Trick in 1939 from Laugharne, one to Margaret Taylor in 1947 from Rapallo, demonstrated this thesis and antithesis in his restless goings. In Laugharne, he wrote, 'I miss the boys and the smoky nights. Here everything is so slow and prettily sad. I'd like to live in a town or a city again for a bit. Let there be one town left, and we'll fill it with ourselves.' Yet, from Italy, he was to write back, 'Oh, anywhere a house. I am lost without one. I am domestic as a slipper, I want somewhere of my own, I'm old enough now, I want a house to shout, sleep, and work in.' So he bounced from home to away, from security to exposure, until the blood ran thin in him as the alcohol rose.

Vernon Watkins, who probably knew Dylan best of all others except for Caitlin, wrote that any study of him must remain totally inadequate. For he prized seriousness and was a born clown. He created an immediate intimacy with strangers and hid his private strict self. 'The entertainer and the intellectual alike were slightly ashamed after meeting him, as he could beat them both at their own game; but if they were humble, they quickly recognised that he was humble too. The prig was his *bête noire*, the pedant a black and white crossword figure whom he didn't despise. The variety of life and its abundance sang in his veins. He was born to praise it and he did so most completely when war distorted it into every manifestation of horror.'

After the war, as Watkins further commented, Dylan's own war continued. His free and easy social life led to the rich comedy of the broadcasts. His isolation and fear and toil wove the intricacy of the later poems. Yet the social mask put on to protect the inward poet was fatal. 'His method was not to retreat from the mask but to advance beyond it, and in that exaggeration remain completely himself. He agreed readily with his detractors and did not mind at all being misunderstood. Then, in the private dark, his exuberance was subjected to the strictest control.'

These were the contradictions of the man who was the finest lyric poet of his age. He had one foot in Eden, the other in Babylon. He had one hand on the Bible, the other under the bedclothes. His heavy head was lifted to the sky, his feet were set on the bar-rail. A frail angel became gross, a self-declared Lucifer took in his aged parents. The sensuous prophet of the adolescent, the generous wastrel of middle age, the fierce mourner of the dead, he passed a Christian name from the *Mabinogion* on to a folk-singer. His last name, however, was so common in Wales that it meant any farmer, railwayman, teacher or housewife. He was the bard of the mysteries of heaven and hell, the poet of the country and the body, the writer of the excessive and the vernacular. His plays shall sound for him, his poems shall speak for him as long as there are ears to hear. Let him be his own last best witness.

Man himself is a work. Today he is a dirty piece of work. But tomorrow he may sprout wings under his serge shoulders, be faced and sided like Aquarius, who is the first sign of the vital year.

So much for Dylan's hope for humanity, and finally, for his hope for himself.

> . . . And every wave of the way
> And gale I tackle, the whole world then,
>   With more triumphant faith
> That ever was since the world was said,
>   Spins its morning of praise.
>
>   I hear the bouncing hills
> Grow larked and greener at berry brown
>   Fall and the dew larks sing
> Taller this thunderclap spring, and how
>   More spanned with angels ride
> The mansouled fiery islands! Oh,
>   Holier than their eyes,
> And my shining men no more alone
>   As I sail out to die.

Appendix

The making of the film of *Under Milk Wood*

———

There is a law in making a decent film in this country. The law is, the impossible must always happen. That is why so few decent films can be made over here, although Britain is full of good film-makers.

The impossible always happened in making *Under Milk Wood*. At times, its luck exceeded incredulity and vanished into Celtic mist. Like a necromancer juggling the elements, any Merlin of the screen has to mix the gold of the backers with the stars in their courses and come up with a horoscope that guarantees fair heavens and a safe return. To go at all, *Under Milk Wood* had to find a time when Richard Burton, Elizabeth Taylor and Peter O'Toole were all available to work and in this island, which was rather like fixing a weekend between Howard Hughes, Elizabeth the Second and Puck. Then the gold had to be conjured in double-quick time from the state and a merchant bank, both of whom were rightly foolish enough to buck the wisdom of Wardour Street and think there could be profit as well as art in the wild warm words of that people's poet, Dylan Thomas. Then there had to be hayfield sun in March in Fishguard, which would be a blessing not seen in thirty years. ('*Wales* in winter!' said the drenched warriors streaming home from Polanski's protracted *Macbeth*. 'Jesus! Not only did Banquo blow off his horse, but the bloody horse blew away too.') Then we had a forty days' budget about as fat as Our Lord's when he had the same schedule in the

[228]

wilderness. What with sixty sets and seventy actors, we had to spend a quarter of our time just shifting from scene to scene; we shot on the run, with the mighty heroes of Lee Electrics humping the hundredweight brute lights as casually as kittens on their shoulders. Everything and everyone had to work too well, beyond normal and half-way to dream. The technicians would mutter about 'Andrew the Luck.' And I would answer, 'Miracles happen daily.' Frankly they had to, so they did.

There is a necessity in a film, once it has begun, which matches the resignation in a Celt, once he has decided to go for broke. There are so many shots to be taken each day, so many actors to play their scenes while they are still available, so many seconds of film to be put successfully in the can each week – or else, the boot. Considerations of art come a bad second to sheer endurance. One makes the script and hopes it works. Any improvisation on the set is a dangerous gift that may save the part, but throw the whole. The important thing, as Beckett once wrote, is to be done, to have done. And to have done well.

For there are no excuses. A film-maker is judged by the final film. He can plead none of his troubles on the way, too little time, bad weather, fractious actors, intervention from the money, accident. But then he gets the credit for the greatness of the others' performance. In *Under Milk Wood*, that ultimate professional O'Toole insisted on wearing milky-blue contact lenses that covered his whole eyeball to play the blind Captain Cat. The trouble was that he could only stand the lenses in his eyes for half an hour at a whack, and then he was really going blind after four days of it. If he had not been such a superb performer capable of five-minute takes hitting an unseen mark without a wrong word, we could never have completed his shots on schedule with him still seeing. As it was, the courage of the man lasted far beyond the good of his eyes until the last four longish shots, which we took from the back or with his lids closed.

Yet endurance and luck are not enough to make a good film. There has to be magic as well. And magic is not on call. For me, *Under Milk Wood* has always been the supreme incantation of my life. However many hundred times I hear the words during the tedious repetitions of editing and dubbing a film, the phrases still reverberate and comfort and tease meanings as only the great sentences do. Richard Burton would complain of being woken o' nights by voices haunting him with Dylan's words; but his own voice with its fits and starts, graduations and gravels, choirs and harmonies is the midnight speech of the lost bards of Wales. The magic began when he recorded the sullen craft of his dead friend's words all in two hours in a Soho cellar before the picture started. We always had that spell to play back to ourselves during the bad days, and every time we heard it, the magic came again and we thought that *Under Milk Wood* might work after all.

Daring to make a classic like Dylan's is a fool's leap into the dark wood. The arrogance of setting forth one's own visual imagination on a screen to compete with the dreams of the many followers of the poet with their own dark-bright visions from the words alone invites the destruction of the gods. Yet our insolence somehow seemed to amuse the Welsh gods. If they did not forgive us, they played with us obscurely, and through their fatal teasing, they brought the magic into the film. If I can try to describe what is beyond sense . . .

The problem of *Under Milk Wood* as a film lay in its bittiness, cross-cutting from voice to voice all the time without knowing whose voice it was. Seventy little stories to tell in ninety minutes in the life of a small fishing-port. The connecting link of Two Voices, their characters and connections with the town unexplained, Voices with the power to conjure up dreams, knowing intimately the private lives of all the sleepers in Cockle Row and Coronation Street, godlike in their comprehension and devilish in their mockery. How to make this counterpoint of words into one visual whole, while being faithful to the text . . . It was daunting.

I had only half solved the problem when we began shooting the film. I had given the Two Voices faces and characters, predominance to the powerful, brooding face and pale, piercing eyes of Richard Burton, foolery to the thin, playful, melancholic skull's head of Ryan Davies, the beloved clown of Welsh television, playing the jester to Burton's King, the imp to Lucifer. I had gone back to an early experience of Dylan's, when he had spent a weekend with a friend in Gower, and the friend's girl with a loose red mouth had swapped beds. I had also gone back to Dylan's other great radio play, *Return Journey*, where the old Dylan travels home to look for the young Dylan, and the final refrain is the same as in Polly Garter's song . . . 'dead, dead, dead.' There was also a story of his called 'Just Like Little Dogs', where two men take out two sisters on the beach and the girls change partners in the night. So I made the reason for the Two Voices going back to Llareggub their quest for a girl, Norma Jane Jenkins, whom they had met way back in the war, and had shared; it made for nice intercutting with the children's kissing games, Billy and Johnnie Cristo and Dicky kissing Gwennie, and with Polly Garter's song as she scrubs the floor of the Welfare Hall.

> Tom, Dick, and Harry were three fine men
> And I'll never have such loving again . . .

Then Norma Jane walks away into a graveyard and the men leave town in their khaki coats, and it is revealed that Norma Jane had been dead a long time, and that these two visible spirits from the sea and the dark wood have come back to relive their life in the timeless town and resurrect their lost love.

This device gave a unity to the film, a visual reason for all the marvellous speeches of the Voices, that orchestration of words which makes *Under Milk Wood* as binding as a spell. But it did not solve the problem of the final coming together of the townspeople, nor did it help the dying fall of the picture, which trailed away into nothing. But we do not always make movies. Sometimes movies make us.

We were filming the night shot of Evans the Death, the undertaker, asleep by an open coffin, laughing in his dreams. The undertaker's shop had been built by us in front of two lavatories on the quayside of Lower Fishguard, which otherwise served naturally as Cockle Row. We had set up the shot through the window of the shop on the first three letters FUN from FUNERALS – beyond the glass, the end of the bed, with Evans the Death's toes curling through a hole in his purple socks. Then a coastguard siren wailed behind us, meaning trouble at sea. And policemen hurried up the quayside, and we stopped work, and a boat set out across the bay. And we looked at the cliffs opposite until the boat came back. In it, the body of a drowned boy. One of our electricians thought it was the body of his child, and he broke down. It turned out to be the child of a local freelance cameraman, who normally worked for television. But in the dead child, we all saw our own deaths and the deaths of our children. So we packed up and went home till the morning.

The funeral was two days later. So I and the associate producer left the scene of Polly Garter singing, 'Little Willy Wee is dead, dead, dead . . .', to pay our respects to the family of the boy and leave wreaths from the company. The father met us, a brave and good man. He said he would not find it easy to leave overnight his wife and other children and his home for some weeks now. So we offered him work in getting us some shots of seals, which we might need. For he knew where the seals were at this time of year.

What we did not know was that the seals lay at the bottom of a thousand foot cliff. Putting his Arriflex on his back, the brave cameraman and two of our party got down that cliff, risking their lives and losing the top of a finger. The father came back with some spectacular shots, including one of a group of seals humping away into the foam.

We went back next week and did the shot of the undertaker laughing by the coffin, although nobody wanted to think of it. Dylan had written it, and it still had to be done. But when I saw the rushes of the seals and I reread *Under Milk Wood* for the hundredth time, I saw where the magic and the end of the picture lay. Celtic myths are full of seals coming back from the sea; their singing voices are meant to be the drowned dead, like the five sailors who come back to Captain Cat in his dreams. 'I lost my step in Nantucket,' says Dancing Williams, now down salt deep into the Davy dark. And endlessly, Dylan refers to dreams coming from the black sea:

> Only you can hear and see, behind the eyes of the sleepers, the
> . . . flight and fall and despairs and big seas of their dreams . . .

> Now behind the eyes and secrets of the dreamers in the streets
> rocked to sleep by the sea, see the . . . wrecks and sprats and
> shells and fishbones, whalejuice and moonshine and small salt
> fry dished up by the hidden sea.

So I filmed a night dream dance in the pouring rain, with a gale blowing the roofs away, while the actors playing the people of Llareggub caracoled around the town pump and danced away into the sea, and they were dissolved into seals, and Satan's jester walked back from the wild drowned caper he had led from the back of a squealing pig to the black Milk Wood, where the devil of Richard Burton was waiting, crossing himself and smiling darkly, with his last incantation sounding, that begins:

> The Wood, whose every tree-foot's cloven in the black
> glad sight of the hunters of lovers . . .

And *Under Milk Wood* had an end, a magical end, that had grown out of its words and its making, out of the life of the welcoming town and the death of the boy that had its sad meaning for us all, out of the rich deep words of the Welsh poet of poets and the tears in Captain Cat's eyes as he remembers Rosie Probert and his lost sailoring days:

> Seas barking like seals,
> Blue seas and green,
> Seas covered with eels
> And mermen and whales.

Richard Burton had said to me that *Under Milk Wood* was all about religion, sex and death, and I did not understand his words until the film was over. My preacher and teacher was not the fond-foolish Reverend Eli Jenkins nor the dark Puritan Jack Black from Dylan's text, but my dandy-dark cameraman Bob Huke, who made me watch the twilights away in his quest for that one shot at evening which he called 'the magic hour'. And in that 'dusk and ceremonial dust, and night's first darkening snow', I sensed the timeless powers of the Gwaun Valley, where the pagan stones still stand at the doorways and the mistletoe hangs from the wind-bent oaks, the powers of light and night, wind and water, stone and hill, crow and cromlech, Celtic cross and bleeding yew, which are still the old gods in that Pembrokeshire where the ancient Celts quarried stones to drag all the way to Stonehenge. And I knew that we only had to resign ourselves to the place and its doings to recapture the spell of Dylan's words and describe Milk waking Wood.

If *Under Milk Wood* works as a film, it will be because we were all the servants of the dead Dylan Thomas, who caught the essence of all Welsh sea-towns and made an incantation of them. The film was the making of us. We were not making the film.

Andrew Sinclair, 1971

CAST

(The cast of the film of *Under Milk Wood* has been called by the Curator of the National Film Archives of Wales 'the Debrett of Welsh acting'. David Jason appeared as Nogood Boyo in his first film role.)

First Voice	RICHARD BURTON
Rosie Probert	ELIZABETH TAYLOR
Captain Cat	PETER O'TOOLE
Myfanwy Price	GLYNIS JOHNS
Mrs Pugh	VIVIEN MERCHANT
Mrs Ogmore-Pritchard	SIAN PHILLIPS
Second Voice	RYAN DAVIS
Mog Edwards	VICTOR SPINETTI
Gossamer Beynon	ANGHARAD REES
Polly Garter	ANN BEACH
Mr Waldo	RAY SMITH
Sinbad Sailors	MICHAEL FORREST
Mr Cherry Owen	GLYNN EDWARDS
Mr Pugh	TALFRYN THOMAS
Mr Willy Nilly	TIM WYLTON
Mrs Willy Nilly	BRONWEN WILLIAMS
The Rev. Eli Jenkins	AUBREY RICHARDS
Nogood Boyo	DAVID JASON
Butcher Beynon	HUBERT REES
Mrs Beynon	MARY JONES
Dai Bread	DUDLEY JONES
Mrs Dai Bread One	DOROTHEA PHILLIPS
Mrs Dai Bread Two	RUTH MADOC
Organ Morgan	RICHARD PARRY

Mrs Organ Morgan	DILYS PRICE
Mae Rose Cottage	SUSAN PENHALIGON
Lily Smalls	MEG WYNN OWEN
Utah Watkins	DAVID DAVIES
Mrs Utah Watkins	MAUDIE EDWARDS
Mr Ogmore	DILLWYN OWEN
Mr Pritchard	RICHARD DAVIES
Lord Cut Glass	DAVYDD HARVARD

with: Mark Jones, John Rees, Rachel Thomas, Bryn Williams, Paul Gist, Peggy Ann Clifford, Bridget Turner, Davyd Harries, Olwen Rees, Griffith Davies, Andree Gaydon, Shane Shelton, Bryn Jones, John Rainer, Olwen Griffiths, Paul Spear, Lucy Griffiths, Nesta Harris, Pamela Miles, Janet Davies, Margaret Courtenay, Gwyneth Owen, Gordon Styles, Brian Osborne, T.H. Evans, Edmond Thomas, Jill Britton, Minnie Collins, Rhoda Lewis, Eira Griffiths, Margaret Lace, Angela Brinkworth and Ienan Rhys Williams.

Chapter Notes

Chapter 1

I was particularly and indirectly informed by Robert Graves in *The White Goddess* (London, 1961) about Welsh bards and minstrels, while D. Parry Jones, *Welsh Country Upbringing* (London, 1948) is most informative. Lady Charlotte Guest's translation of the *Mabinogion* led to the revival of Arthurian and bardic poetry in Victorian Wales.

Chapter 2

The 'Memories of Dylan Thomas by Four of His Friends', sculptor Ronald Cour and painter Alfred Janes and poet Vernon Watkins and artist Mervyn Levy were printed as a special feature in the *South Wales Evening Post*, undated, and are reproduced with grateful thanks, as were the 'Post Impressions' of Daniel Jones, 20 October 1982.

Chapter 3

Thomas Barlowe's testimony on the young Dylan as reporter was printed in the *South Wales Evening Post* on 20 May 1977, while that of Bill Willis was given to the Dylan Thomas special supplement of 27 June 1998. Ethel

Ross's memories of acting with Dylan appeared in the *Evening Post* of 10 November 1978, which also reported Dylan's observations on the gang warfare of poets in December 1934. Vernon Watkins's account of first meeting Dylan has been preserved by Jeff Towns, while the Welsh reviewer of *18 Poems*, A. Spencer Vaughan-Thomas, had his piece printed in the *South Wales Evening Post* on 12 January 1935. For reproducing Dylan's early poems, my thanks to the Poetry Collection of the Lockwood Memorial Library at the State University of New York at Buffalo, 'How Shall My Animal' from the 1930 *Notebook*; 'From Love's First Fever To Her Plague' from the August 1930 *Notebook*; 'Within His Head Revolved A Little World' from the February 1933 *Notebook*. I knew Richard Burton, while making the film of *Under Milk Wood* with him.

Chapter 4

Outside her autobiography and my personal knowledge of her as Lady Snow, I am grateful to Pamela Hansford Johnson for her article on Dylan in *Adam International Review*, No. 236, 1953.

Chapter 5

Dylan's lonely postcard of 17 November 1934 comes from the Jeff Towns Collection. The quotation from George Sterling, the intimate friend of Jack London and a *habitué* of the Bohemias of San Francisco and Greenwich Village in New York, is taken from Alan Churchill, *The Improper Bohemians* (London, 1959). The story about Augustus John paying the bill at the Eiffel Tower comes from Ruthven Todd's *Fitzrovia and the Road to the York Minster, or Down Dean Street* (London, 1973). John Gawsworth's diary entry comes from his Verse Notebook VIII, 5–18 December 1940, MS in possession of Jon Wynne-Tyson, his executor.

Philip O'Connor, *Memoirs of a Public Baby* (intro. Stephen Spender, London, 1958) is a classic of the period, while Nina Hamnett's comments derive from her second autobiographical work, *Is She a Lady?* (London, 1953). Stephen Spender's comments on Peter Watson and David Gascoyne and Dylan Thomas come from 'Some Observations on English Poetry between Two World Wars', *Transformation*, 3, 1945: he has also talked to me about Watson. *The Best Poems of 1934* was edited by Thomas Moult, while Dylan's remarks on writers in gangs, appeared in the *South Wales Evening Post* in December 1934. Geoffrey Grigson wrote of his 'Recollections of Dylan Thomas' in *The London Magazine*, September 1957. Vernon Watkins remembered his first meeting with Dylan in a typewritten letter in the Jeff Towns Collection, while the Welsh reviewer of *18 Poems* was again A. Spencer Vaughan-Thomas. Permission to quote from the works of Gwyn Thomas was kindly granted by David Higham Associates.

Chapter 6

The unique Surrealist sketch of Dylan Thomas is part of the Jeff Towns Collection. The poet's answers to the questionnaire from *New Verse* appeared in 1934.

Chapter 7

The extracts from David Gascoyne's *Journal 1936–37* (London, 1980) are printed by kind permission of the Enitharmon Press. The poem by Ruthven Todd was called 'It Was Easier' and was published in November 1942. George Woodcock's article 'Failures of Promise' on editing *Now* was in the important issue of *Aquarius*, 17/18, published in 1986/7, dealing with the poetry of the 1940s. Michael Hamburger is one of the more discerning analysts of Fitzrovia in his autobiography, *A Mug's Game* (London, 1980), while Jon Wynne-Tyson talked to this author. George Orwell's complaint appeared in his 'As You Please' column in the *Tribune*, 3 December 1943. Before his death, John Davenport advised this author on a stage adaptation of *Adventures in the Skin Trade*.

Chapter 8

Theodora Fitzgibbon's memoirs, *With Love*, were published in 1982 in London. In *Dead as Doornails* (Dublin, 1970), Anthony Cronin proved himself to be one of the more lively and illuminating guides to Fitzrovia. John Heath-Stubbs made his remarks to me. Peter Vansittart's entertaining writer's memoir is called *Paths from a White Horse* (London, 1985). David Wright's account of meeting Dylan Thomas on 17 March 1943 comes from a letter home, printed in *Aquarius*, 17/18, 1986/7. Graham Greene's account of the 'great blitz' of 16 April 1941 comes from his diary, included in his memoir, *Ways of Escape* (London, 1980). Julian Maclaren-Ross, *Memoirs of the Forties*, was published in 1965 in London: it remains the indispensable Baedeker of the place and period. Also essential for the Soho war years is Dan Davin, *Closing Times* (Oxford, 1975) and John Lehmann, *I Am My Brother* (London, 1960), the second volume of his autobiography. The papers of Donald Taylor are preserved in Sterling University. Robert Herring was quoted in *Leaves in the Storm* (London, 1945). Michael Balcon talked to me about the period, and his important comments on 'The British Film During the War' appeared in the Penguin *Film Review* of 1946. I am grateful to Jonathan Cape for permission to quote from Cecil Day Lewis, 'Newsreel', and to Weidenfeld and Nicolson for the extract from Alan Ross, *The Forties*, published in 1950. Mollie Panter-Downes reported the war from London for the *New Yorker*. James Pope-Hennessy was writing to Dorothy Colston-Baynes on 1 January 1943. Julian Symons talks of the division between writers in his autobiography, while Maclaren-Ross confirms the wars of the poets in his *Memoirs of the Forties*. *The Collected Poems of A.S.J. Tessimond* contains his poem on 'The Lesser Artists': it was published in Reading in 1985, while John Heath-Stubbs's poem on Soho, 'Letter to David Wright', was published by the Carcanet Press in his *Collected Poems*. *Picture Post* published 'A Nest of Singing Birds' on 10 August 1946. Dan Davin's *Closing Times* has been cited, while Rayner Heppenstall, *Portrait of the Artist as a Professional Man* was published in 1969 in London. Jocelyn Brooke wrote of his experiences in the BBC in *Coming to London* (John Lehmann ed., London, 1957). William Empson, 'Let it go', was published in his *Collected Poems* (1995), and is reprinted by kind permission of Lady Empson and The Hogarth Press. The evidence of E.C. Jones at the trial of Captain Killick after the gunfire at Majoda in New Quay was reported in the *Welsh Gazette*, 12 April 1945. Ivan Foxwell has talked to me on Dylan's work on *The Little Mermaid*, a script which is lost. I am indebted to *Horizon* for its questionnaire to Dylan in September 1946 on 'The Cost of Letters'.

Chapter 10

Robert Pocock wrote the poem on Dylan Thomas in the Gargoyle in 1950 as a parody of John Betjeman's 'On Seeing an Old Poet in the Café Royal'. Stephen Spender wrote his important booklet in 1946 for the new British Council, 'Poetry since 1939'. Edmund Wilson's comment on England in 1945 came from *Europe Without Baedeker* (London, 1948). I was present when Robert Lowell lectured at Harvard, while George Melly talked to me of Fitzrovia.

Chapter 11

Karl Shapiro wrote of his encounters with Dylan Thomas in his *In Defence of Ignorance* (New York, 1955). The privately printed comic poem by Dylan, 'Letter to Loren', about his experiences in Hollywood and the Ivy League was issued in a limited edition by the Salubrious Press, Swansea, 1993, with an introduction and notes by Jeff Towns.

Chapter 12

I am deeply indebted to the *Texas Quarterly*, IV, Winter 1961 for permission to reproduce the 'Poetic Manifesto' by Dylan Thomas.

Chapter 13

Richard Burton often spoke to me about Dylan when we were making the film of *Under Milk Wood* together. Jeff Towns possesses a dozen unpublished letters from Dylan Thomas including his last one to Liz Reitell. Wynford Vaughan-Thomas told me of the events at Dylan's funeral.

Chapter Notes

Chapter 14

I am grateful to Faber and Faber for permission to quote from George Barker, 'At the Wake of Dylan Thomas'. Mary Sarton wrote to Louise Bogan on 13 November 1953. The Dean of Westminster Abbey told me of the visit of President Jimmy Carter of the United States. Jeff Towns showed me Caitlin Thomas's letter to George Reavey and his wife of 16 December 1953. Aeron Thomas's memories of her father were published in the *South Wales Evening Post*, 27 June 1998.

Index